# Praise for *Buses Are a Comin'*

"An extraordinary document of physical and moral courage. As the youngest of the original thirteen Freedom Riders, Person tells a tale both frightening and empowering. That he survived to relate this tale with his own powerful voice is a blessing for us all."
—Raymond Arsenault, author of *Freedom Riders*

"A compelling narrative, rich in its description of the searing brutality of white racists opposed to the Freedom Rides of 1961, powerful in its depiction of the courage of civil rights protesters."
—William H. Chafe, Alice Mary Baldwin Professor Emeritus of History at Duke University and author of *Civilities and Civil Rights* and *The Rise and Fall of the American Century*

"Charles Person's book is a very personal, poignant, and political account of his life's evolution. It is especially revelatory for young males (of any ethnicity) in their sacred search for 'self, relevance, and calling.' It is a vivid personal snapshot of his coming-of-age. He fully exposes his life's journey: genuinely and movingly. His legacy is well established in this writing. He reminds us of the debt that we owe for the life that we have been given, and that to whom much is given and entrusted, much more is required."
—Rev. Dr. Carolyn M. McKinstry, author of *While the World Watched*

"*Buses Are a Comin'* is the most complete recounting we have of any of the Freedom Riders' experiences during those epochal days of 1961 and is at times lyrical, always insightful, and reveals a true American hero who is humble and appreciative. But Charles Person also subtly wants to exhort others, this and future generations, to 'get on the bus' and challenge inequality and injustice."
—Derek Catsam, professor of history and Kathlyn Cosper Dunagan Professor in the Humanities at the University of Texas Permian Basin and author of *Freedom's Main Line*

"A striking personal history of the 1961 Freedom Rides . . . Shot through with vivid details of beatdowns, arrests, and awe-inspiring bravery, this inspirational account captures the magnitude of what the early Civil Rights Movement was up against."

—*Publishers Weekly* (starred review)

"This dynamic narrative . . . serves as a reflection of what it means to belong in America, then and now. The depth with which the author examines not just his own story but that of his fellow riders gives a multifaceted perspective that clearly demonstrates why each was committed to the cause."

—*Kirkus Reviews* (starred review)

"Person's searing, revelatory, and often inspiring memoir provides a clear, vivid, and eloquent account of the first segment of the pivotal 1961 Freedom Rides." —*New York Journal of Books*

"This is a book you hand to readers too young to remember the Civil Rights Movement. It honors and it sings out names. Read it; *Buses Are a Comin'* will keep you in your seat."

—Terri Schlichenmeyer

"*Buses Are a Comin'* chronicles Person's political coming-of-age during the Civil Rights Movement. [His] memoir is a sobering, first-person account of that historic bus ride."

—*The Atlanta Journal-Constitution*

"Person's engagingly rendered, intimate testimony offers a look at the power of character and conviction among grassroots activists who paid the painful price of direct action to penetrate America's consciousness." —*Library Journal*

"An enthralling account of the American Civil Rights Movement and an impassioned call to action." —*BookBrowse*

# BUSES ARE A COMIN'

## MEMOIR OF A FREEDOM RIDER

## CHARLES PERSON
### WITH RICHARD ROOKER

ST. MARTIN'S
GRIFFIN
NEW YORK

*To Papa.*

*To the other twelve original Freedom Riders and
the 423 subsequent Freedom Riders of 1961.*

*To all who participated in the Atlanta Student Movement.*

*To my wife, JoEtta, and our children Cicely, Cammie, Carmelle,
Brandon, and Keisha.*

*To my special friends Nancy and Zack.*

The Library of Congress has cataloged the hardcover edition as follows:

Names: Person, Charles, author. | Rooker, Richard, author.
Title: Buses are a comin' : memoir of a freedom rider / Charles Person,
    with Richard Rooker.
Other titles: Buses are coming
Description: First edition. | New York : St. Martin's Press, 2021. |
    Includes bibliographical references and index.
Identifiers: LCCN 2020048562 | ISBN 9781250274199 (hardcover) |
    ISBN 9781250274205 (ebook)
Subjects: LCSH: Freedom Rides, 1961. | Person, Charles. | African
    American civil rights workers—Biography. | African Americans—
    Civil rights—History. | Segregation—United States.
Classification: LCC E185.61 .P465 2021 | DDC 323.092 [B]—dc23
LC record available at https://lccn.loc.gov/2020048562

ISBN 978-1-250-83676-2 (trade paperback)

Our books may be purchased in bulk for promotional, educational, or business use. Please contact your local bookseller or the Macmillan Corporate and Premium Sales Department at 1-800-221-7945, extension 5442, or by email at MacmillanSpecialMarkets@macmillan.com.

First St. Martin's Griffin Edition: 2022

10  9  8  7  6  5  4  3  2  1

Freedom Riders huddle around Reverend Fred Shuttlesworth after being attacked in Birmingham, Alabama. Clockwise from the left: Ed Blankenheim (kneeling), Charles Person, Theodore Gaffney, James Peck, Reverend Benjamin Cox, Moses Newson, and Simeon Booker.

(Next page, top) CORE training session, with John Lewis facing Joe Perkins and Albert Bigelow as Jimmy McDonald (background) and Genevieve Hughes (background) observe.

*Johnson Publishing Company Archive. Courtesy Ford Foundation, J. Paul Getty Trust, John D. and Catherine T. MacArthur Foundation, Andrew W. Mellon Foundation, and Smithsonian Institution.*

(Next page, bottom) James Peck and Charles Person.

*Johnson Publishing Company Archive. Courtesy Ford Foundation, J. Paul Getty Trust, John D. and Catherine T. MacArthur Foundation, Andrew W. Mellon Foundation, and Smithsonian Institution.*

Frances Bergman and Charles Person wait to board.

*Johnson Publishing Company Archive. Courtesy Ford Foundation, J. Paul Getty Trust, John D. and Catherine T. MacArthur Foundation, Andrew W. Mellon Foundation, and Smithsonian Institution.*

Left to right: Congress of Racial Equality director James Farmer, Walter Bergman, James Peck (background), unidentified woman, Frances Bergman (background), and Simeon Booker.

*Johnson Publishing Company Archive. Courtesy Ford Foundation, J. Paul Getty Trust, John D. and Catherine T. MacArthur Foundation, Andrew W. Mellon Foundation, and Smithsonian Institution.*

Charles Person and Walter Bergman order lunch at an all-white bus terminal restaurant counter. *Johnson Publishing Company Archive. Courtesy Ford Foundation, J. Paul Getty Trust, John D. and Catherine T. MacArthur Foundation, Andrew W. Mellon Foundation, and Smithsonian Institution.*

Freedom Riders before the journey that left Washington on May 4: Top, left to right: John Lewis, James Peck, Ed Blankenheim, Hank Thomas, Walter Bergman, and James Farmer. Bottom, left to right: Joe Perkins, Charles Person, Frances Bergman, Genevieve Hughes, and Jimmy McDonald. *Johnson Publishing Company Archive. Courtesy Ford Foundation, J. Paul Getty Trust, John D. and Catherine T. MacArthur Foundation, Andrew W. Mellon Foundation, and Smithsonian Institution.*

# CONTENTS

# PROLOGUE

## A Mother's Arms

The arms of mothers are made of tenderness; in them children sleep profoundly.

—*Victor Hugo*[1]

"Let's burn them niggers alive. Let's burn 'em alive," the voice said.[2]

Strong arms held the door of a burning bus closed from the outside. Angry men shouted vile words to the black and the white passengers sitting side by side in the bus—the Greyhound bus traveling from Washington, D.C., to the Deep South through the Bible Belt. The passengers heard the hatred, saw the enmity, felt the venom. Panic mixed with resignation. Panic. No escape apparent. If escape were possible, the route out would lead to men bent on murder. Resignation. So, this is how life ends. With last breaths being smoke, not air.

"If we got off of that bus," remembered my friend Hank Thomas, "there was no doubt in my mind we would have been killed. I decided that the best way to die was by taking a big gulp of poisonous smoke. I thought . . . that would put me to sleep, and that's the way I was going to die."[3]

It was 2:00 P.M., Sunday, May 14, 1961, in Anniston, Alabama.

Two hours later, sixty miles to the west in Birmingham, Alabama, dozens of angry arms and fists and knuckles surrounded and beat a man. In his infancy that man had slept profoundly in the tenderness of his mother's arms. His black mother's arms. It was now white arms of power and violence attacking him. Hadn't those men, too, slept profoundly in their mothers' tender arms?

Years earlier Birmingham's commissioner of public safety had proclaimed, "Damn the law. We don't give a damn about the law. Down here we make our own law."[4] He had assured those bent on hate and violence they could have fifteen uninterrupted minutes this day to do whatever they wanted to the unwanted Black bus riders and their white companions before he and his police force would intervene. Had not the commissioner of public safety also known the tender arms of his mother?

Mothers wrap their babies in blankets and love. They protect them from danger. They gaze into their innocent eyes and see kindness. They stare into their imagined futures and see promise. It is a rare mother who holds her infant in her tender arms and awaits with eager anticipation the day her child will hold a burning bus's door closed trapping people inside, who foresees with hopefulness a bludgeoning, or who dreams of her child having thoughts beginning with the word *Damn*.

Because a mother's love is like no other, we give mothers a day like no other: Mother's Day. Today, we celebrate Mother's Day with store-bought cards, bouquets of flowers, gourmet chocolates, and meals at nice restaurants. In the late 1950s and early 1960s, Mother's Day to me meant making a homemade card and giving Mom a hug. At best, I might give my mom a dainty hanky that cost pennies. When a parent brings home $40 to $50 a week, flowers, chocolates, and restaurants are not on your Mother's Day mind. But whatever the year, wherever the place, we want Mother's Day to be a memorable day.

On the most memorable Mother's Day of my life, arms held a burning bus's door closed. My friends and colleagues, such as Hank Thomas, were on that bus in Anniston.

On that Mother's Day in Birmingham, a circle of anger and hatred rained down fists, feet, and clubs on a black man. I was that black man. And Eugene "Bull" Connor was the commissioner of public safety who assured members of the Ku Klux Klan he would not interfere with their violence for a quarter of an hour.

The year 1961 began with optimism and hope. On January 20, the youngest man elected president in our nation's history took the oath of office. Forty-three-year-old John F. Kennedy opened his inaugural address by calling the day "a celebration of freedom."[5]

Folks such as me were not feeling all that free. But President Kennedy's words inspired us—inspired me—because a moment later he said, "United there is little we cannot do. . . ."

Make no mistake, the young black people who wanted to bring change to the Southern way of life were united. And in our youthful exuberance and our hopeful optimism, we believed there was little we could not do.

The new president said that day, "The energy, the faith, the devotion which we bring to this endeavor will light our country and all who serve it. And the glow from that fire can truly light the world."

Well, we in the Movement—be it the Atlanta Student Movement or the Civil Rights Movement—had energy, had faith, had devotion. In abundance. We believed. We believed we could spark a fire that would be a light unto the country and the world.

In his most famous line President Kennedy challenged us:

"And so, my fellow Americans, ask not what your country can do for you; ask what you can do for your country."

In 1961, we answered that challenge. We fulfilled that call. We did something for our country.

We took to the streets, the establishments, the institutions, the parks, and the playgrounds where we were not welcomed. We made a demand to be seen, acknowledged, heard, and affirmed as human beings. We sat in at restaurants, kneeled in at churches, and waded in at beaches where human beings who somehow thought they were more human than we met us with force, indignation, mockery, and arrest. We sought to educate those who had little tolerance and no acceptance of the idea that because the Declaration of Independence had *declared* "all men are created equal," it was more than time to think those words included us. We marched down streets. We got arrested. We went to jail for our beliefs. We did this because the Fourteenth Amendment to the Constitution told us "all persons born . . . in the United States . . . are citizens of the United States."[6] But we were not being treated the way other citizens were.

We asserted our humanity because it galled us that white men in our communities had not only been cradled in the loving arms of their mothers, but had also been cuddled in the caring arms of black nannies and domestics rearing them as they would rear their own children. Now as adults those former innocent babies held a bus door closed and pounded on people who sought to do something as simple as ride a bus. Might it have been possible that a woman who had held one of those attackers as an infant in her loving arms was now being trapped by the door they held shut? Would they have cared if she had been?

In Anniston, while my Freedom Rider friends were pushing out on the door of the burning bus to escape its flames, they were also pushing in on the consciousness of America to accept their claim to equal treatment under the law.

In Birmingham, while blows rained down on me trying to force me to my knees or my grave, I was trying to stand up and change a country's attitude about how it saw me, defined me, valued me.

How does an infant go from tender, loving arms to hate-filled animosity directed at fellow citizens? "What did that to them?" we wondered in 1961. Our answer was fear. Fear of a terrible *they*. *They* are going to take our schools. *They* are going to take our jobs. *They* are going to take drinks at our drinking fountains. *They* are going to take over our neighborhoods, our department stores, our restaurants, our theaters, our clubs, our swimming pools. In 1961, we were the *they* they feared. For in 1961, we, the students, represented the inch that, if given in to, would lead to the mile white Southerners had no intention of yielding. But we, the students, did not want to *take* anything from anybody. We wanted to receive our rightful seat at the table of full citizenship. A seat in a WHITE ONLY bus terminal restaurant. A seat in a WHITE ONLY waiting room. A seat on a toilet in what should have been a *public* restroom. Somehow, we were not part of the *public*.

To us, full citizenship was far more than that. We wanted acceptance in any restaurant. We wanted the end of all WHITE ONLY this and COLORED that. We wanted full access to any department store. We wanted to be able to try on clothes in a store before we bought the clothes. Who denies that? Could it be only those who think there is something contaminating about the terrible *they* they so feared? We wanted to join our fellow citizens in the enjoyment of their citizenship. We expected it to be our enjoyment, our citizenship, too. We wanted opportunity that those who had opportunity never thought about as opportunity. They thought about it as normal. Sitting at a lunch counter. Normal. Sitting in a waiting area. Normal. Sitting on a toilet. Normal. We, on the other hand, were forced to think of these as opportunities to be fought for and granted to us. Well, the US

Supreme Court did not *grant* us anything. It decided in December 1960 that someone's normal should be everyone's normal. It decided, in *Boynton v. Virginia,* that segregation in all aspects of interstate transportation was unconstitutional. It decided—in the present—that all people *are* created equal when it comes to riding a bus.

Would the country allow such a radical thought as that?

We sought to find out.

Yes, we did something for our country in 1961, but we did it in a way the man pledging to uphold the Constitution of the United States did not mean that cold morning in Washington, D.C., and we did it in a way he did not expect.

President Kennedy was speaking not only to the nation but to the world. Large challenges awaited him. The Bay of Pigs military invasion of Cuba was but three months away. Sooner than that, in early April, the Russian space program would be first to launch a human being—Yuri Gagarin—into space, garnering enormous prestige for the Soviet government and the Communist way of life while NASA scrambled to catch up. Early in the first year of this presidency our new, young leader awaited a meeting with Soviet premier Nikita Khrushchev at a June summit in Vienna, Austria, to discuss pressure points in the world such as the divided city of Berlin. But Kennedy would also have to deal with civil unrest that he could not fathom would happen in the happy domestic days of 1961.

After all, 1961 would be the year Mickey Mantle and Roger Maris would mount their epic assault on the record of 60 home runs in a season by the untouchable Babe Ruth. By season's end, Roger Maris would hit 61 in '61. It was the year Chubby Checker would have young people nationwide doing the Twist on the dance floor, although not as well as we saw him do it on TV.[7] At the movies, *West Side Story, Breakfast at Tiffany's,* and *101*

*Dalmatians* would charm our sensibilities while *The Guns of Navarone* would heighten our patriotism.[8]

In this environment of international tension and seeming domestic tranquility, civil rights were far from President Kennedy's mind. Probably not on his agenda. In an interview in *Look* magazine in March, eight weeks after the new administration took office and five weeks before we took to buses, his brother Attorney General Robert Kennedy answered a question about how his newly inaugurated brother would handle a civil rights crisis like the Little Rock Nine in 1957 during the administration of his predecessor, President Eisenhower. Robert Kennedy responded with confidence, "I cannot conceive of this Administration letting such a situation deteriorate to that level."[9]

Little did the president or attorney general know, little did they anticipate, little did they understand that buses were a comin'. A comin' their way. They were a comin' whether the president and his administration knew it, anticipated it, or understood it. What Robert Kennedy could not conceive, CORE—Congress of Racial Equality—was already planning. We in the Negro community had waited long enough for change to come. In 1961, as in the year before, we were going out and changing things ourselves.

The year before, the change and the challenge to the status quo had come in the form of sit-ins. On February 1, 1960, four African American students at North Carolina Agricultural and Technical College decided enough was enough.[10] They planted themselves on lunch counter stools at Woolworth's department store in Greensboro, North Carolina, seeking the same service any white customer would expect and receive. That planting in Greensboro harvested no food that day, but from those seeds, thousands of sit-ins sprouted across the South. Within a year, food would be served to those who had been denied service and refused meals until a demand made white businesses comply.

Now it was time for the next step in our march toward equality with our white brothers and sisters. Following the 1955–56 Montgomery Bus Boycott, Dr. Martin Luther King, Jr., wrote his first book, entitled *Stride Toward Freedom*. Dr. King was half a generation older than we were. Already holding an undergraduate degree from Morehouse, a divinity degree from Crozer Theological Seminary, and a doctorate degree from Boston University, Dr. King in his first thirty years had led the Montgomery Bus Protest and communicated with President Eisenhower during the Little Rock Nine crisis in Arkansas. He was married with two children and had helped found and was president of the Southern Christian Leadership Conference (SCLC). Already, he was a national and international figure whom we admired and looked up to.

But in 1960 and '61, we felt it was our time and our turn. We were high school and college students, and we were eager to shake, rattle, and roll the country out of its complacency toward our freedom. In the words that fellow student and future congressman John Lewis would say over and over, year after year, "We want our freedom, and we want it now."[11]

We were in a hurry, and we were not going to wait for Democrats or Republicans or the NAACP or the SCLC to trudge along. The time was now, and now was the time to move.

Dr. King was born thirteen years before I was and grew up two and a half blocks from my house in Atlanta. The King family moved three blocks farther away from our house when young Martin was twelve—the year before I was born—so I never knew him as a boy. Everyone would know him by the end of 1956 and the successful conclusion of the Montgomery Bus Protest.[12]

Now it was four and a half years later. Spring 1961. New decade. New president. New demands. In 1955 and '56, Montgomery marched and walked and carpooled until the city's bus system said yes to allowing integrated seating. The court system—*Browder v. Gayle*—decided the issue, but a year's worth of feet on the ground made a difference.[13]

I was thirteen and fourteen years old then and experienced frustrations of unfairness that my early, limited teenage vision could barely discern. By eighteen years of age, my eyesight improved.

My generation saw what Sam Cooke would sing about a few years later: "A Change Is Gonna Come." We intended to be the change. New buses were comin'. Thirteen of us got on those buses in the spring of the first year of President Kennedy's term of office. Freedom Ride 1961 we called it. Hank's bus and my bus were both stopped by forces of violence and hatred on Mother's Day.

By summer's end, though, more than four hundred Americans got on board buses in support of us. Police arrested over three hundred of them as soon as they got off those buses. Into jail and prison many of them went. Trespassing was the charge. Breach of peace was another. Those were the official offenses. But in truth *we* were the offense. Our existence was the offense. The first two buses that summer—including my bus—were stopped before we reached our aim, but the buses a comin' in their places with a visionary FREEDOM inscribed on the destination sign above the windshield made it to the finish line.

When President Kennedy took office on January 20, 1961, signs in the South leading into bus station waiting rooms, restaurants, and restrooms told any of us who by birth looked like me that we were unwanted, unwelcomed, and forbidden to be there. Signs reading WHITE ONLY or COLORED were as common to my eyes as those saying ENTER. Eight months later the Interstate Commerce Commission (ICC) ordered the racist signs down. Within two months of the order, the signs came down. We had won.

It has been sixty years since my Freedom Ride. Today, only

two of our original thirteen survive. Hank Thomas and I remain to tell the tale so that the courage and patriotism of Walter and Frances Bergman, Albert Bigelow, Ed Blankenheim, Elton Cox, James Farmer, Genevieve Hughes, John Lewis, Jimmy McDonald, Joe Perkins, and James Peck might inspire youth of today and tomorrow to get on a bus—their own bus—their own Freedom Ride—to whatever injustice needs addressing, needs fixing in their time. Walter, Frances, Albert, Ed, Elton, James, Genevieve, John, Jimmy, Joe, and James will be cheering from beyond this time and place. Hank and I will one day join their choir in celestial celebration of such striving. For now, we shout and sing and let our voices ring from solid soil in support of such efforts.

So, this is my memoir. It is not my story alone. It is the story of people I admire. People, perhaps, you have never heard of. Not only the original thirteen mentioned above but Herman Harris, Mae Frances Moultrie, Ike Reynolds, and Jerry Moore, who joined us before my Freedom Ride came to an end in Birmingham, Alabama. It is the story of Fred Shuttlesworth and Diane Nash, who stepped into the fray when the struggle seemed lost.

As important, it is the story of Lonnie King, Julian Bond, Herschelle Sullivan, Frank Holloway, and Leon Greene, all of whom led the way into today by leading and serving in the Atlanta Student Movement. It is a today that affords so much more opportunity for African Americans born in the twenty-first century than existed for those born decades ago. It is also a today that has so far—*so far*—to go.

These are people who six decades ago saw injustice and acted to change it. Many of us had relatives who encouraged us, as my grandfather did, to "do something." None of them ever hit a record-breaking home run or danced on national television or won an Academy Award like Roger Maris, Chubby Checker, or Rita Moreno. No, instead, they beat the throw to first. They danced a dangerous dance. They walked a red carpet leading to freedom. They acted on what Dr. King would call "the fierce urgency of now."[14] And choosing to move, they moved a country. When these freedom fighters asked the universal question, "Do I belong?," and the Deep South replied, "No, you do not," they made the country change the answer to "Yes, you do." Not completely. Far from it. But they advanced the answer toward the affirmative as much as anyone might have dared to hope. They made the tapestry of America more beautiful.

I got to be part of that groundswell of change.

To me, these "foot soldiers" in the battle for equality—these friends and colleagues of mine—stand twenty feet tall, not on a silver screen pursuing a gold statuette for themselves, but in reality still pursuing some sixty years later their vision of what this country might mean for all her children, all her dispossessed, all her unjustly and disproportionately incarcerated, all her citizens "yearning to breathe free."

Yes, this is my story, but it is also theirs—these heroes of mine. I'd like them, by the end of this book, to be heroes of yours, too. They are the focus of this memoir as much as I.

In 1961, I got on a bus that was a comin' my way. It was a real bus. Some days a Trailways, others a Greyhound. My bus brought about changes my parents' generation hoped for in their dreams. Equal access in transportation. Equal opportunities in public facilities. It put me in dangers I never imagined. Threats, beatings, and jail. It took me to destinations I did not see on my horizon. A path of service to others. A lifelong commitment to equality.

Some of the heroes I've mentioned above boarded real buses as I did. Freedom Ride buses. All of the above willingly boarded metaphorical buses taking them to and through dark dangers of fear on one side but leading to the bright skies of freedom on the other side.

I know their desire as much as mine is that you will board

your bus when it stops near you, when it opens its door, when it offers a ride. The ride you accept, no matter the risk—in fact, because of the risk—may have the force to lift and uplift millions.

Board the bus. Take the seat denied you. Make the country better for those yet unborn who will never know the seat you took, the ride you rode, the risk you accepted, the fare you paid, the change you made.

Buses of change are always a comin'. Here is the story of the bus I got on.

## Life in the Bottom

Let us look at Jim Crow for the criminal he is and what he had done to one life multiplied millions of times over these United States and the world. He walks us on a tightrope from birth.

*—Rosa Parks*[1]

Our neighbor had a peach tree in his yard. A vegetable garden, too. I loved fruit. So did my cousin, Kenneth Booker. We craved juicy flavors created by sinking our teeth into tree-ripe Georgia peaches.

We felt the fuzz on the fruit and checked our chins to see if we were growing any. Neither Kenneth nor I were yet ten years old. No fuzz.

Our neighbor was—who knew how old? Thirty? Fifty? One hundred twenty? In the early 1950s, kids didn't know the ages of adults. They were adults. They were old. We were kids—young, full of fun, and hungry.

The sun was hot. Summers in Atlanta can be sweltering.

Swelter builds thirst. Thirst builds temptation. Temptation yields to naughty.

Some days Kenneth and I pretended we were marines fighting in Korea in the bitter cold of the recent disaster at Chosin Reservoir. This day we were the US army attacking Nazi Germany as my father had when we were toddlers. We stuck sticks out our sleeves and small twigs out our pant cuffs to camouflage our assault. We crawled on our bellies, then climbed the neighbor's fence to penetrate the "German" perimeter.

The tree had no chance; the garden, no protection. We plucked peaches. We stole vegetables. We escaped. We crawled back. Our bellies hugged the earth until reaching the fence. Our heads moved back and forth keeping watch for the enemy. Our Raid on Peach Tree succeeded.

The plan was to tell Mom we had saved our pennies, walked to the grocery store, and purchased the food so she could make us vegetable soup and peach pie. That made sense to us. So, as we filled Mom's ears with fibs, our mouths dripped peach juice. We were proud. We were happy. We were stupid.

Mom marched us over to the neighbor and made us knock on his door. Hinges creaked. It might have been the old man's joints. The huge door opened. Mom stood behind me. Her eyes bore down on my head. I felt them. Being nine and two years older than Kenneth, I knew she would make me do the talking. I started stuttering.

"We . . ." I paused.

"Go on," Mom commanded in a voice both soft and steel.

"We stole peaches and vegetables from your garden."

I don't know if my quivering voice made my knees knock or my shaking knees made my words tremble.

"Keep going." Mom was not going to make this easy. Her quiet voice echoed enforcement more than volume would have.

Words stumbled out.

"We can repay you for what we've eaten. Here's the rest of what we took."

"Took?" Mom's voice challenged.

"Stole." She made me say the word a second time.

I tilted my head back so my eyes could meet the neighbor's eyes. Mom insisted we make eye contact with people as we spoke. Adding a second offense to stealing would not go well. I knew that. I kept my head tilted.

The neighbor's face was so far up. When you are caught in your guilt, it is a stretch to see beyond your shame. But there he was looking down on me. I didn't like it when people looked down on me.

His face looked stern. Then a miracle happened.

"Boys, thank you. That was the right thing to do. You can keep what you have as a gift. Next time, ask. I might come out and help you pick."

Back home, Mom made us the best peach pie and vegetable soup I can remember eating. Kenneth and I felt as if we had dodged death.

Then Death came home from work.

My dad, Hugh Person, strode through the door in a hurry to get to his second job on time.

"We have a situation that needs . . . attention," Mom said.

She told him what we had done, what she had done, and what the neighbor had done.

Then we found out what Dad was going to do.

"Ruby, I'll take care of it." Dad was a man of few words.

Moments later, as Dad rushed out the door, our shame lingered on our tearstained faces and our sore rear ends. We got our butts spanked. Sometimes I can still feel it today, though I can laugh about it now in a way I could not in 1951.

The Raid on Peach Tree defines the kind of trouble I got into as a youth—the kind of troublemaker I was. That is to say,

I wasn't. Mischievous? Misbehaving? Of course. Every young-
ster is. But troublemaking? I am not built that way. It is not in
my DNA.

Strange, then, that a lifetime later—at age eighteen—
Atlanta city police locked up me and hundreds of others for
the troublemakers we were. Stranger, still, that I could be an
"outside agitator" in my native South because I boarded a bus
in Washington, D.C., and rode it home.

That is what a segregationist mind can convince itself of: a
bus rider is a troublemaker; a native son is an outside agitator.
That is what Jim Crow teaches people to believe: that people's
"disorderly conduct"—one of the offenses Freedom Riders were
charged with—is worthy of their being jailed, beaten, or killed to
"teach them a lesson."

Jim Crow. Segregation. These are aberrations from human
dignity no one should live under. They should never have existed, but since they did, they should be anachronisms of eras
long past. Instead, they are realities conceived from our nation's
original sin of slavery, and they continue today in the hearts of
those who act to ensure whites remain in charge.

As a young child in 1940s Atlanta, I did not know the existence of segregation any more than a fish knows water. Or a bird
air. Or a white child knows whiteness. In my childhood awareness, I wasn't growing up in segregation. I was growing up on
Bradley Street—21 Bradley Street.

I was growing up in a community of folks like me in an area
of Atlanta called Buttermilk Bottom. *Buttermilk* because many
families there survived on buttermilk and corn bread. *Bottom*
because *Heights* doesn't make a lot of sense when life lands you
in the lows.

In the Bottom, life was simple. I thought my family was
wealthy. We weren't. Wealthy in time, food, people, and love?
Sure. I had Mom and Dad, my siblings, my cousin Kenneth, and

my grandparents Papa and Grandma Booker and Mama Arlena. I had abundance in everything that mattered to me.

It's hard to imagine being richer in food than we were at 21 Bradley. Our relatives lived out in the country, and that gave us access to farm food. Pigs alone gave us delicacies in four seasons. We had bacon all year round but much more than that. Mom used pigs' ears, tails, and feet to make food ranging from meals to snacks. She cooked pigs' ears, put them between two pieces of bread, slapped mustard and hot sauce on them, and I had the best sandwich I ever ate. She cooked pigs' tails down till they were so tender the meat fell off easier than the softest puff of wind disperses dandelion seeds. They were better than dark meat on a chicken drumstick. Mom pickled pigs' feet in vinegar, salt, and pickling spice and let them cure in a canning jar for a month. We had a hard time waiting for what was on the other side of those thirty days.

Mom cured hams in a smokehouse for months preparing for the holidays. The same ham that provided Christmas dinner gave us leftovers for sandwiches and food for breakfast. It also gave us redeye gravy. Mmm, mmm. Mom placed pieces of ham in her cast-iron skillet and browned them on both sides. I watched with "Is it ready yet?" eagerness as she turned the ham over, careful not to burn it, but turn it into a beautiful rich brown. Mom's self-control outmatched my eagerness. After placing the ham on a plate, and sometimes slapping my hand to keep me away from it, she poured leftover coffee into the skillet. The coffee loosened the residue from the pan to make pure magic. My nose knew before my eyes did—breakfast was ready. And I was ready for breakfast. I rushed to my seat, pushed my spoon into my grits, and dug a reservoir for Mom's gravy. She would say, "Tony"—Mom sometimes called me Tony from my middle name, Anthony—"Tony, slow down. Be patient." It was hard for me to be patient. I wanted what I wanted, and I wanted it now. She poured the steaming sauce into the basin I'd created in my bowl and . . . slapped my hand to keep me away from it. I grabbed one of her piping hot homemade biscuits and placed a piece of the ham inside. Biscuits. Grits. Redeye gravy. Ham. Me. It was Christmas Day all over again every day for a week.

Had I enjoyed an abundance of awareness of the physical world around me, I might have noticed the Bottom reeked. Decay permeated nostrils. I did not smell it. Coal-burning trains spewed black sewage skyward. I did not detect it. Fulton Bag and Cotton Mills billowed clouds of cumulous gray. I never noticed it. The black soot climbing into the blue had to fall somewhere. It fell on us—on me. I did not feel it. The smell of chitlins cooking and the smell of collard, turnip, and mustard greens with ham hocks jarred our sense of smell, but they tasted good. Drunken old men smelled of liquor and urine. They smelled of whiskers and wrinkles, too. They, like us kids, lived oblivious of the obvious—the Bottom offended human senses if you were aware enough to notice.

Wide, unpainted, rotting clapboard houses hugged Bradley Street. Slatted-wood porches held rickety chairs. Rickety people sat in those chairs. At least that's what Kenneth and I thought. Rusted tin roofs repelled the rain except where holes had worn through. In the Bottom, it rained inside and outside.

Unpaved streets meant that the few cars in the Bottom bounced and bumbled at speeds kids could outrun because speed raised dust. The dust of clouds was one more thing to fall on us. We didn't need anything more falling on us.

In the Bottom, everyone had exquisite dark skin—shades that ranged from light brown to dark chocolate—except for a small minority. The milkman was white. The laundry owners, Asian. The owners of the ice cream shop, Greek. The insurance man stood out to Kenneth and me because he had chalky-white skin, straight hair, thin lips, and a thinner nose. We made fun of that.

"Press your nostrils together and inhale," I coaxed Kenneth. He did, but it didn't last.

"You do it," Kenneth said.

"I'd rather look like Satchmo." I flared my nostrils out.

That didn't last either. We laughed longer than either of our nose contortions lasted. I guess we learned we have the noses we're born with.

Years later a man I did not know and would never meet again decided to reshape my nose for me because he did not care for where I chose to sit on a bus. Why my nose and the rest of me mattered so much to him I do not know, but it did.

On Bradley Street we lived in a two-room, second-story apartment in an eight-apartment wooden building. Six small upstairs apartments sat atop two large apartments at ground level. This was the one time in my early life I got to be on top. To get home, we climbed an outside staircase and proceeded down a street-facing balcony past other apartments till we reached 5B.

The words *apartment building* are accurate, but they do not capture 21 Bradley. Warped planks formed the floors, the walls, the ceilings. I remember the balcony felt solid, but its railing looked more like rolling waves than leveled wood. Most windows in the apartments were glass. A few were holes in the walls boarded up with nailed, horizontal slats of pine. Gaps in the slats allowed daylight in and kept most rain out. No foundation existed. Every eight feet or so, blocks of stacked bricks propped the building three feet off the ground. A lot of brick was missing from those supports that held up 21 Bradley, but the building still stood. It tilted a little, but stood.

The front door of our home opened to a combined living room and bedroom. That's where Mom and Dad and my younger sisters Norma Jean and Carole slept. The second room was a combined kitchen, dining room, and bedroom for Mama Arlena (we called her Malena), my brother Jimmy Dale, and me.

My younger three siblings had not yet come along, so there was plenty of room for the seven of us in the two rooms of 5B. Our toilet was outside on the back balcony. We shared it with the other families in the upstairs units of our building.

Today, I know life was small on Bradley Street, but a few blocks away life was big. Ebenezer Baptist Church. Bethel AME Church. Wheat Street Baptist Church. Big sanctuaries. Big steeples. Big congregations. Big voices from the pulpits and choirs. Preachers with big personalities.

Martin Luther King, Jr., grew up on Auburn Avenue all of four hundred steps from my home. Auburn was known as "the richest Negro street in the world." But today I know "richest Negro street" meant poor and undesirable by white standards.

A half mile down Auburn Avenue from the King home, the Royal Peacock nightclub brought national talent to "Sweet Auburn Avenue." Muddy Waters, Fats Domino, Dizzy Gillespie, Big Mama Thornton transformed that lounge into a volcanic celebration of music. In our young teens, Kenneth and I sneaked there at night. We crouched outside and heard the music, felt the vibrations, and imagined what we were missing. Every kid we knew wanted to be old enough to enter the Royal Peacock.

This was our world.

Men worked jobs paying $40 to $50 a week. Women worked as domestics. That brought another $5 a day. It's hard when a woman is mother to two sets of children—her own four kids (eventually seven) and her white family's children. Ruby Person hid the hardness. My siblings and I were not aware of Mom's world—a world where Jim Crow sat on her as she and Dad tried to make it up from the Bottom.

After a long day of working for someone else's family and a long evening of tending to her own, Mom gathered Jimmy Dale, Norma Jean, Carole, and me to her bedside. She sat on the bed.

We sat on the living room floor next to the bed and listened to the Bible reading. Sometimes, we got to pick the story.

"Tell us about Shadrach, Meshach, and Abednego," we said in chorus. Like most kids, we wanted to hear the same story over and over.

"Here's a story of brave people just like the four of you," she said.

Still at nine, that made me proud. I wanted to be brave like Bible heroes, like Dad fighting Nazis, like Mom.

We finished Bible-reading time by memorizing verses together. This night it was Joshua 1:9:

*Have not I commanded thee? Be strong and of a good courage; be not afraid, neither be thou dismayed: for the LORD thy God is with thee whithersoever thou goest.*[2]

"Be strong." "Be not afraid." Those were words I wanted to live by. Where would I be without Mom?

At bedtime, Jimmy Dale and I slept in the same bed and fought over who got to sleep next to the wall. Somehow that felt more private. I won. Sleep took its time setting in. It was hard falling asleep because home had two rooms, seven people, and three of them were adults talking late into the evening. I remember hearing them say things that made me wonder. Things like "They aren't old enough. They don't need to know that yet" or "It doesn't have to be that way for them, so why tell them?" I'd try to stay awake to find out what the "that" and "that way" were, but sleep did come, and when I awoke, it was a new day on Bradley Street.

Yonge Street Elementary School was a half mile west of our place—a ten-minute walk there and a faster run home for Mom's blackberry pie or hot, roasted peanuts. When I got close enough for my nose to figure out what was in the oven, my ears could hear what was on Mom's mind that day.

Some days, plaintive melodies accompanied the yearning

words *Swing low, sweet char-reee-ahht, Com-in' for to car-ry me ho-o-o-o-me.* Other days, the cheerful buoyancy of *Lord, I want to be a Christian in my heart, in my heart* . . . spilled out of the apartment. I was too young to know what troubles Mom had seen and was too caught up in other things to wonder about Mom's faith, but her singing was a constant during my grow-ing-up years. When I think of my mom, I think of her working and singing.

As early as elementary school, math and science fascinated me. By nine I knew about the illusive dream of a perpetual mo-tion machine. It captivated me. I learned it was an impossible idea because the expenditure of energy exhausts the source. I re-member thinking my teachers must not have known my mom. She was always working, always producing, always moving . . . perpetually.

I know now our school was nothing like schools in other sections of Atlanta. Desks were hand-me downs—worn and bat-tered. Classroom sets of books were rare. Teachers gave us expe-riences more than book learning. Experiences such as watching caterpillars grow into butterflies.

"Caterpillars are like you," my fourth-grade teacher told us one day. "They start off crawling and learn to fly."

That was all I needed. Back home I practiced. Wrapped in a blanket for a cocoon, I stood on the first step of the apartment building going up to 5B, struggled to get free of the blanket, and jumped. Rewrapped in the blanket, I tried the second step. Then the third. I didn't get past the third one.

I didn't learn to fly, but I did learn to love school and love learning. In elementary and high school our teachers knew what it took to be successful, so they disciplined us and placed high expectations on us. They were kind, and they were tough. They paved a path to our future prosperity by believing like the poet

Robert Browning that nothing was beyond our grasp except our reach. They expected us—expected me—to reach. So, I did.

Some days I didn't run home as soon as school was dismissed to fill my stomach. Some days my friends T.C., Felix, and I walked to Fire Station 6 on Auburn Avenue—a few houses west of the King home. The firemen let us sit in chairs inside the station and watch them. Maybe we were a curiosity to them. Maybe they were being friendly. Maybe they let us pretend being firemen because they knew we could never be one. No black firemen existed in Atlanta when T.C., Felix, and I sat in those chairs. But we loved to watch. And dream. Just like flying.

Firemen slid down the pole. We wanted to do that. Fire Station 6 had a dalmatian. I wanted a dalmatian. The firemen cleaned the station till it was spotless. They moved with purpose when an emergency came. All that—the fire pole, the dog, the sparkle, the character—intrigued me. It was something I wanted to be a part of.

When the firemen came back from a fire, the smell of smoke stoked my imagination. The smell of coffee in Station 6 made me want to be an adult. The heavy coats, the hard helmets with curved rims, and the big rubber boots made me forget about butterflies.

Some nights in bed next to Jimmy Dale, I tried to dream about being an Atlanta fireman. My dream seemed impossible. I told my dream to Mom. She embraced my dream and did not share my opinion.

"You can do anything you want to do, Charles. Anything."

It was as if Ruby Person could see the future. It was a wideopen future even though her life had been closed. For Jimmy Dale and me, she spoke the language of possibility. As I did not see the soot or smell the foul odors of Bradley Street, Mom did not see current limitations. She chose to smell the cooking inside the doors of 5B, not the decay outside them. Becoming a fire-man *was* possible. At a time when society denied so much, she encouraged me to imagine and believe and fly. She envisioned a future that society could not yet see. She ignited a flame in me even though her flame had been doused as a fireman pours water on a burning building or as Atlanta drowned the dreams of 40 percent of its citizenry.

I never became a fireman. I never sat in those then-forbidden seats, but Mom's unalterable belief in achievement would direct me in a future year to take another forbidden seat I could not have imagined when longing to be a fireman. It was not a seat on a fire truck, but on a bus. A freedom bus. A Freedom Ride.

Mom was an anchor in my life and a hero. So was Papa. But Papa was not my dad. Papa was the name I called my mom's dad. Edward Booker lived on Irwin Street, two blocks north of Bradley Street. At that point in life, I walked everywhere I needed to be—friends' houses, school, church, store. And Papa and Grandma's.

Kenneth lived with Papa and Grandma. He knew sorrows I did not. Kenneth never knew his real father, and his mother died on his fifth birthday. So, Papa time, for me, was also Kenneth time.

I'd knock on Papa's door and let myself in. There Papa would be in his blue-and-gray plaid flannel shirt with his ribbed undershirt peeking through as he rocked away in his chair. His crossed legs held the book he was reading, and the bottom of a laced brogan shoe showed a small hole revealing Papa to be a man who not only wore his clothing stylishly, he wore his cloth-ing out. The barbershop smell of bay-rum aftershave splashed on Papa made me want to sink my nose into his cheek. I gave him a hello hug.

"Hey, Bo," he said. I was Charles to my teachers, Tony to Mom, Bo to Papa. Where Bo came from is a mystery, but it's what he called me, and it stuck.

"Hey, Papa," I replied. "What are we going to do today?"

Kenneth joined us.

Papa was a carpenter by vocation, a coin collector by avocation, and a voracious reader. The first thing Papa did in the morning was open his Bible and read. Papa loved his Bible. He loved teaching Kenneth and me the role Africa played in the Bible—Moses and Zipporah, Abraham and Hagar, and the kings and queens of Africa. I think Africa was as important to Papa as Jesus.

"Well, Bo," he said, "I want to teach you and Kenneth more about Haile Selassie."

We already knew Haile Selassie was the current emperor of Ethiopia and that Papa revered him. Haile Selassie painted a picture in Papa's mind of the wealth and power the ancient royalty of Africa possessed before imperialism came and took the riches—and the people—for their own. Haile Selassie in his regal robes, proud posture, strong face, and determination was as important a person for me to learn about as President Roosevelt.

"You are like Haile Selassie, Bo, because people called him many names—Jah, Janhoy, Abba Tekel, and HIM."

I liked *HIM* the most because it stood for His Imperial Majesty. I could imagine *me* being *HIM* someday.

"Does having lots of names sound like anyone you know?" Papa asked me.

"Me." I beamed. "Me, Papa."

After we talked about leadership and being strong and imagining our futures, Papa turned to woodworking.

"Let's make more progress on the birdhouse," he said.

Another time I went to Papa's, Kenneth opened the door with a curled smile that ignited excitement in me. His shoulders rose in the giddiness that says in a secretive way, "I know something you don't know."

"What?" I asked. "What?"

"Wait till you see."

I entered Papa's house.

"Papa says it's time."

Papa joined us in the doorway. His hand held out a small gold piece of metal.

"Boys, here's the key."

As soon as we saw it, we knew where to head. We ran to the black trunk in the corner of Papa's living room. Bulbous silver metal protected each of its eight corners like shoulder pads on a football player. Tarnished, scraped banding along each edge spoke to its age. We inserted the key into the lock and turned. The clasp fell open. Kenneth and I each unlatched one of the two metal hasps on either side of the lock.

We lifted the lid. It seemed like forever I had wanted to know the answer, and a million times I had asked, "What's in the trunk, Papa?"

"It's not time," Papa would say.

And the now I wanted would be postponed again.

The shallow tray covering the lower and larger portion of the trunk contained commemorative coins and old books that looked as fragile as brittle autumn leaves. Papa lifted the tray out of the trunk to set it on a table. That was the mistake.

"Boys, look at these. Look at these coins. These are colored folks on here. These are our people. This is our money."

He tried to capture our interest. Kenneth and I tried to obey. But our eyes wandered from his lesson on the table to the bottom of the trunk.

"This is Booker T. Washington, and his coin came out just a few years ago."

We did not care.

"Someday, it will be worth a lot more than fifty cents."

Our eyes could not stay on the money he was trying to show us.

"This coin goes back one hundred years. One hundred years," he repeated to punctuate the importance.

On it a kneeling woman lifted her chained arms in prayer.

"You need to learn about this coin," Papa told us.

But all we could see were the two rifles lying diagonally across the trunk's bottom. The barrels were oiled to a sheen. The stocks looked older, the wood marred and smoothed with the passage of time and the hold of hands.

My mind exploded. I had no idea what Kenneth was thinking. To me, he wasn't there. It was just those guns and me. Papa was saying something—most likely about the coins. I did not hear him. My eyes deafened me. My imagination heard only the bolt action of my right hand turning the lever to release a spent shell.

Papa must have figured out the futility of trying to keep our minds on the contents of the trunk's tray. He took a different tack.

"Would you like to shoot those .22s?"

I don't remember being able to speak, but somehow we communicated yes.

"Well," Papa said, "it's time."

He taught us how to hold the rifles when walking.

"Cradle the stock in your right arm. Keep the barrel pointing straight ahead and down."

We obeyed with exaggerated care. He might have told us, "Well, not that far down."

Papa led us out to his backyard, where he had constructed a shooting range within Atlanta's city limits. Here we were surrounded by houses and people, and we were about to fire rifles into embanked ground at the back of Papa's yard.

He had rectangular pieces of cardboard and crayons.

"Draw the roundest circles you can." He modeled an example

for us. I'm sure we thought our circles were round, but I expect they looked more like concentric squiggles than circles.

Papa walked us to the elevated mounds of dirt that would be the backstop for our targets. We put the cardboard in place.

Back at our rifles, Papa took great care to teach us how to hold the gun and how to squeeze the trigger.

"When the gun goes off, you are going to jerk. You have to be ready for the noise and the kickback."

Papa fired his rifle, and just as he said, we jumped. Neither of us had ever been so close to a fired weapon. He fired more rounds till we stopped reacting to the noise.

"Bo, you first," Papa said, and my heart swelled with pride as much as my nerves made me scared. My now was here. Papa's patience balanced my anticipation. He helped me hold the gun, and I'm sure he helped direct the barrel.

"Slow," he said. And I tried to be slow.

The gun went off. I jumped up as the gunstock pushed my shoulder back. It was as if we had never practiced not jumping. The cardboard was untouched.

Then it was Kenneth's turn. Same lesson. Same result. The safest place for that cardboard that day may have been in the sight lines of Kenneth's and my rifles.

But Papa was patient. After lots of sessions of practice, Kenneth and I were able to hit the bull's-eye with regularity. Papa was proud. So were we. But it never occurred to me to ask Papa why he kept those guns, and why he thought we needed to learn to shoot.

During the workweek, Papa was more present in my life than my dad. Sixteen-hour days working two jobs meant Dad was gone before I got up, and I was asleep when he got home. In summer, I saw Dad between his jobs. The rest of the year, I was at school, and Dad was at work.

Dad worked as an orderly in two locations. His day started at 7:00 A.M. at Emory University Hospital. At 3:00 P.M. his shift ended, and he headed to Georgia Baptist Hospital to work from 3:30 to 11:00 P.M. All that work brought barely enough for us to live on. Mom's ironing and Dad's odd jobs such as raking autumn leaves and working on engines and motors brought us a bit more. Engine work gave Dad a mechanical smell like transmission oil. It's funny. He worked such long hours in sterile facilities, but the memory I have of him is the aroma of an automotive engineer trying to wash the smell off with Lava soap's pumice harshness.

Where Papa seemed quiet and serene to me, slow of foot and methodical in his work, Dad was always in a hurry. His hair, brushed straight back and held in place with Royal Crown pomade, formed embedded lines. He would take both hands and sweep his hair backward as his feet moved forward. A cigarette— Pall Mall Red, no filter—constantly hung on his lips and pointed downward as if it were about to fall from his mouth, but the smoke from it seemed to me to be trailing him like smoke from a train. He was on the move because life required it. To make ends meet, Dad needed to be moving forward no matter how far behind he was.

Dad and Mom got married in 1942—the year I was born— and then Dad went off to World War II. So, Dad was away from home even at my birth. More than a million African Americans served a country and a military that did not see them as equal to white Americans. Georgia was the state with the highest percentage of its citizenry enlisted in the war effort. I don't know how Dad knew that, but he took pride in that fact, and it added to his sense of purpose, dignity, and service.

In my teens I came to know that segregation in the army kept Dad behind the front lines. He had signed up to fight. Instead, his unit provided supply and maintenance to those who did the fighting. Learning that put a pang in my heart. I came to know my Raid on Peach Tree adventures with Kenneth were based on the reality of white boys' fathers, not mine. The whipping Dad gave me that day when I was nine was real. My imaginings of Dad's heroism in war were fiction. How much fiction? Maybe Dad cleaned latrines in the war but told me he was a supply officer so he could be bigger in my eyes than in the country's army that made him small.

I hate racism. It even steals your imagination.

As the war moved on to German soil, so did Dad. Dad told us that "kinky hair" fascinated German kids in towns occupied by the Allies. They wanted to touch Dad's hair to see if it was real. Sometimes the Germans wanted to touch black skin to see if it felt the same as theirs. Sometimes they maneuvered around black soldiers to see if they had tails. White Americans were not the only racists on the planet.

These fascinations—kinky hair, the feel of flesh, the possibility of tails—sound bizarre and inappropriate to us today, but the times *were* bizarre and inappropriate. A German monster tried to capture all of Europe and put it under Aryan rule. That same German devil sought to exterminate an entire race and religion from the European continent.

I think each generation lives in its own bizarreness. That bizarreness makes such perfect sense to the people of that time that the majority live by it, even laugh about it in its time. We make jokes about certain nationalities. We talk in stereotypical voices to diminish those of a different race or sexual orientation from our own. We make insulting gestures mimicking people with disabilities. We snicker when women want to wrestle or box or in earlier times vote. But the bizarreness of any time needs confronting. It needs to be stopped in its tracks. The horror that was Adolf Hitler had to be confronted and stopped. My dad's generation of men walked or drove or got on buses and reported for duty to stand up to it and stop it.

When my time came to confront a bizarreness of my day—the denial of equal access to restaurants, theaters, beaches, voting booths, and public transportation—we walked, we marched, we got on buses, and we reported for duty just as our fathers had. Theirs was a more popular fight even if they were not allowed to fight it.

No, Dad was not present at my birth, and I saw little of him throughout the workweek. Those were the circumstances of his and our lives. On weekends, though, I got some Dad time. He took me fishing, and he taught me how to sit and be quiet. That was hard.

Other weekends Dad took me hiking in the green-capped hills of northern Georgia. Dad loved the outdoors, and he wanted me to love it, too. Usually we walked in Georgia forests full of pine trees and north-Georgia rhododendrons. I'd follow his blue overalls and long-sleeved (even in summer) white shirt up the hills, every now and then stepping on the words *Pall Mall* to make sure the stub of his cigarette was as out as he thought it was. Little kids take things more seriously than adults do sometimes. Springtime hikes led us through tunnels of rhododendron bushes ablaze in brilliant purple and white. I loved the rare days when I had Dad all to myself.

Once, instead of taking me to forested paths, Dad brought me to Stone Mountain, the enormous, bald bluff famous (and infamous today) for the giant sculpture of Confederate "heroes" Jefferson Davis, Robert E. Lee, and Stonewall Jackson. The front side of Stone Mountain looks like a giant, eight-hundred-foot-tall loaf of granite bread sitting on the flat ground around it. The back side is a stone quarry. Granite from the Stone Mountain quarry made the steps of the US Capitol and the locks of the

Panama Canal. Cars in Washington, D.C., drive across bridges made of this Georgia stone, and guests staying at the Imperial Hotel in Japan reside inside it. Stone Mountain is famous for its granite.

It is also famous for the Ku Klux Klan. I've come to learn in my adult life that following D. W. Griffith's 1915 film, *Birth of a Nation,* the KKK rose from near extinction.[3] It rose on Stone Mountain. There on Thanksgiving Eve 1915, a few handfuls of men burned a cross atop it.[4] The next decades saw hoods and robes gather in increasing numbers at Stone Mountain's "Klan Shack" to reinforce their idea of the Southern way of life.[5] They all looked the same in their getups, and they all had the same name: Jim Crow.

Dad knew Stone Mountain was a Ku Klux Klan location on the day he took me on a hike to the top, but he knew they operated there at night. I don't remember how old I was that day, but I know I had no idea what the Klan was.

It was an easy climb even though there was no path. We simply wandered up the hillside littered with stone-size bits of granite and downed tree trunks left behind as victims to the need for harvested rock. In some places, the cut chunks of granite were the size of steps. The closer we got to the top, the bigger the steps became until they turned into walls. Then we had to find a pathway between or around the walls. We made it to the top and didn't encounter the Klan. What we did encounter was a firepit, and I noticed lots of cigarette butts on the ground.

"Do people camp up here, Dad? Can we?"

Dad diverted my attention by making a strange observation. "The folks up here don't smoke my brand," I remember him telling me as if he were protecting me from people who didn't smoke Pall Malls. When I got older, I realized he *was* protecting me, but not from Marlboro or Salem or Camel smokers.

Visiting our relatives in the country was always fun. One

weekend I remember us kids picking blackberries and peaches and ending up in the watermelon patch. Mom raided Great-Grandma's garden and picked tomatoes, green beans, collards, and sweet corn. The soil was so rich you could grow anything in that ground.

The kids fed the chickens and the pigs, and we played all day. There was no television in the country, so we went to bed early.

Sunday afternoon we left for home. We packed all the goodies Great-Grandma gave us along with the vegetables Mom had picked. That day, I watched in horror as my uncle wrung the necks of two chickens. They flopped around the yard till they died. When I saw that, I could not eat those chickens. I told Mom I wanted a chicken that came from the grocery store.

After the chickens were fried and the tea cakes were done, we loaded the car and headed back to Atlanta. I remember being tired and eager to get home.

When the sun went down that night, my dad saw something down the road that made him turn off the road we were on and head across the railroad tracks.

"Where are we going, Dad?" I asked. I wanted to get home.

Dad stopped the car in a neighborhood of shotgun houses. Like 21 Bradley, they had tin roofs, but these homes were built on stilts, not stacks of brick. We didn't know a soul, but porches were full of folks staring at the road from where we had just come.

"Kids, come here. Now."

Dad was not messing around, but I could not figure out why we were stopping at a home with people we did not know. They welcomed us and gave us their porch to share.

I looked down the road and saw a large caravan of cars with strange lights coming from them. Crosses ablaze in fire were fixed on the front of their hoods. They lit the night sky like fireworks.

It was strange, and it was beautiful. I thought a religious service might be starting. The people in the cars were all wearing the same robes. Bright white like the crosses on their cars, and they had cone-shaped hoods that covered their faces with big holes for their eyes but nothing for their noses or mouths. They mostly looked like a group heading to church in their robes, but the hoods made them look like Halloween costumes, not church outfits.

I could tell the adults we were staying with were frightened. Dad and Mom, too. I wanted Dad to explain.

"What is it, Dad?"

The adults talked in whispers I could not hear. The caravan drove right down the street. Car after car looked the same. Churchgoer after churchgoer looked the same.

I did not know the word *surreal* at that age, but if I had, this was that. Mixed emotions filled me: the excitement of the parade; the curiosity of the new; the bright crosses filling the dark sky; the funny church outfits we never wore at our church. All this mixed with a sense of danger and a mood of dread. The adults were not acting the way I was. Their whispers contrasted with my enthusiasm. I felt the way Kenneth looked when he invited me inside Papa's to open the trunk, but I could tell I was not supposed to.

The parade ended. We waited without saying a word. I wanted to scream.

"Why won't anyone tell me what is going on?" my mind yelled.

But when everyone is hushed, you hush up, too. I didn't say a word.

After about thirty minutes—who knows how long it really was, kids can't judge time in any meaningful way—we got back on the road. Dad drove cautiously and in silence. It seemed to me his face and his eyes spent as much time looking into the rear-view mirror as they did looking ahead at the road.

I was confused because Dad was not afraid of anybody, but I knew he was scared. He was concerned for me, for him, for us. Silence. The whole way home to Atlanta.

It's hard to see your father fearful. Like any boy, I looked up to my dad, and I saw him as strong. As the strongest man I knew. I was so proud to be his son. That day, I remember seeing him afraid—physically afraid. That was a difficult day in my life. I did not like seeing Dad scared. No child does.

Dad was a man of few words. That day he gave me no words. So I did not know the meaning of what I was experiencing except that it had a lot to do with fear. Soon enough I would learn—I don't remember how—these men with their crosses and flames and costumes were not Christians, and they scared the hell out of black people. That was my first encounter with the KKK. It would not be my last.

Both of those days—on the weekend hike up Stone Mountain and the drive down the country road—the Klan was nearby and threatening. Neither day brought immediate harm, but both instilled fear. I had no way of knowing that another day would come when I would be face-to-face with the Klan and learn what they were capable of doing. I'm glad that in the days of my youth—the days in the Bottom—I was too young, too innocent, to understand the bizarreness of my times.

Hugh Person's life was hard. In the military, he served his country. At home, he served his family. But work wore Dad out. Dad had to leave work at sixty-four in 1986 after suffering a degenerative disease. He was in the hospital less than a week. Nobody expected him to die, but he did. I think Dad died of being worn-out by the hardship of this life. I think this world was unkind to my father. I miss the Pall Mall Reds, no filter. I miss the transmission-oil smell. I miss the hair combed back. I miss the man I saw so little of and can never see again.

These are the people—Kenneth and Mom and Papa and Dad—who shaped me as a boy. The Bottom is the place that taught me how fortunate and rich I was and am. From Mom, I learned kindness, forgiveness, hard work, and singing. All these gifts I tried to carry with me through life, though singing would get me into trouble a few years down the road.

From Papa I learned the love of learning and precision and patience and waiting. Within a few years, waiting would become more challenging than looking at Papa's coin collection, but patience would serve me well in solitary confinement.

From Dad I learned perseverance through difficulty. Difficulties this Bradley Street boy could not imagine would become reality before long. Difficulty likes to persevere in life, so I would have to persevere to overcome it. I learned that from Dad.

From Bradley Street I learned to be proud of where I came from. I learned how to be decent. I loved living on Bradley Street. And I love that I came from the Bottom. The poorest part of Atlanta protected and sheltered me from a world of which I was unaware, but a world I would come to realize did not value me the way Mom and Dad and Papa and Bradley Street did. Soon I would wake up from the cocoon my Bradley Street blanket wrapped me in during my youngest years. The chrysalis would first get cracks, fissures, and fractures; then it would fall off, and the real world would reveal itself to me. My slumber would come to an end. My awakening was at hand. Soon I would stretch my wings and try to fly.

## Awakenings

My parents handled race by not handling race. They taught us to be human. They taught us to be fair, taught us the value of hard work and responsibility. We were all taught to be of service.

—*David Forbes, cofounder of SNCC*[1]

The cracks in the chrysalis of my youth first appeared when I took my first real job at age twelve at a bowling alley. My uncle George was the maintenance manager at Briarcliff Lanes, and he got me hired to help tidy up the place after he finished his shift and went home each night. My job was to pick up soda bottles, empty wastebaskets, and remove debris when customers completed their games. That was okay, but I could see the future in working at Briarcliff was being a pinboy. Pinboys had spunk. Pinboys, at least in their minds, were the stars of the place. They were a team. They were cool. They were it. And pinboys made more money than I did. As soon as I learned the ins and outs of Briarcliff Lanes, my dreams of sliding down that fire pole at

Fire Station 6 were put on hold. What I wanted to be in life was a pinboy.

The bowling alley was in Briarcliff Plaza in Virginia-Highland—an exclusive white section of Atlanta two miles north of 21 Bradley. All pinboys at Briarcliff were black. Most were high school students. When I started my pinboy career, I was not only the youngest, but also the shortest. Being four feet eleven and weighing eighty-five pounds earned me new names. Here I wasn't Charles or Tony or Bo, I was Shrimp, Mouse, Atom. Everybody knew I liked science in school, so they turned that into a negative. Growing up has growing pains. Growing up small has special ones. Friends and classmates found fun in making fun of me. I suppose I did the same to them. I just don't remember. The pain inflicted on me sticks in my memory. The pain I inflicted on them I've long forgotten.

Picture a bowling alley today. Briarcliff is not that picture. No automatic pin returns. No elevated screens projecting scores. No bright lights illuminating lanes. Or splashy images of falling giant bowling pins on distant walls. No bright digital displays with enticing advertisements. Or shiny waxed lanes reflecting lights, pins, balls, and prosperity. No. Each of twelve dull lanes ended at a small pit that collected downed pins. Behind each pit, a four-foot brown padded-leather cushion smothered flying projectiles and dropped them into the pit for us to retrieve. A slender wooden railing divided each lane and created a perch for us. We pinboys sat atop these railings ready to spring into action after each rolled ball. Our job was to reset the pins, recover the ball, and slide it down one of the ball returns as fast as we could. Sometimes bowlers rolled the second ball to speed up play before we were back on our perch, so agility and quickness mattered. Some boys straddled the wooden railing; others sat with both legs on one side. I straddled. That meant I needed to swing only one leg over the divider to get to work. To me, that created efficiency. Customers admired my hustle and my efficiency.

Bowlers, in those days, came right from work, so they wore business clothes—long-sleeved white shirts, trousers, and ties. In other words, the clientele at Briarcliff was mostly male. And pinboys—being boys—were male, too. No pingirls at Briarcliff. The customers let us know we were boys in the way they talked to us. Sometimes *boy* was used as a common noun, as in "I like it when this boy sets my pins. He's good."

Mostly though, it was used as a proper noun, in place of our names.

"Boy, get to work."

"That's the way to do it, Boy."

That felt different, and the older pinboys didn't like it.

"My name's not Boy," they would tell me, "but I can't say anything if I want to keep this job."

I started to think of the way I did not know the kids where Mom worked as a domestic, and they did not know me. I knew their names, and they knew ours, but none of us knew each other in any meaningful way. Mom spent as much time with them as she spent with us, so you might think we would know them the way we knew, say, cousins. But we were no cousins to them, nor they to us. And Mom was no aunt. An aunt would not have her own particular plate and bowl, as Mom told us she had at the home of her employer. They told her these were "special" dishes for her, and Mom pretended to accept that as reasonable. It must have sounded reasonable to them. The dog where Mom served as a domestic had a bowl of its own, too. But not because he was "special." He had his own bowl because he was a dog. It didn't take much for Mom to understand just how "special" her dishes were or why.

As I became aware of my name at Briarcliff and Mom's table-ware at work, I began to realize there were two different worlds in Atlanta—defined by color—where we knew of each other and liked each other—at least we said we did. I liked my bowlers, and they liked me; Mom liked her second "family," and they liked her. But they did not care about us, and I was at an age when it was becoming apparent to me they never would. No matter how much the family appreciated Mom mothering their children, she always had her "special" bowl and plate. No matter how much a bowler liked me setting his pins for him, he never saw me as Charles or Tony or Bo. He saw me as Boy.

Mr. O'Neill, the owner, expected us to match the customers in dress, so like them we wore long-sleeved dress shirts buttoned all the way up to our necks and dark slacks. Some even wore suspenders. Our looking our best was important to Mr. O'Neill. I didn't understand why, but it helped prepare me years later when we dressed our best during our protests in the Atlanta Student Movement or on the Freedom Rides so we looked like gentlemen and ladies, not like radicals and reactionaries that society wanted to believe we were. Dress mattered at work. It would mean something on the streets of Atlanta and seats of Greyhound and Trailways, too.

Work at Briarcliff for me started at four in the afternoon following school and went till ten, but we had to wait for Mr. O'Neill to finish the books each night because he took us home in his car. Mr. O'Neill was a good man who cared about his pinboys.

I made friends at Briarcliff. Charles Patterson would be on one side of me; Flu Ellen on the other. Pinboys started off working one lane, but once experienced, we serviced two lanes, so more often than not, Flu, Charles, and I were hopping between lanes and not sitting down on the job. Our first priority after each bowled ball was to protect ourselves from airborne trouble. We dodged and ducked. Hands formed our last line of defense to divert the hurt coming our way. Attentiveness, I learned, was an asset in a pinboy.

Next, we needed to get the ball back to the customer. Fast. We set the ball on its way down the railing by giving it the impetus to make it all the way back. Sometimes we failed to put enough oomph on our return. The ball stopped partway. We'd have to walk up the alley to recover our mistake. That was embarrassing. While the ball returned and the customer prepared for his next roll, we cleared the alley of pins that had not made it into the pit. When a strike was bowled or after the bowlers rolled a second ball, we reset the tenpins. The pins had small holes— short, hollow shafts really—in the bottom of them. Each pit had a lever that pinboys depressed with one foot. That brought ten spikes up from the floor upon which we placed the pins. The spikes identified the proper location for each pin. After resetting the pins, we let up on the lever and either hopped over to the adjacent lane or hopped atop the railing for a moment before the next lane was ready to be reset.

Customers tipped us when they were done for the evening by sliding coins—nickels, dimes, quarters—down the alley. We'd rush and gather up whatever they sent our way with the enthusiasm of a child waking up to snow in Atlanta. Tips at Briarcliff were far more common than Southern snow, but every time those coins headed our way, they might as well have been the first flakes of winter.

My days as a pinboy at Briarcliff brought two youthful awakenings to me. The first was one that occurs in the life of almost every American child. The older boys informed me—that would be putting it kindly—there was no Santa Claus. No Santa Claus? I could not believe it. It may be hard to comprehend that at twelve I still believed in Santa, but I did. Their "informing" me came as mockery and belittling. *They* could not believe *I* still believed.

"Mouse believes in San-ta. Mouse believes in San-ta," they would taunt.

"Hey, Mouse, just because the Easter Bunny is real, doesn't mean everything is," they teased.

"Mouse, how can someone as smart as you be as dumb as that," they needled.

I went home and cried my eyes out. I implored Mom to tell me it wasn't so. She didn't.

Discovering the truth about Santa is part of life. Seems like almost everybody, in America at least, goes through that awakening. Santa is part of our culture.

The other awakening I experienced working at Briarcliff was a truth that happened only to Negroes. Down South, it was as much a part of the culture as Santa Claus.

One day, the other pinboys and I stepped out to get dinner on our break. Most days I ate a bologna-and-cheese sandwich Mom had made for me. The first time Mom did not make me a sandwich, Flu and Charles led me next door to the Majestic diner. We walked under its red neon lights proclaiming FOOD TO TAKE HOME, past a wall of glass bricks making it impossible to see inside, till we reached the cutaway corner creating the entrance of the restaurant. Above us a giant, horizontal line of bright red letters spelling MAJESTIC curved around the building. Above them, a glowing vertical sign proclaimed FOOD THAT PLEASES. That place sucked you in with illumination and glitz. Today, the bowling alley is long gone, but you can still sit down for a meal at the Majestic. I learned that night I could not.

We entered. Inside, a long, narrow aisle separated a seemingly endless counter from a row of four-person booths that also stretched as far as twelve-year-old eyes could see. The place was abuzz with business. With every stool occupied, I headed for one of the booths.

"What are you doing?" said Flu.

I looked at him. "What do you mean?"

"We can't eat here."

"Why?" I didn't have a clue.

"We can't eat here. Negroes can't eat here. Don't you know that?"

It was another Santa Claus moment. "We can't?"

"You boys ordering something?" the woman at the counter asked.

We told her what we wanted and stood at the front of the restaurant waiting for it. Not far from us, students not that much older than Flu and Charles were seated on stools and in booths.

"Why can they sit down?" I pointed to college students wearing Georgia Tech clothes. "They have dark skin."

"They aren't Negroes," Flu said. "They're Iranian, I think. Somewhere in the Middle East."

"That doesn't make sense. Their skin is almost as . . ."

The woman delivered our food bagged up. We paid. We left. We ate outside.

That was the day I learned something called se-gre-ga-tion meant we could order food, pay for food, get food, but not eat food inside the premises. We were not sitting down at the Majestic or any of the other nearby diners—the Miss Georgia Dairy, the Deli, the Rexall counter. Instead, at every eatery, we stood in the small entrance, gave the waitress our order, and had to clear the way for non-Negro customers making their way to the counter or booths.

"Just the way it is," Flu Ellen told me.

Those students studying at Georgia Tech intrigued me. They came almost every week, and they always came as a group. I never understood how these international students, many of them as dark as me, were allowed to sit down in a Majestic booth, and I was not.

FOOD THAT PLEASES the sign said. It was a relative term.

Just the way it was.

First no Santa. Next, no seat. These awakenings in my life

were more like Mom trying to get me out of bed on Saturday morning.

"Why can't I just sleep a little longer?" I'd complain. Then I would roll over for a few minutes more of unconsciousness.

Two subsequent events in my young life startled me right out of bed from the slumber of childhood into asking sociological questions I had never considered. One question was "Why?" The other was "How?"

Let's take "Why?" first. That event happened on a bus. On my way to Briarcliff.

For African Americans in the segregated South, the idea of a startling event happening on a bus was not surprising. Buses represented segregation. Everyone knows that now. Rosa Parks brought that to the country's—even the world's—attention with her defiant act on December 1, 1955, in Montgomery, Alabama. What the world learned then, Southerners already knew. The signs made it clear. Whites in front. Blacks in back. In some Southern cities, Negroes paid their fares at the front of the bus, disembarked, walked to the back door, and reentered so as not to "offend" the white folks in front by the mere act of walking past them. Buses in some Southern cities had movable signs. Drivers could move the COLORED sign back a row or two if the white section filled. Moving the sign made more seats available to whites. It also made those behind the sign—that would be us—give up seats. Seats that moments before were perfectly comfortable and perfectly capable of supporting pairs of pants that black men filled or dresses that black women wore, but then, somehow, those seats needed pants and dresses with white skin pressing against the fabric. Peculiar things, bus seats.

Yes, Rosa's singular act taught the world what blacks already knew: We (black human beings) must sit here; they (white human beings) can sit there. Except that Rosa's singular act was not singular. In Montgomery alone, in 1955 alone, teenager

Claudette Colvin defied the segregated seating in March—nine months before Rosa did. Mary Louise Smith did the same in October. Many Negros had personal bus stories, often at a young age, that opened their eyes, taught them a lesson, puzzled their minds, and led them toward their awakenings.

Fifteen years before Rosa Parks defied the laws and customs of Montgomery, thirty-year-old Pauli Murray violated the segregation laws of Richmond, Virginia, by refusing to give up her seat in the front of a bus in 1940. When Murray was also denied admittance to Harvard Law School in 1944 because of her gender, she coined the term *Jane Crow*.[2]

That same year, on July 6, 1944, exactly one month after D-Day, Lieutenant Jack Robinson found himself in custody at what is now Fort Hood, Texas. The Negro lieutenant objected in strong language and forceful posture when the driver of his bus demanded he vacate his seat next to the light-skinned wife of a fellow African American officer. Military police escorted Robinson off the bus, leading to a general court-martial trial a month later. Had the trial ended in a guilty verdict, the world might never have known the man who became the most important figure in the history of baseball. For Lieutenant Jack Robinson went on to become #42 for the Brooklyn Dodgers, Jackie Robinson.[3]

Marcelite Jordan Harris, a 1964 Spelman graduate who became the first African American female major general in the US Air Force, grew up in Houston.[4] Her bus story happened because she was a young girl who simply followed leadership. To Marcelite and her sister, the driver of a bus was the leader of the bus, so she and her sister wanted to sit right behind the driver—right behind the leader—so they could follow him. When they did that one day—when they sat in the first seat on their city bus—an African American woman in the back came up front and kindly led them to the back where they "belonged."[5]

"Mar-ce-lite," society said, "wake up."

And she did. Marcelite learned at a young age this world did not operate for her the way it operated for whites.

My bus story—my awakening—came on a day I had a headache. It happened the year before Claudette and Mary Louise and Rosa experienced their bus stories. It happened in 1954. I was twelve.

I stood at the bus stop with my head pounding. I boarded the bus and paid my fare. I was headed to Briarcliff for work. But I was also headed where I had been taught to head. To the back of the bus. Back to the back I walked to sit where we all sat. The bus pulled away from the curb. Normal day. Normal bus. As the bus picked up speed, it began to make odd sounds in the back. Mechanical noises. Clanging noises. Headache expanding noises. The noises got louder and louder. They exacerbated the pain pounding in my head. They intensified the throbbing. They tweaked my normal complacency into defiance. I needed to get away. I needed to move from the rear of the bus. I rose from my seat, and I walked forward—as far forward as I could—to settle into a seat that gave as much space as possible between me and the harsh sounds.

Like Marcelite's older African American woman, a concerned elderly woman—almost grandmotherly—intervened. She looked at me all the way from the back with eyes conveying something between worry and anger. Probably both.

"What are you doing?" her eyes counseled in silent inquiry. "You'll get us in trouble!" her face warned. "Come back," her body language beseeched.

But I was young. Younger than Claudette, younger than Mary Louise. I was . . . twelve. Just trying to get to my pinboy job at Briarcliff. Just trying to get away from a headache.

"Why should I?" my return gaze asked.

That was the question: *Why?*

"Why should anyone care where I sit?" my twelve-year-old, headstrong self conveyed to her.

The bus driver cared. He glared in the mirror giving me as much of his attention as he did the road ahead of us. He glared as if his eyes would move me on their own.

I was going to stay where I was. There was no reason to do otherwise. I stayed put.

Then a strange thing happened.

Nothing.

Based on my reading of that woman's face, I had thought everything would happen. Everything bad. But nothing happened. Nothing. I rode the rest of the way to Briarcliff and got off the bus. Except for my headache hammering to the vibration of the bus's noise, it was a normal day on a normal bus.

In the larger scope of my life, though, it was not normal.

That was the first event, the first episode I remember that made me think something was wrong. It opened my eyes wide enough to start noticing the reality of the world around me.

The look in that woman's eyes, the pronouncement of her face, the misgiving in her alerted posture, said loudly and clearly, *"Stop!"* Even if I did not have ears or sense to hear it, a sliver of the sound penetrated something in me at that age telling me things were not as I believed them to be, a sliver that pricked me enough to look at the sliver and wonder why it bothered me so much. What did that woman know that I did not? What did she understand that I would come to learn? She shook my norms. She tapped on the concrete innocence of my youth. It had a ring of *hmmmm* that made me question my boyish certainties. My job at Briarcliff was moving me beyond the Bottom. On the way to work, segregation. At dinnertime at the Majestic, segregation. Even in the safe environs Mr. O'Neill insisted upon in the alley itself, it was starting to sink in. Separation. Customers were white; pinboys black. The foul line that bowlers could not cross and the length of the bowling alley between us created a breach not to be bridged.

At twelve, I was ready to see things invisible to me till then. Santa does not exist. Color matters. Lines are drawn that cannot be crossed. Twelve, for me, was the age questions needed real answers. "Why?" was making its way to the front of my thinking. It took a headache on a bus ride and a meal at the Majestic to make that question meaningful.

Bus story after bus story is known today only to the individual teller of each tale. Its meaning specific to the indignity to that person. My guess is Claudette and Mary Louise and Rosa had earlier bus stories in their lives when they, in their innocent youth, sat unwittingly behind the driver of a bus. Or when they changed seats to a row denied them because they had a headache. Bus stories were as common as straws on the camel's back. It was the final straw—Rosa's straw—that began the breaking of the camel. Pauli Murray's straw, Lieutenant Jack Robinson's straw, Marcelite's straw, Claudette's, Mary Louise's, and my straws were just straws. Common as hay. Ordinary as dust. Sending each of us a message that we individually were "other" so that we collectively were substandard. The world was not ours; the world was theirs. The question was "Why?" Why couldn't we belong? Why couldn't it be our world, too?

My next awakening sought the answer to "How?" More to the point, I wanted to know "How could I not know this?" or "How could this be?"

That awakening came in tenth grade.

Tenth-grade civics class taught us citizenship, politics, government, voting duties, and civil debate. It also taught us the impact on society of demographic issues such as age and gender and race. And it taught us about affluent and impoverished populations. I knew about race in America. I got more civics education on race riding that bus to Briarcliff than I did from any classroom. But I didn't know much about poverty and prosperity or scarcity and abundance. I thought what I think every kid thinks. Everyone is like me, isn't he? Everyone is like us, aren't they?

In civics class, we reached a chapter on something called blight. Blight in the context of the lesson was new to me. I associated blight with agriculture—infestation, disease, wilting, dying. My image of blight was of arid soil—barren, cracked, dry, dusty, dirty, gray, lifeless. Now a textbook was broadening my understanding. This chapter on blight had nothing to do with the images in my head. In fact, this application of *blight* had an adjective in front of it: *urban*. Urban blight. I had never heard of it. Urban blight spoke of deterioration of city centers. It told of decline in infrastructure and the decimation of prosperity. Urban blight, I learned, meant that certain populations grow together in distress—economic distress, criminal distress, educational distress—becoming areas of metaphorical plague, pestilence, and . . . blight. Two or three pages into this chapter, a picture slapped me awake. The picture was of *my* neighborhood. Right before my eyes—Bradley Street. *My* street. There it was. The gravel street. The close apartment houses. *Tenements* it called them. My home wasn't a home. It wasn't an apartment. It was a tenement. A footnote on that word taught me *tenement* meant "a house broken up into apartments in a poor section of town." That's where *I* lived. I lived in "a house broken up into apartments in a poor section of town."

The picture stared back at me. It jolted me like a first sip of Scotch. It tasted of a first drink as well. An involuntary sideways snap of my head tried to shake the image from my eyes. I was poor. My family was poor. My friends were poor. We lived in a section of Atlanta seen as infested, decrepit, diseased.

How?

How, I wondered, could I not know this? How could I be fifteen years old when I discovered that my lifelong neighborhood was an example—*the* example—of poverty? Of deterioration? Of crime? Of uneducation? Of . . . of . . . of . . . tenement?

As long as I can remember, I've liked to tinker and build and invent. When I was much younger than a sophomore reading a civics book learning about urban blight, I assembled model toys. Inventors construct prototypes—the original version or representative example of something. It occurred to me that day in that class that to all who read that book—regardless where they were in the United States—my neighborhood, my street, my home, my . . . tenement, would be *the* prototype of urban blight for that reader. Embarrassment made me want to shrink to invisibility. Shame warmed my face to discomfort. A change came into me that day.

Was my living in urban blight connected to my not being welcomed in the front of that bus three years earlier? Was my poverty—my tenementness—the deciding factor in where I could sit on that bus then? On any bus this day in tenth grade? Was it my color alone? Or was it both? I needed to know. I felt as if I needed to do something. But high school was a world unto itself. What could a high school kid do to stand up against the frustrations of the world?

Two more years would pass. The fifties would change to the sixties. Eisenhower would change to Kennedy. Old would turn to young. By decade's end, by high school's end, change was in the air. As I finished high school in the spring of 1960, winds of dissatisfaction roiled. Waters of unrest boiled. Drums of protest were a drummin'. Buses of change were a comin'.

Almost unknown to me, students at the black colleges of Atlanta—Morehouse, Spelman, Clark, Morris Brown, Atlanta University, and the Interdenominational Theological Center— had had enough.

Our parents in their time of awakening had handled race one way: Life is difficult, but it could be a whole lot worse. Get along. They had taught us to work hard in order to be valued and respected. My job at Briarcliff taught me hard work, and Mr. O'Neill showed me respect. Those between our parents' ages and us—Dr. King and his contemporaries—handled race a different way: Enough is enough. Not gonna take it anymore. Gonna stand up by sitting down. Gonna *stride toward freedom.*

Soon it would be our turn to handle race. We, too, would stand by sitting. We, too, would march to gain our freedom. But our answer would also be in song—"Ain't Gonna Let Nobody Turn Me 'Round," "We Shall Not Be Moved." Our answer would be in chants of demand: "What do we want? Freedom! When do we want it? Now!" Unlike our parents, we were not inclined to get along; unlike our icons, we were not waiting till age forty-two (Rosa Parks) or age twenty-six (Dr. King). We, the college-aged Negroes of America, believed our time was now. The day was upon us. I was awake and up for the day.

# 3

## Do Something

What are you going to do about it?

—*Edward Booker (Papa), 1960*

Mom and Dad taught me to take school seriously. Education was important to them, and they expected it to be important to all their children. I was not only to be a good student, but I was to find an academic area of interest and dive into it like a squirrel into a mound of acorns. Like Mom into her faith. Like me into roasted peanuts. Science turned out to be the peanuts.

One thing I remember learning early in science is the concept of metamorphosis. The cadence of the word alone was rhythmic. And it was big—five syllables big. As early as Yonge Elementary School, small me latched onto that big word and its bigger idea: undergoing a complete conversion while moving to a different stage of life.

Science taught me, for example, the caterpillar does not live forever in its chrysalis. As it hangs upside down in its protective shell—its temporary home—a caterpillar has space and time to grow and change. Inside its rigid, safe enclosure, it begins a transformation that starts with digesting itself. Amazing. It literally consumes itself. What kid would not find that fascinating? I know I did.

What the caterpillar has been to that point in its life becomes food to nurture and shape distinct wings, antennae, and legs so different from what it was. It loses itself to become something different and beautiful. Something it is meant to be. Metamorphosis occurs. As it struggles and flaps, the wings fill with fluid and expand to their full size, preparing it to take flight. Even then, the butterfly does not spring forth into the world. It pushes and presses and nudges and stresses the boundaries of its environment.

My chrysalis was 21 Bradley. At Briarcliff, I got a view of life—Caucasian, Negro; customer, employee; bowler, pinboy. On that bus ride I got a feel of reality—them, us; fear, boldness; separation, relegation. From the Majestic, I got a taste of society—ins, outs; welcomed, unwelcomed; sit, stand; stay, leave.

My years in high school, I still needed my chrysalis, as all young people do. There was plenty to digest, more nutrients to form me. I was not ready to shed the shell, not prepared to emerge into the world. Lessons remained. High school tried to teach them. It tried to teach me I was too small to play sports. Fortunately, in some things, I was a slow learner.

I may have been small, but I did not lack for determination. On the David T. Howard baseball team, I played catcher, the position guarding the most important spot on the field. Catchers know they are going to get clobbered because they are the only barrier left keeping opposing players from getting where they want to be. Catchers have to be willing to sacrifice their bodies to protect home base. My four feet eleven inches and my eighty-five pounds did not make much of a barrier. I knew that. I had to prove what was inside me far exceeded my outside.

"Charles, some of these guys play football. You'll get creamed," our coach argued, attempting to dissuade me. Or perhaps save me. In my teen years, that thought did not cross my mind.

"Let me try, Coach," I argued. "Let me show you what I can do."

Coach put me in. He gave me a chance. And he was right.

But so was I.

In one of the first games of my first year on varsity, I got my chance. Man on third. Ball hit to outfield. Catch made. Runner tags. Fielder winds. Runner sprints. Fielder throws. Runner nears home. Ball on way. Eyes on both. Going to be close. Thoughts rush.

"Here it comes."

"Hold on."

"Gonna hurt."

"Hold . . ."

At 21 Bradley, sometimes we'd have creamed corn, sometimes creamed potatoes. On rare occasions, Mom served creamed chipped beef. I looked forward to all three with the anticipation hunger amplifies. That day on that ball field, we got creamed Charles. That was something I never looked forward to after that day, but in my baseball life that something came around with a frequency more like corn and potatoes than chipped beef.

I held on.

That play and that moment gave me a reputation. I may have been small, but I could not be run over without consequence. I could hold my ground. Coach could depend on me. That was important for him to know. It was important for me to know, too. My "gonna hurt" moment taught me that Mom's and Dad's and Papa's influences had metamorphosed me. Their nurture had turned into my nature.

Within two years, other concerns would matter more than

a runner on third coming home. I would be part of a much-bigger team staking our ground, making our stand. When that time came, despite my size I was not going to let people push me around. "Gonna hurt" would be a thought familiar to my future self.

Baseball in high school gave me camaraderie, teamwork, and competition. It was not going to give me a college education. We had talented athletes on our team. My cousin, for instance, got drafted for the pros. I taught him the game, and he excelled. As a Negro, I looked up to Roy Campanella, the first great African American catcher in Major League Baseball. I was good—I batted .400 every year of high school—but I was no Roy Campanella. Brainpower, not athletic prowess, would be my ticket to college. My love of science fueled an aspiration to be an engineer. I knew Massachusetts Institute of Technology (MIT) and Georgia Tech each had a nuclear reactor. In 1960, a nuclear reactor meant state-of-the-art learning. To my mind, the idea of learning about nuclear physics would be roasted peanuts deluxe.

MIT had a program where juniors in high school submitted PSAT scores. Based on that, MIT granted preliminary acceptance. Then, senior year SAT scores and GPA solidified acceptance.

"Mom, I think my scores are going to be good enough."

"Of course, they will be, Tony. You can go to any school you set your mind to."

I sent in my scores and GPA. They were good enough, and at MIT, race was not an issue. As far back as the 1800s, blacks attended MIT. My hurdle was not my intellect. My hurdle was not even my race.

"Mom, I did it. My scores were good enough. MIT accepted."

"Of course, they did, Tony. I'm so proud of you."

"But, Mom, I don't think I can afford to go."

"Tony, you know we can't help you with college. You're going to have to make it on your own."

My mind scrambled to calculate how many odd jobs I would need to pick up to save the money needed. But MIT was beyond my means.

Tuition was almost $2,000 a year. Even if I could have managed that, the expense of room and board and the cost of travel from Atlanta meant my dreams exceeded my reality.

Georgia Tech had outstanding academics, too. It was affordable as well. Just $375 a semester. What Georgia Tech did not have were black students. Soon Georgia Tech would become the first university in the Deep South to admit Negroes without a court order. A proud claim. Unfortunately for me, Georgia Tech achieved that in 1961; I entered college in 1960. A year later my friend Ralph Long would be one of the first three black students to matriculate to Georgia Tech. I was a year too early. But Georgia Tech would teach me a lesson—provide digestible stuff—that would sustain me throughout the trials coming my way. Actually, Papa would do it for them.

Here I was qualified to attend Georgia Tech. I had the grades. I had extracurricular activities—baseball, French Club, Math Club. I had the standing—second in my class and president of National Honor Society. I had the resources to afford it. All that, and I could not attend because of the color of my skin. By every meaningful measure, I was a yes. Yet Georgia Tech said no. That enraged me. It felt unfair because it *was* unfair.

That's when Papa took me aside. "Bo, how are you going to deal with this? What's your next move?"

I did not have an answer. Self-pity immobilized me. Dejection depressed me.

*What's my next move? What does that even mean? I'm supposed to have a "next move"?*

"How should I know what my next move is? There is no next move!" I shouted. "Next move," I repeated in sarcastic frustration. Here I was, shouting at Papa. I had never done such a thing. I could barely believe it possible. My anger at Georgia Tech screamed in the direction of my grandfather. I was furious. Furious about unfairness. Furious about injustice. Furious about being "colored." I fumed.

*If I were white, I'd be going to Georgia Tech.*

I didn't dare express that thought aloud. Papa would have slapped me across the face before the exclamation found voice. And I'd have taken the slap. I would have had to take it. He was my grandfather. He was my Papa. I loved him and, in that moment, hated all things black. Hated all things white. All things.

I didn't have to express it aloud. Papa knew what I was thinking, and he would have none of it.

"Bo!" Papa's voice hardened, his face soured, his posture stiffened, his volume rose. "What are you going to do about it!" It was more exclamation than question. It was more slap than hug.

Papa had never before treated me this way. By nature, he was quiet. Calm. My inaction and my self-directed commiseration angered him as I had not seen in seventeen years. But I had never treated him this way. And I had never expressed such defeat and defeatism.

There are moments in life when you realize you are the problem in your life more than the problem is the problem. *I* was holding *me* back. Papa did not like that and would not tolerate it.

"Do something. Do. Something!"

Something, to me, meant apply to Morehouse College in Atlanta, three miles from home. Morehouse was all-male and one of six institutions—Morehouse, Spelman College (all-female), Clark College, Morris Brown College, Atlanta University, and the Interdenominational Theological Center (ITC)—composing the Atlanta University Center (AUC), a consortium providing African Americans affordable post-high-school educational opportunity. More important, Morehouse was and remains today one of the HBCUs (historically black colleges and universities)

created after the Civil War in collaboration with religious organizations sympathetic to the plight and circumstances that freed
slaves faced. Wealthy white benefactors of faith sought to help
the dispossessed participate in the promise of America, so they
made education possible for African Americans. Industrialist,
philanthropist, and devout Baptist John D. Rockefeller donated
the land for Morehouse's current location. HBCUs worked to in-
still tradition and pride, confidence and conviction, worth and
worthiness in their students. Not a haughty worthiness, but a
worthiness based on equality. A person's humanity made him
or her of equal worth to any other person. Morehouse wanted its
men to know that, believe that, and live that.

That resonated in me. It appealed to me. Papa had never
had the chance to go to college though he was smart enough and
would have been determined enough to do so. But his "What are
you going to do about it?" reverberated in my thinking.

Morehouse, at $350 a semester and an academic scholar-
ship, was even more affordable than Georgia Tech. Its faculty
had some of the best math-science talent—particularly Dr. James
Birnie, a brilliant biologist who worked with the Atomic Energy
Commission—in the South, perhaps the country. Its president,
Dr. Benjamin Mays, was internationally known as a leader in the
Civil Rights Movement and as mentor to Martin Luther King, Jr.

My "do something" moment came in January 1960. Half-
way through my senior year, my next year was set. What was
I going to do about it, Papa? I was going to become a man of
Morehouse.

I did not know that when Papa was issuing his "do something" demand to me, thousands of Negro college students
across the South were already "doing something." I did not
know, for example, the Reverend James Lawson had been conducting Gandhian nonviolent, direct-action workshops at Van-
derbilt University in Nashville at the exact moment Papa was

pushing me to quit feeling sorry for myself. I did not know that thirty-seven-year-old Reverend Fred Shuttlesworth in Birmingham was encouraging students half his age to stand up nonviolently for their dignity and their rights as he was standing up for them at great risk to his life. And I did not know that four freshmen in Scott Hall at North Carolina A&T were becoming annoyed enough to "do something" soon.

Soon came less than a month after my decision to attend Morehouse. While I was deciding my future that January of my senior year at David T. Howard, three hundred miles to the northeast in Greensboro, North Carolina, Ezell Blair, Jr., David Richmond, Franklin McCain, and Joseph McNeil were meeting in their dorm rooms to discuss issues that mattered to them. A common topic for them was their frustration over segregation. Across the fall semester of my senior year when I was saying no to MIT and Georgia Tech was saying no to me, they were saying "Yes" and "Amen" and sometimes "Good Lord" to each other.

On February 1, 1960, the unknown-to-the-world "Greensboro Four" gathered outside Bluford Library following afternoon classes. They knelt. They prayed. They rose. Then they walked. Deliberately. Slowly. Silently. They traversed the one-mile route to F. W. Woolworth & Company.

Department stores in 1960 were the Amazon of today. Everyone used them because they had everything you could want. Including food. McNeil, McCain, Blair, and Richmond, in that order, entered the store. They purchased items—a notebook, a comb, toothpaste—and kept their receipts so they had proof they were paying customers before heading to the lunch counter.[1] Then they made their bold move. Sitting down at 4:30 P.M. in a "white" seat at a lunch counter for the first time in the history of both the store and the city was an act of liberation to each of them. They felt free.

Until they didn't.

They asked for service and were denied. The store manager, Curly Harris, came over and informed the four if they did not leave, he would call the police. Unlike Rosa Parks, who at her arrest—at her freedom moment—told the policeman in Montgomery, "You may do that," the four remained silent.[2] And seated. A policeman came. He walked the aisle behind the four students. They held fast. Uncertainty filled their minds, but no hesitation inhabited their bodies. The policeman took out his billy club.[3] Fear, but no surrender. If he was going to club them, he would just have to club them.

He didn't.

Stalemate.

No service. No succumbing.

They stayed on their stools till closing time at 5:30 P.M. Then the four rose from their stools and left as they had entered. Single file. McNeil. McCain. Blair. Richmond.

It is easy now to believe their actions on that day were a simple—almost quaint—act of civil disobedience because in retrospect we know how the story played out. They were not arrested, not brutalized, not killed. So, six decades later in the twenty-first century, we might think, "What was the big deal?"

It was a big deal in 1960. Five years earlier, fourteen-year-old Emmett Till had been killed for something as insignificant as whistling at a white woman in a grocery store. Small acts deemed inappropriate for people of color had big consequences. McNeil, McCain, Blair, and Richmond knew that and sat at a "white" counter anyway. They did what millions of others could have done but didn't. Getting along, accepting your place in life, and following the rules was what society pressured us all to do. Most didn't want to be the disrupter. The troublemaker. The one who upset the system that was working. It was easier to get along than push against injustice. Getting along let you live. Defying the system could get you killed.

I did not know of their actions on February 1. I was too consumed with my "do something" issue about my own future. What was happening at a lunch counter in Greensboro, North Carolina, on February 1, did not get much attention in Atlanta, Georgia.

Then came February 2. McNeil, McCain, Blair, and Richmond returned. Twenty other students joined them. That got attention. White patrons showed up to confront unwanted black patrons. It turned into a clash of wants. The Greensboro students wanted what the whites acquired at birth. The students wanted inclusion into the life of privilege that whites did not perceive as privilege. They wanted admittance into society as full participants as I wanted admittance to Georgia Tech. And the students wanted acceptance, not rejection or tolerance, of their expectations. For whites, acceptance represented destruction of their way of life. It meant infiltration, mongrelization, loss. Loss of comfort, hierarchy, power. Loss of their pursuit of happiness. Whites, it seemed, had to maintain separation. Lunch counters represented a battle line that was not to be breached. If Negroes were allowed to eat at lunch counters, it would not stop there. "Coloreds" would want to move into white communities, recreate at white parks, marry white women, take white jobs. So, whites barricaded themselves inside walls of fear and possession. Entitlement taught them the world was theirs, and they were not letting anyone else in. Greensboro students wanted in, but not to destroy a way of life. Their desires were for equal access to that way of life. Their desire was to belong.

Police showed up to calm fears and enforce customs, norms, and laws. Media showed up to report and record whatever might transpire. Despite being badgered and bullied, insulted and harassed, the Greensboro students sat in silence expecting to be served and ended up studying instead of eating.

Then came February 3. Sixty students showed up. So did

the Ku Klux Klan.[4] White robes loomed. White hoods hovered. White patrons jeered and mocked and gaped. Tensions rose. Now national media was on hand to tell the story.

And then came February 4. Important in my life, not so much because of what happened in Greensboro, where three hundred students joined the protest, but because of what happened in Atlanta. In Atlanta, three students showed up. They showed up at Yates and Milton Drugstore. Only one of them knew what was going to happen. His name was Lonnie King.

Yates and Milton was a typical drugstore in many ways, but it was a legend to all the students in the Atlanta University Center. Located on a corner across from Morehouse, Clark, and Spelman Colleges, Yates and Milton attracted students like no other establishment. It lived up to its name—*drugstore*—with shelf upon shelf crowded with medicines, drugs, herbs, elixirs, and remedies. Except for a front counter filled with gumballs, chocolates, soda bottles, and a cash register, Yates and Milton seemed more Middle Ages apothecary than modern business. The front of the store was not what attracted students. It was the back. The back had a lunch counter and tables, food and music. Jazz music. Pulsating tunes such as Horace Silver's "Señor Blues" and Miles Davis's "So What" drifted over the tables and penetrated through the customers. Cuts such as "Finger Poppin'" and "Milestones" flew across the air, crisp and clean. Trumpets trilling. Keyboards nimble. And, of course, Coltrane.

These were the sounds in the back of Yates and Milton. And students thronged there to drink the music as much as to eat the food. But Yates and Milton was a wonderful place for guys to meet and just talk. Talk about girls, classes, sports, cars. On February 4, 1960, Lonnie King came to talk about Greensboro.[5]

He sat down at a table—Formica surface, grooved aluminum edge, single metal post supporting it all. He pulled up his chair—four spidery metal legs, a cushioned seat covered in taut vinyl, a sturdy back but split plastic with bits of fiber oozing out. His friend Joe Pierce was waiting for him. Lonnie told Joe what he had in mind, and the two invited Julian Bond to join them at the table.

Lonnie and Julian were a contrast. Not a contrast like apples and oranges. More like a contrast between a knife and a dictionary. Lonnie was a star athlete. Rugged. Stocky. Solid. Strength personified. If you patted Lonnie on the shoulder, your palm hit granite. Your hand hurt. Julian was a writer. Refined. Sophisticated. Erudite. Dignity personified. If you matched wits with Julian without being careful, your brain hit brilliance. Your intellect got hurt.

Lonnie's eyes intimidated. Julian's eyes probed.

Lonnie filled out a suit. A sweater hung on Julian.

If you picked a teammate for football or tug-of-war, you chose Lonnie. If you picked a teammate for a chess match or Scrabble tournament, you went with Julian. It's not that Lonnie was unintellectual or Julian unathletic. They each had multiple strengths. But if you were in Yates and Milton looking for an athlete, you'd move toward Lonnie; if you sought a diplomat, you'd end up with Julian.

"Hey, Lonnie," Julian greeted him.

Agitated elbows struck the tabletop. Two hands formed a single fist in front of King's face. He leaned into the center of the table, his face excited, eyes intense. Typical Lonnie. Typical Julian, too. Relaxed, nonchalant, unexcitable, sipping, not gulping, the coffee he had already ordered.

"Did you see what happened in Greensboro?" King asked.

"I did." Julian's eyes were indifferent, his expression plain.

"Someone ought to do something like that here."

"Someone probably will," Julian said between sips. He set his cup back on the table.

"It's going to be us," Lonnie proclaimed.

That got Julian's attention.

"It's going to be us."[6]

That one sentence started the Atlanta Student Movement. And the earth under Yates and Milton shook.

On February 4, 1960, I could not know Lonnie King meant me when he said "us." Nor could he. I did not know him; he did not know me. What he meant—elbows on table, fist in front of face, face in middle of table—was that he was ready to lead, he was eager to act, he was determined to move. He intended to push and press and nudge and stress the boundaries of Atlanta's environment. At twenty-three years of age.

Lonnie King's movement would need hundreds, perhaps thousands, of followers. It would need the students of Atlanta University and Clark and Morris Brown and the ITC. It would need the women of Spelman and the men of Morehouse. I did not hear him say those words—"It's going to be us"—to Julian Bond in Yates and Milton. But when Lonnie King told Julian Bond that someone should "do something," he was talking my language even though I was three miles away at 21 Bradley Street and four months away from leaving David T. Howard High School. But now I knew where I would be the coming school year. I would be at Morehouse. The streets I would walk from home to Morehouse would take me not only on a path to college, they would put me on the road to my future. A road to Lonnie King, to Fulton County Jail, to the Freedom Ride. All because Georgia Tech said, "No," and Papa said, "Do something."

# 4

## The Leader of the Pack

Raise a glass to the four of us. Tomorrow there'll be
more of us.

—*Lin-Manuel Miranda, "The Story of Tonight," Hamilton*[1]

So there it was. February 4, 1960. The original four students—
McCain, McNeil, Richmond, and Blair—sat on stools at Wool-
worth's drugstore in Greensboro, North Carolina, now with
three hundred students seeking to be served along with them.
King and Pierce and Bond sat at a table in Yates and Milton in
Atlanta, Georgia, just the three of them. I sat in science class at
David T., just the one of me. All happened simultaneously and
independently, but in the mystery of the universe, connectedly.
Because if there were no Greensboro Four, there would be no
three hundred others. No three hundred others, no Lonnie King.
No Lonnie King, leader of the Atlanta Student Movement, no
Charles Person, future Freedom Rider.

The visible image common to all three settings was a stool
or a chair. All of us seated. To me, though, looking back, the

correct image was a bus. F. W. Woolworth & Company was literally at the corner of South Elm Street and Sycamore Street. Metaphorically, the Greensboro Four were at the intersection of Future and Freedom. A bus to their destiny arrived. They got on.

Literally, Yates and Milton was at the corner of Fair Street and Chestnut Street (today James P. Brawley Drive). Metaphorically, King and Bond were at the junction of Integration and Soon. A bus to their futures arrived. They got on.

David T. Howard High School was literally located at the corner of Houston (now John Wesley Dobbs) and Randolph Streets. Metaphorically, I was at the crossing of Graduation and Matriculation. A bus to Morehouse arrived. I got on.

For me, there would be no student activism, no arrest, no jail, no solitary confinement, no Freedom Ride, and no reason to tell this story if not for Lonnie King. Lonnie King determined my future. He determined the future lives of hundreds of others who attended the Atlanta University Center colleges and were moved to activism just as he was moved to action because of Greensboro. In my life, he became the echo of Papa's "Do something." So, it is appropriate to take a moment—a chapter—and add into this memoir a memorial. A memorial to a man who died on March 5, 2019, and who, though well-known in Atlanta, is largely unknown to the rest of the world and to history. But Lonnie King was a giant in the civil rights story of America and in the struggle for freedom, equality, and justice. And Lonnie King was my friend.

While I was living out my high school senior year, Lonnie had set about to "do something." Through the force of his personality, charisma, and determination, King created a movement that shook Atlanta's ground and shifted Atlanta's landscape. In shifting Atlanta, Lonnie King was integral in shifting America. Here is his story.[2]

---

Six years before my birth in Atlanta on September 27, 1942, Arlington, Georgia, gave birth to Lonnie King on August 30, 1936. While I grew up in Buttermilk Bottom, King grew up, as he liked to say, "looking up at the bottom." Born of a mother who was one of seventeen children and a father who was one of eight, King knew family. Until age two. His parents divorced. Then he knew poverty, want, and hardship in abundance. Neither parent was able to care for Lonnie, so he moved in with his grandfather Joseph Smith.

"The bottom was up there," King liked to tell audiences as he pointed an index finger upward. Way upward.[3]

But Lonnie had other things in abundance as well. Desire for freedom. Passion. Commitment. Endurance. Perseverance. Strength. For those qualities, he credited his grandfather.

Like philosopher John Locke, Lonnie King believed what you teach children in the first six years of their lives influences how they're going to be the rest of their lives. He was a disciple of Locke's idea of the blank slate.

"I guess my granddad wrote a few things on my blank slate," he would say. "I know he wrote on my blank slate . . . that 'one day we have to change the system.'"[4]

King knew at an early age the system needed changing because of an event that happened to him in 1942, the year I was born. King was in first grade then. A crop duster flew overhead in Arlington dropping leaflets for the upcoming election for governor. No television ads and no social media campaigns existed back then to get the word out to vote. In rural Georgia, crop dusters were the medium to spread the message. Lonnie wasn't going to vote. He was six years old. And he was black. That's two reasons he couldn't vote. There was just one reason Granddad couldn't or wouldn't vote. His well-being depended on not voting.

Lonnie picked up a leaflet.

Because Granddad Smith valued education, Lonnie knew how to read before going to school. He read the flyer. There was only one phrase on it he did not understand.

"Granddaddy, what is 'the nigger'?" Lonnie asked. "A plane just dropped this, and I picked it up. I can understand everything, but I've never heard of a—what is a 'nigger'? Why do we need to 'keep a nigger in its place'?"[5]

Granddad put Lonnie on his knee and spoke words King remembered to the day he died as "You know, we're still in a form of slavery. The difference is that we can go home at night. We don't have anybody who is an assigned overseer. But . . . the system we're in is one that is oppressive."[6]

*Oppressive.* That was another word first-grader Lonnie needed help with.

Lonnie got an early vocabulary lesson on a word we dance around today by calling it the N-word. Blacks don't get to dance around it. It's a word every young African American encounters and learns and wonders about. You hear the snort of an angry white: "Nigger, don't you ever look at me like that again." You see the sneer of disgust, the narrowed eyes, the lines of hatred carved in a face. You feel tension straining the voice and suspicion aimed at you.

It is meant to hurt.

Hurt in the way a paper cut hurts. At first, it stuns and surprises and causes an involuntary reaction—retraction, really. Then it throbs. You want to shake it off, but it doesn't cooperate. So, you rub it for a while till it stops. Then you forget about it till the next time. The difference is paper cuts are few and far between. As you age, they become rare because you learn how to avoid them. In 1950s Atlanta, there was no avoiding *nigger.* In 1950s Atlanta, the older you got, the more frequent came the cut.

In my life, Grandma Booker talked to me about it. She soothed the paper cut:

"*Nigger* is a word white folks made up because they need to feel good about themselves. It's got nothing to do with you. Or anyone you know. *Nigger* is about whoever says it. It comes from ignorance. You come from forgiveness. When someone says it to you, do what the Great Teacher would do. Forgive him. That's what *nigger* means, Bo. It means it's time to forgive."

That was a lesson I would have ample opportunity to employ across my life because when that word is directed at me or anyone I know, forgiveness is not my first inclination.

Whenever I heard Lonnie tell his airplane-leaflet story across my life, it made me think of Grandma Booker and paper cuts.

Lonnie's granddad recruited members for the National Association for the Advancement of Colored People (NAACP). He told Lonnie as he moved toward school age, "Son, one day, this organization is going to set us free."[7] King believed messages such as that were his granddad painting on Lonnie's blank slate an attitude of resistance to racism and discrimination.

Granddad Smith died when Lonnie was eight, so Lonnie moved to Atlanta to live with his mother again. In Atlanta they attended Ebenezer Baptist Church, Martin Luther King, Jr.'s church, where Martin's father, Daddy King, was pastor. When Lonnie reached high school, Daddy King saw leadership qualities in Lonnie and asked Lonnie to create and lead something—anything—for his classmates. Lonnie formed the Ebenezer Youth Organization. Martin was seven years older than Lonnie and was upstairs in the church practicing preaching while Lonnie held youth meetings downstairs. Martin's younger brother, A.D., and Lonnie became good friends at those meetings.

Because Lonnie's mom did not get off work as a maid till 6:00 P.M., Lonnie hung out at Atlanta's historic and legendary Butler Street YMCA and worked there doing odd jobs for fifty cents a day. Those small jobs introduced Lonnie to the movers and shakers in the black community in Atlanta. King felt these formative things—Grandpa Smith writing on his blank slate, meeting adults at Butler Street YMCA—were God preparing him for what lay ahead when four students in Greensboro decided to take their seats at a forbidden lunch counter and when Yates and Milton would meld his mind with Julian Bond's.

Lonnie started at Morehouse after high school, but he didn't have enough money to stay, so he grabbed an offer from the navy to enlist in what was called a Kiddie Cruise. That meant if you entered before reaching eighteen, the navy would discharge you one day before you reached age twenty-one. In the navy, King was a champion boxer. His boxing brought him esteem; his blackness made him demeaned. Despite having the highest test scores of the recruits, he cleaned restrooms belowdecks for two hundred people who worked up on deck. But Lonnie remembered what Dr. Mays, the president of Morehouse, had told him: "Whatever job you do, do it better than anybody else other than God. And if it's your fate to be a lawyer, be the best lawyer, be the best preacher, best doctor. But if fate falls upon you where you have to be a ditchdigger, be the best ditchdigger there has ever been."[8] So, Lonnie determined to be the best toilet cleaner in the navy.

As he approached his twenty-first birthday in 1957, Lonnie's friend Everett Render, who managed Lonnie's prizefighting career in the navy, encouraged King to settle in San Francisco, where Render was moving. Lonnie's response was "I'm going back to Atlanta and finish Morehouse, Everett. There's going to come a time, I believe, that we are going to throw off the shackles of segregation down there, and I want to be there."

King's Kiddie Cruise ended. He headed back to Morehouse as a twenty-one-year-old freshman in 1958. The star boxer in the navy now became the starting quarterback for Morehouse football. That gave Lonnie a team, a position of leadership, a community of friends, and a multitude of admirers. By February 4, 1960, three days after McCain, McNeil, Richmond, and Blair made their move in Woolworth's, Morehouse junior Lonnie King made his move in Yates and Milton.

King and Bond called for a meeting that day at Sale Hall Annex, a common gathering place for students. Twenty showed up.

"We need numbers to make this work," Lonnie said. "Look what they're doing in Greensboro. We can do it here, too."

Abraham Lincoln's birthday, Friday, February 12, would be the day of action and protest. Lincoln's birthday came. And passed. No protest. Insufficient numbers numbed the effort. A new date—February 19—was set.

Where would Lonnie get the people? That was the pressing issue. King appealed to the people he knew best—his teammates, specifically the players who blocked for him on Saturdays. They responded. Bond appealed to his friends— English majors. They responded. From there it spread out like a sprinkler casting its spray from a single small spot on a lawn and reaching all corners of a yard. Or campus. Or campuses. Morehouse got word. Clark College got word. Spelman got word. So did the presidents of each institution.

Lonnie's phone rang on Wednesday, February 17.

"Mr. King, I'm Mrs. Hill, Dr. Mays's secretary. Dr. Mays wants to see you at three o'clock in the conference room at Harkness Hall."

Julian got a call, too.

"We're in trouble now," Lonnie said to Julian.

The meeting convened. Not just the college presidents and King and Bond, but Student Government Association representatives from all the schools.

"You need to let the NAACP handle this," Dr. Rufus Clement, president of Atlanta University and chairman of the council, said. "Your parents did not send you to Morehouse to start a revolution. They sent you here to get an education. You can lead the revolution later on."[9]

Dr. Mays concurred. Here was a man sympathetic to their cause, a man who had fought a lonely battle against segregation on his own against the very things Lonnie and Julian were railing against. And yet. As president of a college responsible for his students' safety, he could not endorse action that could bring those students into conflict with police and with Klansmen and with police who were Klansmen with the potential for beatings, bloodshed, even death. Fear froze Dr. Mays. Wisdom compelled him to advise caution and delay.

But Lonnie King and Julian Bond were not seeking advice. Or permission.

Dr. King had said in Montgomery in 1955, "There comes a time when people get tired of being trampled over by the iron feet of oppression. There comes a time . . . when people get tired of being plunged across the abyss of humiliation, where they experience the bleakness of nagging despair. There comes a time when people get tired of being pushed out of the glittering sunlight of life's July and left standing amid the piercing chill of an alpine November. There comes a time."[10]

For Lonnie King, that time was now. Now was the time to act and march and sit in and push and press and nudge and stress the boundaries of Atlanta's segregated society. Now was the time to belong in the same society with the same rights and privileges that whites enjoyed, that whites took for granted, that whites denied Negroes. Now was the time.

Then a tremor hit the room.

Dr. Harry Richardson, president of the Interdenominational Theological Center, agreed with the students. The students in his view were right. "I have a Ph.D. I am president of a major institution. I can go downtown and spend my money, buy clothes, buy anything I want down there. But if I want to stop in a nice restaurant to have lunch, I can't go in there. Is there something wrong with that picture? I support the students."[11]

Richardson's words shocked the students and inspired them and affirmed them. King in particular. Richardson gave King hope. Gave him confidence. Made him ready to move. Right then.

Morris Brown College's president, Dr. Frank Cunningham, concurred with Richardson. The vibrations in the room were knocking down fear in freedom's favor. Clement asked who would speak for the students. Everyone knew it would be Lonnie.

"I will," King said. "Atlanta University Center has always been a citadel of higher learning for Negroes, and there is no reason why we should be left behind in the struggle. I will lead the struggle."

With that, the presidents had two pieces of advice they hoped the students would consider and then agree to.

"You need to let the NAACP handle the legal issues," Dr. Clement told them. "They know what they are doing. You don't."

Then came the key moment. The second piece of advice was the moment that made the movement. The Atlanta Student Movement.

"Before you demonstrate, you need to write a manifesto to the Atlanta community explaining why you are doing this and what your grievances are. Put a full-page ad in all the papers. I will raise the money for it."

Agreed. The meeting adjourned.

Back to Yates and Milton.

This time King gathered a larger group at the same table where he had said to Pierce and Bond, "It's going to be us." Now "us" included Charles Black, Morris Dillard, Albert Brinson, and Roslyn Pope. King assigned them the task of accomplishing Dr. Clement's charge: write a manifesto.

Roslyn Pope.

There are names history ignores and students never learn because we monumentalize leaders into giants. Ask almost anyone in America about Dr. King or Rosa Parks. Before they are of school age, most know Dr. King had a dream and Rosa Parks refused to give up her seat on a bus. Nothing wrong with that. Nothing wrong with building monuments to the giants. The monuments give us heroes calling out the best in us. But in seeing the monuments, we miss the cement that is the groundmass and the binding material making the monument possible.

We miss the Roslyn Popes.

Roslyn Pope listened to the ideas of the others at the table. Then she went off by herself and within twenty-four hours authored "An Appeal for Human Rights."[12]

*We, the students of the six affiliated institutions forming the Atlanta University Center—Clark, Morehouse, Morris Brown, and Spelman Colleges, Atlanta University, and the Interdenominational Theological Center—have joined our hearts, minds, and bodies in the cause of gaining those rights which are inherently ours as members of the human race and as citizens of these United States.*

She continued:

*We pledge our unqualified support to those students in this nation who have recently been engaged in the significant movement to secure certain long-awaited rights and privileges. This protest, like the bus boycott in Montgomery, has shocked many people throughout the world. Why? Because they had not quite realized the unanimity of spirit and purpose which motivates the thinking and action of the great majority of the Negro people.*

Buses had come in 1955 Montgomery. Rosa got on. Then got off. And stayed off. So did fifty thousand others in Montgomery. For 381 days. The groundmass rose. The cement held. Desegregation won.

*The students who instigate and participate in these sit-down protests are dissatisfied, not only with the existing conditions, but with the snail-like speed at which they are being ameliorated. Every being wants to walk the earth with dignity and abhors any and all proscriptions placed upon him because of race or color. In essence, this is the meaning of the sit-down protests that are sweeping this nation today.*

Say it, Roslyn. Another bus is a comin'. This time in Atlanta.

*We do not intend to wait placidly for those rights* which *are already legally and morally ours to be meted out to us one at a time.*

The time is now.

*Today's youth will not sit by submissively, while being denied all of the rights, privileges, and joys of life.*

This is the natural cry of every generation of youth to rise and be heard, be acknowledged, and be respected. A change is going to come. This is the call of Parkland students tired of active-shooter drills, tired of fear, tired of death. This is the notification by Black Lives Matter that they are tired of the disproportionate lethal violence against African Americans at the hands of police. They are tired of the Dontre Hamiltons (shot fourteen times by a single police officer) and Eric Garners (killed by choke hold while pleading, "I can't breathe"), the Michael Browns (killed while unarmed by a police officer in Ferguson, Missouri) and Tamir Rices (killed at age twelve while brandishing an Airsoft toy pistol in a park in Cleveland, Ohio), the Walter Scotts (killed while running away from a police officer after being stopped for a broken taillight) and Freddie Grays (injured in a police van in Baltimore, Maryland, and later dying), the Philando Castiles (shot fatally in his car in Falcon Heights, Minnesota, despite informing an officer he was not reaching for his registered handgun) and Jemel Robersons (killed while working as a security guard and pinning down an active gunman in a bar in suburban Chicago), the Ahmaud Arberys (gunned down while jogging), Breonna Taylors (shot eight times in her bed), and George Floyds (killed under the knee of authority).[13]

*We want to state clearly and unequivocally that **we cannot***

**tolerate** in a nation professing democracy and among people professing democracy, and among people professing Christianity, the **discriminatory conditions** under which the Negro is living today in Atlanta, Georgia—supposedly one of the most progressive cities in the South.

We want our freedom, and we want it now.

This was but the start of Roslyn Pope's magnificent appeal, her inspired contribution, her monumental call to all with ears to hear. Education. Jobs. Housing. Voting. Hospitals. Movies. Concerts. Restaurants. Law Enforcement. Pope addressed each area of grievance with demands as radical, as revolutionary, and as normal as Jefferson's core premise: "All men are created equal."[14]

*The practice of racial segregation is not in keeping with the ideals of Democracy and Christianity.*

It is not.

*Racial segregation is robbing not only the segregated but the segregator of his human dignity.*

It is.

*In times of war, the Negro has fought and died for his country.*

He has.

*Yet he still has not been accorded first-class citizenship.*

He has not.

*In spite of the fact that the Negro pays his share of taxes, he does not enjoy participation in city, county, and state government at the level where laws are enacted.*

Sing it, Roslyn.

And she did. Roslyn Pope concluded:

*We, therefore, **call upon** all people in authority—State, County, and City officials; all leaders in civic life—ministers, teachers, and business men; and **all people of good will to** assert themselves and **abolish these injustices.***

Injustice. What is the objection to abolishing injustice? How could Jefferson's words—"created equal . . . unalienable rights . . .

Life, Liberty, the pursuit of Happiness"—be radical and revolutionary almost two centuries after his penning of them? For us, they could not be. Jefferson said it: "created equal." Roslyn Pope appealed for it. For us.

*We must say in all candor that* **we plan to use every legal and nonviolent means** *at our disposal* **to secure full citizenship rights** *as members of this great Democracy of ours.*

Yes, we do.

Take the parts of Roslyn's thinking I have highlighted above in bold text. Read them as an abridged version of her hopes and expectations:

*We, the students, pledge our unqualified support to walk the earth with dignity. We do not intend to wait placidly for those rights. Today's youth will not sit by submissively, while being denied all of the rights, privileges, and joys of life. We cannot tolerate discriminatory conditions.*

*We call upon all people of good will to abolish these injustices. We plan to use every legal and nonviolent means to secure full citizenship rights.*

That sounded reasonable to the students of the Atlanta University Center in 1960. It sounds reasonable to me today. It sounds like the cry of students seeking an end to the Vietnam War, a war I fought in. It sounds like the shout of students in Tiananmen Square, or the silent roar of a single man in Tiananmen Square standing up to a row of tanks. It sounds the way students look atop a crumbling Berlin Wall. It sounds like the scream of Black Lives Matter. It sounds like the activism of Parkland high school students. It sounds like the eternal cry of youth ascendant. Always insistent. Never welcomed.

Her words were not welcomed. Georgia governor Ernest Vandiver went on television the night the "Appeal" was published to denounce it. He claimed Roslyn's document "did not read like it was written in this country." He said the "Appeal" had been written "to breed dissatisfaction, discontent, discord, and evil," and that it could "gain no good for anyone." He said, "The statement was skillfully prepared [and] obviously . . . not written by students." He said, "It has the same overtones which are usually found in anti-American propaganda pieces."[15]

With his televised address, Governor Vandiver sought not only to malign the intelligence and abilities of AU Center students, but to have his audience draw false conclusions. In this case, that Roslyn's "Appeal" had a Communist intent behind it.

It is sixty years later, and politicians do the same today when they devalue and disrespect important African American societal concerns by turning Black Lives Matter into All Lives Matter. Of course, all lives matter. No one argues against that, but changing the issue from "Black" to "All" steals the legitimacy of a vital concern that needs political attention and a political solution. The intentional and insidious shifting of an issue through language is a calculated move. It was by Vandiver in 1960, and it is today. It avoids and insults at the same time. Today, it reemerges in what has been done to Colin Kaepernick. Kaepernick's protest by taking a knee during the national anthem at NFL games has sought to compel our country to focus on the disproportionate violence toward African Americans by police. By making it about patriotism, those opposed to Kaepernick divert attention from a serious matter. Kaepernick's knee had no more to do with patriotism than Roslyn's "Appeal" had to do with Communism. But protest is seldom welcomed, never convenient, always criticized.

Consider Roslyn's words:

"Walk the earth with dignity." What's wrong with that? Yet, the powers that be saw harm in that thought.

Refusing to wait "placidly for those rights." And the problem with that is . . . ? Yet, the powers that be said, "Wait a bit longer."

"Abolish . . . injustices." The Bible I read teaches me to "act justly." The Constitution I read proclaims, "We the People of the

United States, in order to form a more perfect Union, establish Justice. . . ."[16] Nothing wrong with a "more perfect Union" in my book.

Working for "a more perfect Union" sounds to me like Lincoln abolishing slavery. It sounds like women gaining the vote. It sounds like my dad wanting to fight for his country or Lonnie King wanting to sit at a lunch counter. It sounds like a bus picking up passengers on the way to tomorrow.

Lonnie King. Julian Bond. Roslyn Pope. A bus came. A movement started. Representatives of each of the six institutions in the Atlanta University system—Willie Mays (Atlanta University), James Felder (Clark College), Marion D. Bennett (ITC), Don Clarke (Morehouse), Mary Ann Smith (Morris Brown), and Roslyn Pope (Spelman) put their John Hancocks to the document. The ground shook.

"An Appeal for Human Rights" appeared in every Atlanta newspaper—*The Atlanta Journal, The Atlanta Constitution,* the *Atlanta Daily World*—on March 9.[17] *The New York Times, The Nation,* and *The Harvard Crimson* all published it soon thereafter.[18] New York senator Jacob Javits entered it into the *Congressional Record.* The Movement was on the move. Sometimes organized. Sometimes not.

A buzz filled the AU Center campuses. Excitement flowed in anticipation of the enthusiasm of the Greensboro sit-ins coming to Atlanta. Students prepared to start demonstrating; some staff, too. And some before the organizers planned or anticipated. While Lonnie King was forming a united coalition of AU Center students, Atlanta University mathematics professor Dr. Lonnie Cross jumped the gun and led a half-dozen students on a small sit-in at Rich's Department Store.[19] Rich's was considered the prime target of Movement organizers. It had the Magnolia Room, the exquisite, be-all and end-all segregated destination for diners. Negro servers worked in the Magnolia Room, but no Negroes were served there. Negro women wore black dresses with stiffly starched white aprons. Polite deference to the whims of the white female clientele was the expectation. Win at Rich's, the thinking went, integrate the Magnolia Room, and segregation in the rest of Atlanta's stores and restaurants would fall in quick order.

King objected to Dr. Cross moving ahead of schedule. "This will divide us," he complained to Dr. Clement. "We can't have one school demonstrate one day, and another the next day. That's a divide and conquer. Who will store owners and city officials negotiate with? We need to have one voice. One voice only. The common denominator is that we are all being subjected to the same kind of discrimination by the same institutions downtown. We need unity."

Clement agreed. Dr. Cross relented. The students would lead the way.

On March 15—the ides of March—Lonnie led 250 students from all six AU Center campuses to peaceful sit-ins at ten Atlanta restaurants. Seventy-seven arrests followed. The next day the Committee on Appeal for Human Rights (COAHR) came into existence to provide leadership for the Movement. Three students represented each of the six campuses. Those representatives elected Lonnie King chairman.

Across the next month—mid-March to mid-April 1960— problems arose. The largest problem was insufficient support from students. Lonnie King went to his mother.

"Mama, I need your help. I need more students. We're only getting twenty, thirty, forty at a time at our meetings. That won't work. How do I get more?"

"People are afraid," she replied. "Here's what you do. Go to Spelman. The women there know you, Lonnie. They like you. They cheer for you. Appeal to them. Get them on your side. Do that—*do that*—and Morehouse men will come by the busload. Clark will follow. So will Morris Brown."

King's mother was right. He appealed. Women came. Men followed.

The big march was set for Tuesday, May 17, the sixth anniversary of *Brown v. Board of Education*. The press got wind. May 16, *The Atlanta Constitution* headline read, "Student Leader Announces Massive March on Capitol."[20] Hairs on the back of Atlanta's neck rose. Governor Vandiver called out the state police. Law enforcement surrounded the capitol, billy clubs in hand.

Would students show or back down?

The day came, and thirty-seven hundred students came with it. Spelman. Empty. Morehouse. Empty. Atlanta streets. Filled. Lonnie King. Ecstatic. The marchers would march. The enforcers would enforce.

King met with Dr. Mays. "Police Chief Jenkins's jurisdiction ends at the capitol. He's not in charge of state police and cannot protect you on those grounds," Mays said. Mays urged King to back down and cancel the demonstration.

King reminded the Morehouse president of a speech he had given Morehouse men during King's sophomore year. "Your speech was entitled 'Never Sacrifice a Principle for Peace.' You are asking me to sacrifice this principle to end this segregation because I might get killed. In other words, in order to have peace, I've got to leave it alone."

Dr. Mays replied, "Mr. King, where are you going to end up? Sadie and I will be there."

"Ebenezer Baptist Church."[21]

The two men—college president, college student—departed. King returned to the AU Center library grounds, where the students congregated.

"There are people downtown who want to hurt you," King told his fellow students. "This is a nonviolent movement. If you cannot take the blows, do not go. If you cannot afford to be spat on, don't go." If they could not agree to nonviolence as a tactic, he told them not to go. He was not asking them to be nonviolent in their lives, but to use nonviolence as a tactic.[22]

Everyone stayed. No one dropped out. The march was on.

Two by two students made their way toward the capitol, toward Rich's, toward the Magnolia Room. Chief Jenkins met up with Lonnie at the head of the line and started walking with him so he could talk to him.

"It's going to be dangerous at the capitol," Jenkins said.

"I know. Dr. Mays told me you two talked."

"Mr. King, I think you ought not to do this."

"I think we have to do this."

They kept walking.

"Chief, if you give me a direct order as a chief law enforcement in this city, at Whitehall Street, I will turn. I'm not trying to get anyone hurt. We are making a point."[23]

Jenkins gave King the order. King complied.

Why?

King's march scared adults who cared about the students. Parents, professors, college presidents, even police who did not seek conflict, sought a way out of the crisis. Lonnie King had to decide.

"If one student gets killed, I've played into the arms of the enemies of what we are trying to do," King thought.

He backed down.

He had made his point. To save the Movement, King chose caution over confrontation. The march halted at Whitehall. Except for about two hundred students under Charles Black, who did not get the message. They kept marching to the capitol. Violence did not break out, but verbal abuse, threats, and tension did.

That Saturday, May 21, Lonnie called for a boycott of Mann Brothers food stores because of their hiring practices. Blacks as janitors. Fine. Negroes as stock clerks. Sure. But African Americans as managers, assistant managers, or cashiers? Never. Even in Black neighborhoods, in a Mann Brothers store, no blacks in charge. Newspaper articles preceded the boycott linking King's name to Hitler to warn residents of who was on his way to disrupt their lives.

King showed up. Students showed up. Three hundred whites showed up to heckle. One of them charged at Lonnie and threw a canister of solvent on him, burning his eyes, eating through his clothes. King's friends Frank Holloway and Charles Black rushed him to a service station to wash Lonnie's eyes out.[24] No service offered. Now, a black pool hall emptied into the street to meet the three hundred whites. No violence broke out, but again, tension, threat, menace, all hung in the air.

May turned to June. With June, AU Center campuses emptied for summer, bringing an end to the protests. The genesis of February's sit-ins had led to the climax of May's march. But neither sit-ins nor marches had brought desegregation. And now students were gone. And the largest African American newspaper in Atlanta, *the Atlanta Daily World,* stood in direct opposition to the ideals of the protests because white businesses threatened to remove their advertising dollars. With no students and no media support, Lonnie's movement was in danger of collapse.

But Lonnie King was a military veteran. When defeat seemed imminent, when retreat seemed wise, his training taught him to advance. Summer would bring opportunity for the Movement, not an obituary for it. Discrimination had to be defeated. To Lonnie, Atlanta would be segregation's Yorktown. It was time to attack.

First, Lonnie hired Julian to create a new publication, *The Student Movement and You,* to replace the lack of support from the *Atlanta Daily World.* Across the summer, Julian's handbill called for Atlantans to "not spend money anyplace where services, facilites [*sic*], and employment are segregated."[25] Soon, twenty thousand copies of *The Student Movement and You* were being published and distributed on Sundays, until office supply store owner Kossut Hill came to Lonnie with money and a printing press. Hill sought to start a black newspaper to compete with the *Daily World* because of his disgust with its publishers choosing dollars over human dignity. *The Atlanta Inquirer* was born to give voice to the push for equality.

Next came the strategy for the fall campaign. With the *Inquirer* up and running and serving as a mouthpiece for the Movement, people started joining and rejoining the effort. Boycotts would be added to sit-ins and marches. Refusing to buy segregation would force businesses to change. Economic impact would turn the tide. But Lonnie butted heads with others because he thought a strategic delay necessary. Lonnie King delay? Lonnie King pause?

He had his reasons, and they were political.

Lonnie wanted to wait till October to have the first large march of the new school year because of the presidential election. The polls had the election even between John Kennedy and Richard Nixon. Lonnie had some ideas: Wait until late October, invite Martin Luther King, Jr., to join them on the protest lines, and, here was the key, have Dr. King submit to arrest. The attention Atlanta would bring to national politics would compel movement by city fathers and businesspeople. The Atlanta Student Movement needed Dr. King's participation and, more important, his arrest. King called King. Lonnie asked. Martin agreed. Lonnie King was on his way to pulling an "October surprise" before sociologists coined the term.[26]

Finally, Lonnie scheduled to meet with Chief Jenkins and the owner of Rich's. This time instead of talking on the streets of Atlanta, they would converse in the Magnolia Room of Rich's Department Store. Rich's was the king of Atlanta stores; the

Magnolia Room was the queen of the city's banquet rooms. *Look* magazine had written that summer, "As goes Atlanta, so goes the South."[27] Lonnie's thinking was "As Rich's goes, so goes Atlanta." If Rich's would agree to desegregate, the battle would be won. His meeting with Chief Jenkins would be a first attempt at terms of segregation's surrender. Lonnie tried to be seated in the Magnolia Room in an act of singular demonstration when he arrived at Rich's. Rich's closed the room instead of seating Lonnie. No protest could be made, no offense could be taken, if the room happened to be closed for the day.

Lonnie got hot about that. "Big Rich," as the department store owner was known to the students, got hotter: "I've been the best business owner in Atlanta for Negro citizens. I've supported the AU Center. I was the first to ever put *Mr.* and *Mrs.* on the names of Negro customers when we send our bills out. I was the first one to give Negroes charge plates. You need to go back to class. Take your fellow students with you."

"No," Lonnie replied. "You need to change."

"No. You need to leave. I'm going to lock you up and throw the keys away."

"Mr. Richards, I will be back in the fall, and when I come back, I'm going to bring thousands with me."[28]

Fall came. So did the thousands. I was one of them.

## 5

### Man of Morehouse

We have pledged our lives to thee.

—*Morehouse College hymn*[1]

My college marching began the first day of fall semester, 1960. It was not in protest of anything. It was to get to Morehouse. I was not going to live on campus, so I would not be moving into Graves Hall, the oldest dormitory on campus. I would not be experiencing dorm life or making dorm friends for life. I would be walking three miles—Bradley Street to Edgewood Avenue to Hunter Street (now Martin Luther King Jr. Drive) to Morehouse—and back. Living at home would save money and make college affordable, and walking would give me time to think. Two hours of extra thinking time each day. But it would also make me feel lonely and apart. I wanted to be a Man of Morehouse. Commuting to school made me feel more like a Man *at* Morehouse.

I remember wanting to dive into Morehouse waters to see if I belonged in a large pool of stronger swimmers than high school offered. Instead, I was a pedestrian treading my way there. My mom and siblings gave me a hug at the door of 21 Bradley and tried to let me know I'd be fine. Dad had long gone to work. On that first day's walk, my mind shifted from excitement to anxiety, from confidence to questioning. When I arrived at Morehouse, it seemed as if most parents had accompanied their freshmen sons to school, moved them into Graves, and said their goodbyes with hugs and tears on campus.

I was so alone. Morehouse was so big. Tall brick buildings. Deep tradition. Hundreds of fellow freshmen. I looked up at the steeple of Graves Hall. I felt tiny. I looked down at Morehouse ground and felt unsteady. I looked around at all the other students and wondered, "Where do I fit? Do I fit?" It would have been nice to have Mom with me. Dad, too.

Dots are so much easier to connect from a distance of six decades. As I look back, a single bus ride to a bowling alley at twelve years old prepared me for bus rides to freedom at eighteen; a seat denied me at the Majestic in grammar school prepared me for seats that would be denied me in a few months at Sprayberry's and Rich's and Davison's and Kessler's in college; walking to an education at Morehouse prepared me for marching toward desegregation in Atlanta's downtown when I would join the thousands that Lonnie would lead. In retrospect, the dots all connect.

But in the present, I was a typical, nervous freshman. Here was an institution committed to building men of strength and character. Morehouse looked me straight in the face and expected those qualities in me. Here was a call and a charge and a commitment to something beyond me. Here was Morehouse. I hoped I belonged. Arriving with three miles behind me to think about it, I wasn't sure I did. What if I failed? How could I walk back home and tell my family?

"Mom, I'm not enough."

"Papa, I don't have what it takes."

"Grandma, I don't belong there."

"Dad, I'm sorry."

I had challenged myself in high school with preparation for my next steps in life, and this first morning of this first day, I was walking those steps. It was beautiful and exhilarating. It was terrifying. It was Morehouse.

Somewhere on campus, an unknown future friend and current student leader, Lonnie King, was planning events that would invite me in and challenge me in ways the Morehouse curriculum would not. That would challenge me to become a part of the thousands so that an irresistible force would hit an immovable object and prevail. That first day I did not see myself marching toward freedom; I saw myself competing against hundreds of bright kids from all over the country.

First-day testing, I discovered, would determine who would get first-tier professors. I had no idea what made a first-, second-, or third-tier instructor, but I knew what a first-string catcher was, so I wanted to be accepted to first. A reading test determined placement. I was slow, methodical, and deliberate in my reading because I was accustomed to reading scientific material. That took time, and this was a timed test. Slow, methodical, and deliberate landed me in Tier Two. It was Day One at Morehouse. I had already failed in my own expectations for myself.

Compulsory chapel five days a week at 8:00 A.M. introduced us to lecturers who challenged us to conduct ourselves in a Morehouse manner. I remember chapel as being more about building character than deepening faith.

In the classroom, Composition 101 challenged each of us to write like a Morehouse Man. In 1960, every freshman knew Martin Luther King, Jr., had been a Morehouse Man. Class of '48. Everyone knew how Dr. King spoke and that his speaking came from his writing. Writing like Dr. King? Me? I did not think that was in me at all.

Like everyone else, I learned my way around campus and

located the best places to eat lunch. The Atlanta University Center colleges—Morehouse, Clark, Spelman, Atlanta University, Morris Brown, and the Interdenominational Theological Center—were all within walking distance of each other, allowing students to mingle over food. Yates and Milton Drugstore, between Morehouse, Clark, and Spelman, back then had the best chili dogs, milkshakes, burgers, and fries. It also cooked up the best servings of student activism. By the fall of 1960, the tables were alive with students from all corners of AU Center. Many frequented Yates and Milton to plan strategies to be implemented first semester. The hunger they brought with them was not satisfied by anything on the menu. My first visits to Yates and Milton, all I wanted was a hamburger.

The more I hung out at Yates and Milton, the more I learned something was stirring. I heard stories of what had taken place during spring semester and summer months: the ides of March demonstration, the May 17 march, the pool hall confrontation. I began to read Julian's *Student Movement and You*. I saw upperclassmen possess a vitality I did not have, but wanted.

As I heard specific complaints, my frustration with the status quo grew. My desire to join gained urgency. Yates and Milton rumblings of dissatisfaction awakened me more as students expressed infuriating anger over injustices that punctured their self-respect: a sign at the fairgrounds reading NIGGERS AND DOGS NOT ALLOWED with the signature of the mayor, William Hartsfield, below it; a policeman confronting a Morris Brown student, "Nigger, don't you touch my car."[2] *Nigger* stories alone were sufficient cause for us to say, "Enough!" They felt like boils filling with pus. The upperclassmen wanted to lance the infection. They wanted to rid the face of Atlanta from the disgust they felt. Now, I did, too.

Their disgust would show itself in the new semester at the restaurants and theaters, the lunch counters and cash registers. The lance would be economic. They would drive a stake into the financial heart of the city. In the spring, they had taken to the streets and sidewalks to "do something." In the fall, the inactivity of their wallets combined with the movement of their feet would make their voices blare and the system falter.

We freshmen heard, and we saw. But we were not invited in.

A big fall semester demonstration was being planned, and the leaders wanted experienced students, not newcomers, to handle the event. In early October, Lonnie and Julian called an assembly of upperclassmen who wanted to continue the spring demands. Students would conduct sit-ins and kneel-ins. The crowd was large and eager to start.

The date was set: October 19. Lonnie knew he had to raise the stakes or the fall effort would be a repeat of the spring, and nothing would change. To raise the stakes, Lonnie invited Martin Luther King, Jr., to join the marches. Dr. King was back in Atlanta from his six-year pastorate at Dexter Avenue Baptist Church in Montgomery and was serving as assistant pastor to his father at Ebenezer Baptist Church. It was normal for Dr. King to encourage us in our efforts, but with his international fame, he had to measure with care the activism in which he would participate.

On Tuesday, October 18, Lonnie received word Dr. King would not be participating because he would be breaking probation from a traffic ticket. A traffic ticket? A follow-up offense to that small violation of the law could give authorities reason enough to put him in prison for years. That is how the politics of preserving Jim Crow worked in 1960.

Lonnie placed a call to Dr. King. He reminded ML— that's what Lonnie called Dr. King—that Dr. King's father had preached a sermon years earlier entitled "You Can't Lead from the Back." Lonnie pressed Dr. King to join AU Center students.

"Well, ML, you can't lead from the back. You got to lead from the front."

That pricked Dr. King's conscience. "Well, LC"—Dr. King's

nickname for Lonnie C. King—"what time should I come tomorrow?"

"Ten o'clock on the bridge."

"I'll be there."[3]

The next day the march, the pickets, the boycott, and the sit-ins came to Atlanta streets and businesses.

Students dressed in their Sunday finest—suits, ties, white shirts, dresses, scarves—to show the seriousness and the dignity the protest warranted. Placards as tall as dresses, long signs from shoulders to knees, made the demands known:

WE WANT TO SIT DOWN LIKE ANYONE ELSE

JIM CROW MUST GO!

DON'T SHOP HERE

EQUALITY NOW!

Upperclassmen marched two abreast, while we freshmen watched and learned. Dignity and discipline required. Eyes ahead. Calm demeanor. Courtesy. Respect. Determination. Keep marching forward. Forward.

At 10:00 A.M., Dr. King came. He and Lonnie marched side by side. They marched into Rich's. The department store's awning had a taut cloth banner with thick alternating red and white horizontal lines stretched across the marquee that identified Rich's with large serif letters on the white field. Triangular red tassels with white balls at the ends hung from the bottom of the canopy and resembled inverted jokers' hats. In 1960, it was an elegant look. Lonnie and Dr. King entered under the marquee and took the elevator up to the Magnolia Room, a dining room with white tablecloths, white china, white patrons, white everything. Negroes need not enter. Rich's liked money even if it came from black hands. So, we could shop at Rich's as long as we didn't try on clothes, try to use the restroom, or try to eat.

When Lonnie and Dr. King invited themselves to the white opportunities at Rich's, police arrested and jailed them. Then, in the middle of the night, they moved Dr. King from his cell. Alone. In the middle of the night. They said to Reidsville State Prison, two hundred miles away.

But who knew where they were really taking Dr. King? A drive—alone—in the middle of the night—sent terror through the Movement.

The solitary transfer of Dr. King to Reidsville in darkness for a possible four months of hard labor was a moment filled with such peril that presidential candidates—Vice President Richard Nixon and Senator John Kennedy—were contacted to see if they might intervene. Only Kennedy's campaign acted. Senator Kennedy called Mrs. King, who was pregnant with her and Martin's third child, to console her, assure her he was thinking of their family, and let her know she could reach out to him if he could be of help.

That phone call—that one phone call of concern two weeks prior to the presidential election—turned the King family's votes from Republican to Democrat, turned the city of Chicago for Kennedy, and in the view of many, turned one of the closest elections in US history in Kennedy's favor.[4] Such was the impact of Lonnie's strategy to up the stakes in the battle for Atlanta.

October's protest brought immediate compromise but not capitulation. Business leaders called for a monthlong truce to seek a solution to the conflict. Hope filled the air. We lived with a hope that society would come to its senses, but no solution came. The day after Thanksgiving with the start of the Christmas shopping season, the AU Center demonstrations resumed. Rich's. Woolworth's. Davison's. H. L. Green's. Rexall's. McCrory's. Kress. Newberry. All maintained segregation against us. All remained committed to discrimination. All stood in the crosshairs of our aim. But the student focus was on Rich's. If we could break

Rich's, we thought, all the others would succumb. Sign after sign marched down Forsyth Street:

DON'T SHOP SEGREGATION
CAN'T EAT. DON'T BUY
DON'T BUY WHERE YOU CAN'T WORK
END LUNCH COUNTER DISCRIMINATION
WEAR OLD CLOTHES WITH NEW DIGNITY

Across the street from Rich's, white robes, white hoods, white capes, and white crosses in black circles on the left chest marched against us. The Klan was not about to let this be a one-sided affair.

The Christmas boycotts brought decreased sales for Atlanta's stores and increased tension in the city. And now, Lonnie, Julian, Herschelle Sullivan, and the rest of the leadership encouraged freshmen to get involved. I signed up. I showed up. Every day. Every event. Every rally. Some students were part-timers. Their hearts seemed to beat at a slow pulse for change. Others beat faster. My pulse bordered on a get-this-guy-to-the-hospital rate. I took the Atlanta Student Movement personally. I had applied to Georgia Tech and been denied for no legitimate reason. Papa had said, "Do something." This was something I could do. I could see the purpose and effect of my movement in the Movement.

My "doing something" was more than the action of my feet and placing myself on lunch counter stools. It involved reading Gandhi's thoughts on satyagraha (holding on to the truth of nonviolent resistance). It involved committing to our "Oath to Non-Violence" and acknowledging "non-violence does not seek to defeat or humiliate the opponent, but to win his friendship."[5] I vowed to direct my activism against the "forces of evil rather than against the persons who happen to be doing the evil."[6] Reading, discussing, committing, were all integral to our Atlanta Student Movement training and preparation for the struggle ahead.

And my "doing something" meant moving more toward the center of the action. At Yates and Milton, I shifted tables. Now I sat with upperclassman Frank Holloway and fellow freshman Leon Greene. What a contrast Frank was from me. He was six feet four inches and built like the football player he was. When Frank crossed his massive arms and looked down on five-foot-six-inch me, I felt menaced. His crossed arms and fists were about head level on me. I felt as if I should duck. And Frank was my friend. It made me wonder how his physical presence made strangers feel. Frank was someone I wanted to stand with, march with, and be with because he could knock anyone's block off who would try to hurt me. That, in itself, was a crazy notion because we all committed ourselves to nonviolence. But the idea that he could defend me was reassuring.

Leon stood halfway between Frank and me in height. He was so different from Frank. Frank's stoic, stern, serious exterior intimidated. Leon's perpetual smile, jovial nature, constant laughter, and good humor invited. Frank scared me though his voice was marshmallow soft and his spirit as gentle as a rabbit's fur. Leon made me chortle though his conviction was stone.

"Imagine what it's going to be like when we can be clerks and tellers instead of janitors," I remember Frank saying. He, like Mom, was always visualizing a future of possibility.

"Teller?" Leon replied. "That's going to take more marching than we have years left in college." And he laughed and shook his head at Frank's lunacy.

"Then we better get marching," Frank replied, his velvety voice quiet but resolute.

Frank, Leon, and I became known as "the guerrillas." We liked the name because we felt it fit us—a group of unpredictable soldiers harassing the opposition with surprise raids. The three of us could close down any establishment. We would enter a lunch counter and plant ourselves on stools with seats in between us. No white wanted to sit next to a black, so our effort was more effective if we did not sit together. Sitting together would leave only two empty seats—one on either side of us. Spreading out, we could guarantee at least six empty stools.

Once seated, we would ignore any offense taken at our presence. We were determined. We were defiant. Most of all, we were steadfast. We. Would. Not. Be. Moved. Not by threat. Not by intimidation. That does not mean we sat in place till police dragged us from our stools. When we were ordered by officers to get up, we got up. It was important to be obedient to law enforcement. But it was as important to insist on service from the establishment and, like Rosa in 1955, stand up to the denial of our patronage by sitting down.

On one occasion, a manager approached and gave all three of us an opening line common in any establishment we tried to integrate: "You niggers best be moving on."

We stayed. He left. We each picked up a menu expecting to be served as any white person would. Nothing abnormal about that.

Then he returned with a meat cleaver. I had never seen a white customer approached that way. All three of us sat stone-faced holding fast to our menus. I know I was determined to hang on to mine and keep my seat, but I can't say I wasn't relieved when the manager picked Leon to threaten.

"Get your hands off that menu or I'll take them off for you." The manager raised the cleaver to emphasize his point.[7]

Leon sat pat, clenching the menu perhaps out of determination, but I have to think somewhat out of fear. I know I felt sweat forming on my brow, and I was half a counter down from Leon.

The manager grabbed the menu and tried to wrestle it away. Leon succeeded in keeping it in his grasp. The manager raised the cleaver again.[8] Right about then, I think, I might have ducked or at least flinched. But Leon was unshakable. I don't think he so much as blinked. That was the second time within minutes I was glad the manager had picked Leon.

The cleaver stormed off with the manager's hand attached to it, and Leon stayed seated with his hands still attached to him. That was a satisfying moment.

We, all three, put our menus down, pulled out our books, and got to work on our studies. We studied till the restaurant closed, then we left to start again the next day.

At every location we entered, we knew we would not be served, so we used the counters as desks and did our schoolwork. That required a response of some sort from the stores. Before long, the establishments Frank, Leon, and I entered did what many Southern school districts did after the 1954 *Brown v. Board of Education* decision. Instead of serving their clientele, they shut down. In 1955, multiple communities closed their public schools rather than educate Negro children. In 1961, in Atlanta, the same thinking went into action in response to the threat of integration. If we insisted on being served in restaurants, then no one would be served. We demanded. They closed.

But unlike the closed schools of 1955, Atlanta's restaurants had no intention of staying closed. Their tactic was to wait until we left, remain closed for a while, then reopen to their normal— meaning white—customers.

As their tactics changed, so did ours. The Movement brought in walkie-talkies. A car traveled around downtown Atlanta with a two-way radio. As soon as it spotted a reopened store, it called into headquarters and let them know the location. Frank, Leon, and I moved there and occupied yet another lunch counter. Every time a store employed its tactic of closing down and reopening, we employed ours, and a team of our people went into action.

We returned.

They shut down.

Back and forth it went—our presence, their CLOSED signs. Our tactic cost us nothing but our time. Their tactic cost them money. A lot of money. Ten million dollars at Christmastime alone.[9] Our first choice was equal treatment. Shy of that, we wanted them to feel the economic impact of their segregationist policies.

Neither side budged through the fall and through the winter. In spite of huge financial losses, the merchants refused to negotiate with the student leaders.

No one, at least among the students, thought the deadlock could go on an entire year. But it did. February 1961 brought the one-year anniversary of the Atlanta Student Movement. Frustration built as progress stalled. More pressure needed to be placed on the Atlanta business community if we were to defeat segregation. It was time for another bold stroke.

The first demonstration we conducted second semester was a march from the AU Center to downtown Atlanta on February 7. Some of us went to department stores; some went to drugstores; some went to lunch counters. I wanted to go where I had a legitimate reason. For Frank, Leon, and me, that meant the Federal Building on Peachtree Street where eighteen-year-old males had to register for the draft. Sprayberry's restaurant occupied the lower level of the building. Great aromas and tables crowded with white customers pegged Sprayberry's as a place I wanted to experience more than in my imagination. When it came to food and me, dreams were no match for real flavors in my real stomach. I wanted in. So did about twenty more of my Movement friends.

Harold Sprayberry, the owner, was a character. In the October protest, he had pulled out two cans of insect spray and emptied the contents into the air in a double-fisted show of obstinance. On February 7, he simply called Chief Jenkins. The police chief asked us to leave. This time, we refused. That brought arrest. Disturb-

ing the peace was the charge. Standing in line for the lunch buf-
fet. Disturbing the peace. Holding trays of food. Disturbing the
peace. Trying to pay the cashier. Disturbing the peace. Lunching
with friends. Disturbing the peace. The whites in Sprayberry's
were doing everything we were hungry to do. And they weren't
disturbing any peace. It seemed to us that the ones actually disturbing the peace were the officers arresting us.

Paddy wagons carted seventeen of us off to the jail on Decatur Street. Frank and Leon and I climbed inside the shiny black
vehicle resembling a large hearse except for the barred windows.
The door closed. We sat across from one another and our fellow
"criminals" in the dark interior on two benches. The shadows of
the bars cast on us looked like prison stripes. I remember sitting
in silence content to be facing conviction for our convictions.
The wagon stopped. The door opened. Single file we marched out
of the wagon into the jail. We didn't know what lay ahead. It was
as if we were caught in a current sweeping us to whatever was
about to come next down the stream.

Decatur Street jail was a holding area, a drunk tank. It
smelled of urine and sweaty bodies. It was horrendous. I started
feeling nauseated. Maybe if I'd had food in my stomach, it would
have been different, but, then, if Sprayberry's had served us, none
of us would have been in jail to smell the stench. The rot settled
on my empty stomach. I thought I was going to vomit, but that
would only add to the stink plaguing the place. I held it in.

That evening we were escorted into court. We were represented by Attorney Donald Hollowell, who had successfully
sued to have Charlayne Hunter and Hamilton Holmes admitted
to the University of Georgia a month earlier. Police charged us
with trespassing. I don't remember what the bail was, but it did
not matter. We refused it, and we were bound over to the Jefferson Street Jail, a new facility brightly lit with pastel colors and
Muzak to round out the "ambience."

Jail. I could hardly believe it. I had started the day by walking to Morehouse. After morning classes, walking turned to marching. Now marching was turning to stepping inside confinement. What would Mom say if she knew? She thought I was inside a classroom door, and here I was being shown the inside of a door made of bars. She would find out soon enough. There was no mention of a length of sentence. We would know the answer to that when they let us out. The current moved us along.

Between sentencing and incarceration, interesting things happened. The most interesting being the strip search. *That* was an eye-opener. You're a kid. You don't know what jail is like. All of a sudden, they're saying, "Spread 'em." You're thinking, "Spread what?"—because in your mind they could not mean what you think they might mean. But that is exactly what they mean. Humiliation. Degradation. These are the names of the first wardens you encounter.

A police officer led me to my jail cell. I did not know where Frank and Leon were. Down another branch of the stream, I supposed. My cell was 1-E9. Some numbers in life just stick with you. At first, I was the only student in a cell with two other regular inmates. The cell was three solid walls, one of them with the door in it. The back wall of the cell was bars with a catwalk outside for the guards to patrol and watch what we were doing. Stacked bunks—three high—meant I'd be sleeping between my cellmates. Top and bottom were preferred bunks. The bottom for easy access. The top for at least a modicum of freedom. Nothing above you but the ceiling. The men tried to be helpful. They taught me how to roll cigarettes, even though I didn't smoke. They were puzzled why I voluntarily decided to stay in jail.

"Just post bond and get out of here," one of them said.

"That's not the idea. The idea is to fill this place up until there's no more room for us," I replied. Bursting jail cells, we felt, would force a concession from city officials.

I had no way to communicate with my parents directly to let them know my circumstances, but Lonnie and Herschelle could. Both had been arrested. Both had been jailed. But both had bonded out to provide the leadership we needed. They kept tabs on every jailed student and brought us our schoolwork. Along with clergy, Lonnie and Herschelle were the only ones allowed contact with us.

I can't know exactly how my parents reacted when Lonnie and Herschelle told them the news of my jailing. Bars and distance separated us. My sister Carole told me later that tears flowed out of and worry filled up my mom and my two grandmothers. Dad and Papa, Carole said, assured them I was fine. They had no way of knowing that one way or the other, but Mom needed reassurance. Dad provided it, accurate or not.

Each day the cell door opened. More students joined us. A dozen one day. Three dozen another. In a few days, we found ourselves joined by seventy-five other students. Any moderate-size room with dozens of people in it makes for tight quarters. Jail makes it feel more compressed, but we had happy-go-lucky attitudes and high hopes that enough students in jail would force the changes we sought. So, we sang. We sang freedom songs—"We Shall Not Be Moved," "Ain't Gonna Let Nobody Turn Me 'Round"—and we sang songs to let kids know what the count was for that day's arrests: "And before I'll be a slave, I'll be buried in my gra-a-a-a-ve. There are thirty-nine more of us toda-a-ay."

After a while the two regular inmates joined in on our freedom songs. In any emotive situation there is always someone a bit more engaged, a bit more enraptured, a bit more caught up in that particular moment. And a bit more oblivious. That person stands out in the crowd. Six days into the jail sentence, that person was me. Everyone was singing, but one of us was singing too exuberantly. Somehow, they singled me out and decided, "I'm going to show you." I would be made an example. It would be solitary for me.

The guard led me to my new cell on the back side of the jail. He opened the door and gave the slightest nod of his head. The signal was clear. He stopped. I had a few steps to go. I entered in silence. I offered my back to him. There was no sense in turning around. I could have been polite and pleasant and said something insincere such as "Thank you," but I thought a view of my backside was my best form of speech, my sincerest words to him.

The door rang shut. Sang shut for the jailer. The extra force with which he closed the bars intoned a crescendo from his arms. It might as well have been his lungs yelling at me, letting me know the loudness of my singing could not surpass the clamor of his jail cell door. My volume had irritated; his reverberated. I turned to see him disappear to the left, and I was left alone. Just me, a bed, a stool, three solid walls, bars, and a lock. The lock drew my eyes. My focus. I stared at it. It was all I could see. No peripheral vision registered. Just the lock. And by staring at it, it enlarged. Almost as if it were the cell itself. The three walls and bars were not keeping me from my freedom. It was the lock. The damned lock.

There's no way to tell how long I stared at the lock, but the lock was up to the challenge. It seemed like forever, or more like the forever you feel when as a child you get in a staring contest with a sibling or a friend. It was probably a short forever. In my staring contests with Jimmy Dale or Kenneth, one of us would cave and say to the other, "Okay, you win. Let's do it again."

The lock never did that. It never lost the contest. Never blinked. Never moved. It just stared back. Inanimate. Impassionate. Cold.

Moments before I had been with two men who, though threatening in their appearance, expressed support for my incarceration and encouragement for our cause. Now I was alone. My small body felt even smaller here. The purpose of solitary is to make you feel small, make you feel alone. Make you feel abandoned. And, on me, it worked almost instantly. I thought it might be fun, but it wasn't. I remember wishing for Papa because he seemed like a giant to me. That's what I needed now. Size and a companion. Thoughts kept repeating in my head.

"Papa, what am I to do?"

"Will you come see me?"

"Do you even know I'm here?"

"Papa, are you disappointed in me?"

"Did I blow the family's dream of college?"

"Did I 'do something,' Papa? Did I?"

My new cell was about eight feet by ten feet with a single bunk and no windows, so I could not see out. A stainless-steel toilet sat in a back corner. The shine was still on it, but so were brown stains that sent a message they did not care about the comfort of a disturber of the peace. The sight of the steel made me shiver; the sight of the feces made me mad.

One long electrical cord with a single light bulb at the end dangled from the ceiling. It reminded me of a rope with a noose and a head. I wondered if that was intentional. The wattage of the bulb must have been low because the light it emitted was faint. I wondered if that was intentional, too.

The bunk in my previous cell had a mattress cover, but in solitary all I had was a naked mattress and a naked pillow with no casing. No sheets or anything. Just a stained, smelly mattress and pillow. Stained with what? Smelly, why? I didn't want to think about that. But I was there with my thoughts for whatever period of time they decided. Ten days they told me.

After the initial shock, solitary was meaningless. For a while. What was this to me? I had plenty of assets on my side—exercise, imagination, recall of fond memories, mental math, finger-strumming on the bars. That all satisfied for a time, but soon enough solitary returned to agonizing. No reading material; no nothing. Just me. And time. I could spend some time singing, but singing had landed me here. More singing might mean more something I did not want. I didn't think they had any place worse than solitary to send me, but they had as much time as they decided. I kept my singing in my mind. Other things sing in your mind in solitary. At times, I thought I could hear my own heart beating. It wasn't Papa, but at least it let me know I was still alive.

In solitary, the currents of your mind are like tides. Sense of abandonment rises, then falls. Isolation gets to you, then diminishes. Over the days, my confinement turned to a source of strength. It became a contest of me against. Against loneliness. Against doubt. Against uncertainty. Against that damned lock. Thinking it would end in ten days helped.

Mail delivery helped, too. It surprised me that a punishment meant to ostracize allowed for connection. At least one-way connection. I could not send letters. Pens and pencils—not allowed. But mail came in. The most precious one to me said, in part, in all caps:

WE LOVE YOU

WE HONOR YOU

WE RESPECT YOU . . .

*Warmly,*
*Lonnie C. King*

It meant the world. I felt seen. I felt embraced. It was so Lonnie. That letter alone turned punishment into mission. I've kept that letter six decades.

Our leadership decided to get us out of jail on February 23, 1961. The plan was for us to stay in for the duration of our sentences, whatever that proved to be, but because of our excessive absence from classes and the pressure those absences were putting on our leadership, Lonnie and Herschelle decided it was time to post bond. And the merchants had finally agreed to negotiate with the student leaders. That concession from them required a good-faith concession from our side.

The afternoon we were released from jail, many of us went to Paschal's restaurant on West Hunter Street (what is today Martin Luther King Jr. Drive Southwest) in the heart of the Atlanta University Center colleges. Robert and James Paschal were brothers who ran the most popular restaurant in Atlanta serving black clientele. They did much more than that. They gave us food to carry while protesting, money, refuge, and energy. They served us free meals, posted bond when we accepted it, and made their restaurant available for parents to gather when we were in jail. On top of it all, they had the best chicken recipe in Atlanta. In a city that denied us so much, James and Robert denied us nothing and gave us everything they had to give.[10]

Lonnie, Herschelle, and Julian greeted us all. Frank, Leon, I, and others delighted in being reunited. We shared stories of what our time had been like. Our cells, our jailers, our stained stainless-steel stools. Laughter abounded. Tears flowed. And then there was the food. Fried chicken. Corn bread. Peach cobbler. I think we never felt freer than when enjoying food and companionship at Paschal's. We were out of jail. We were at Paschal's. We were free at last.

Solitary confinement proved to be the most challenging

assignment, the most difficult test, of my freshman year to date. But the ten days passed. So did I. A+ I thought. Didn't know how I could have done better. On my release I felt older, stronger, taller. I felt prouder than ever before in my life. I had endured. A year earlier it had been Lonnie and Julian and Herschelle and their fellow upperclassmen. By following the lead of Greensboro, they were leading Atlanta toward a future they demanded. Now the freshmen of AU Center had joined the fight for right. In that fight, my time in solitary felt like a rite of passage. I was ready to do more.

I needed a task. I wanted an objective. I felt like a ballplayer waiting on the sidelines. A "Put me in, Coach" attitude consumed me. The more I thought about the Movement, the less I thought about my studies. School's destination for me was so far off. Desegregating Atlanta seemed so close. Jail had taken me out of school for half a month, and truth be known, I did not focus on catching up. The Movement provided so much more purpose.

Then news broke.

Lonnie and Herschelle called a meeting at Warren Memorial United Methodist Church on March 10. Rumor. Excitement. Anticipation. Not knowing what to expect, two thousand of us showed up and crammed into a space built for half as many. Our protest had prevailed, they told us. A roar rose from deep within us to far above us. The merchants had agreed to open up their lunch counters and also their hiring practices. Smiles. Laughter. Cheers. Dance. Impatience. We wanted to go and check everything immediately.

Then came the "but."

The agreement came with compromise. We quieted. Desegregation would not come until September at the start of fall semester for public schools. If we would stop protesting for six months, the downtown merchants promised, they would desegregate the restaurants and lunch counters. Approval turned to disillusionment. Six more months of waiting. Of exclusion. Of inequality. Stares of disbelief. Why wait? Gradualism again. Always gradualism. Why not now? We felt as if we had been had. A collective groan of rebellion rose.

Lonnie and Herschelle understood. It was not what they wanted, but it was the best they could do. They looked crestfallen. These two beautiful souls epitomized whom we sought to be and what we wanted. They personified courage and determination and perseverance and resilience and grace. They were no disappointment to us. Our grumbling was not directed at them. It was at the postponement of victory. But Lonnie and Herschelle felt what we projected. In their minds, they had failed. They announced their resignations as leaders of the Movement.

We refused to accept. Unanimously.

Their looks said they did not agree and did not understand.

Daddy King, Dr. King's father, tried to address us, and we booed him back to his seat.

He said something like, "I've lived with segregation all my life."

And a woman shouted out, "That's what's wrong!"[11]

Then Dr. King came forward. He wanted to speak to us. But he also wanted to be a shield to his father. As he walked to the front of the church, we parted like the Red Sea. We changed from raucous disrespect for the older, slower generation preaching patience again to a mesmerized, curious quiet to hear what Martin had to say.

First, he greeted us. Then he rebuked us.

He was ashamed of us for how we were acting. Whatever sound was left in the church vacated the premises. Pure silence.

He spoke in metaphors and messages that reached every member present.

Sports. We were on the two-yard line, he told us, pushing for the winning score. The only way we could lose would be to fumble the ball. We were going to score a touchdown for justice.

Health. Why would we succumb to "the cancerous disease of disunity"?[12]

Respect. The older generation offered us wisdom; students offered them courage and energy. We should recognize the value of both.

Legal. If the merchants were to break the sacred contract they made with us, he would march with us in six months' time. We would keep our word. If anyone broke the promises made in the agreement, it would be the white man, not us.[13]

Lonnie would say for the rest of his life, Dr. King's speech that night was the greatest speech he ever made. We would be wise, Dr. King told us, if we made the change gradually. I remember him saying the changes we were making were life changing, and they would be as new to the white community as they would be to us. He had told the people of Montgomery the same thing.

His oratory that night took us from the depths of our despair to the stratospheric heights of our long-awaited freedom. Tears filled his eyes. His arms stretched out to us. As only Martin Luther King, Jr., could, he reminded us of the travails of our travels, and he predicted the promising path ahead. He agreed with us. The compromise was not what we hoped for or wanted, but, he told us, we would reach the promised land. That night we witnessed a preview of what the country would experience in his "I Have a Dream" speech at the March on Washington two years later. His soaring words calmed us down as they raised our spirits. His passion energized our patience. His appeals to us told me the sixteen days I'd spent in jail were worth it. This night told me I was ready for more.

More, it turned out, came on a bulletin board.

In the center of the six Atlanta University Center schools stands a small redbrick church, strong in construction, quiet in appearance, loud in influence. Its name is Rush Memorial

Congregational Church. While Warren Memorial Church had the size to accommodate the thousands who showed up for Lonnie and Herschelle's compromise announcement, Rush had room for hundreds. If people squeezed in. But Rush Memorial was hub and heart of the Atlanta Student Movement. Location made it hub; the Reverend Joseph E. Boone made it heart. When I remember Reverend Boone, I think big, broad, strong, with hands so large there could not help but be fight in his fists. It was his generosity that meant the most. Reverend Boone opened his church's office space to Lonnie, Herschelle, and Julian to conduct the business of desegregating Atlanta. He offered spiritual growth, support, and refuge to students entering the church's doors. His church provided room for us to meet and plan. And Rush Memorial had bulletin boards where students in the Atlanta Student Movement posted notices of upcoming activities— dances, meetings at Paschal's, gatherings at the quadrangle, worship-group opportunities.

Some students used the bulletin boards to vent. I did that a couple of times. I posted my rejection letter from Georgia Tech to let off some steam. I also posted a pamphlet from the KKK to white parents about why they should reject integration. Anything to help keep the spirit alive in us, I thought, was fair game.

Following the March 10 settlement, Frank and I were checking out the bulletin board at Rush when our eyes settled on this:

### FREEDOM RIDE

Freedom Ride, 1961, sponsored by CORE, will be a dramatic move to complete the integration of bus service and accommodations in the deep South. The ride will begin in Washington, D.C. about May 1 and end in New Orleans on May 17. Traveling via Greyhound and

Trailways, the Ride will test the recent Supreme Court decision banning segregation of interstate passengers in lunch room facilities operated as an integral part of a bus terminal. Cost for Freedom Ride, 1961, will be borne by CORE. Participants will need to pay only incidental expenses. For further information, write Gordon R. Carey, Field Director, Congress of Racial Equality.[14]

The notice looked as if it had been cut out of something. On a table near the bulletin board, two mimeographed publications sat in stacks for students to take. One was Julian's *Student Movement and You*. The other was SNCC's *Student Voice*.

I knew about SNCC. The Student Nonviolent Coordinating Committee formed at Shaw University in Raleigh, North Carolina, after the Greensboro sit-ins and meant it when it said "student." SNCC was student driven, action oriented, and impatient for change. It insisted on a consensus model of leadership. Everyone had an equal voice and was free to express it. It acted by 100 percent consensus by hashing out decisions till all agreed. Its headquarters were in Atlanta.

Frank and I picked up copies of each publication and leafed through them. There it was in *The Student Voice*. The same article posted on the bulletin board. *Freedom Ride, 1961, sponsored by CORE, will be a dramatic move to . . .*

"What do you think?" I asked Frank.

"I think I'm going to write Gordon R. Carey."

"Me, too. Do you think he'd take both of us?"

"Maybe. It doesn't say how many they need. It could be they take neither of us, but the best way to find out is to contact CORE."

CORE was new to me. The Congress of Racial Equality, a generation older than SNCC, based its principles on Gandhian pacifism and nonviolence as did SNCC, but with a leader-led hierarchy. CORE focused on national initiatives, where SNCC worked at the local level.

We didn't have a CORE chapter in Atlanta, but we did have an SNCC office. Lonnie was involved in SNCC, and since we had been successful in the Atlanta protests, he encouraged Frank and me to submit our applications.

The application was simple enough. One page long, it explained the ride and touched on the dangers:

> I wish to apply for acceptance as a participant in CORE's Freedom Ride 1961 to travel via bus from Washington, DC, to New Orleans, Louisiana and to test and challenge segregated facilities enroute. I understand that I shall be participating in a nonviolent protest against racial discrimination, that arrest or personal injury to me might result, and that, by signing this application, I waive all rights to damage against CORE—the Congress of Racial Equality, its directors, its officers, any other sponsoring organization, and all others in any way connected with Freedom Ride.[15]

It sounded exciting. It sounded risky. It sounded purposeful. We knew we could handle "protest." We thought we could handle "nonviolent." Jefferson Street Jail had taught me I could handle "arrest."

We filled in the personal information—name, address, age, race, sex, college. The most important part was the qualification part. What experience did we have with nonviolent action? That was easy for both of us. Frank had spent the entire past year marching nonviolently for freedom with the Movement. I'd been involved less than half that time, but had spent ten days in solitary with six more in jail as an appetizer. We both thought we were strong on qualifications.

The one problem of the application for me was the signature part. Anyone under twenty-one needed parental permission. Frank didn't see that as a difficulty. I did. There was no way Mom or Dad would grant me permission at eighteen to stop attending Morehouse, miss final exams, and leave Georgia on a segregated bus in pursuit of another arrest or worse. I had never been out of Georgia with family members. Why would my parents agree to my leaving Georgia on my own? "What are you thinking?" I imagined both their reactions would be.

I needed a response to their refusal, and I didn't have one.

It was time to lie.

I didn't bother going to Mom. She would see right through my lies and would not sign even if she accepted them. Dad was my ticket, if there was to be a ticket found at 21 Bradley.

I told him about the Washington to New Orleans bus trip. I could not avoid that. But I said nothing to him about testing facilities to see if segregationists would abide by a Supreme Court decision most had not heard of and none would agree with. I offered nothing about sitting with a white colleague to see if other whites—passengers, drivers, depot employees, and police officers—would be okay with that. I skipped bringing up traveling through Alabama, Mississippi, and Louisiana with our dignity and our bodies intact. Dad had to know I could not get to New Orleans by bus without going through states that he would prefer I stay out of. But eighteen-year-old brains don't comprehend that adults can see right through their manipulations. And is it a lie if everything you tell your father is true, but you just decide not to tell him everything? Well, it is, but I wanted what I wanted, and I wanted to go on this trip. I wanted to be a part of this effort to make a demand for my generation. This was the "more" I needed after getting out of jail, and it wasn't going to happen if I told the whole truth.

"It's not going to be dangerous," I told my father. "It's going to be an opportunity to go to Washington, D.C., and get advanced training in nonviolent, passive resistance. Nonviolent, Dad. It's the opposite of what you're thinking."

That was the first lie. I had no idea if it was going to be dangerous, but I was willing to find out.

"I'll only be gone two and a half weeks. I can make up the schoolwork."

That was the second lie. No one had told me I could make up my missed exams.

"Like Papa, you've told me to 'do something.' That's why I spent sixteen days in jail. I want to do more. You should want me to do more."

That felt like the truth. I think that's what got Dad to agree. I think Dad looked back on the absence his two jobs created in his family life and the cost of that income. I think he thought about getting me off Stone Mountain before dark and watching for cars with "churchgoers" in funny robes in his rearview mirror. I think he thought about his generation's forced acquiescence to living diminished lives at the insistence of others who had no expectation of diminishing their own.

Dad signed the application.

"If they accept you," he told me. "Get on the bus."

## 6

### On My Way

This will be the last time you ride in the back of the bus.

—*Julian Bond*

Somehow, they selected me. Who knows why? I've never known the answer. My best guess is that CORE wanted someone squeaky-clean. Someone whose idea of trouble was stealing peaches from a neighbor's orchard. Someone who ends up in solitary confinement for singing too loud.

April 25, 1961

Dear Mr. Person:

We are more than happy that you will be a participant in CORE's Freedom Ride 1961. In one week we shall be meeting for a few days of training, planning and orientation in Washington, D.C. We shall stay at:

Fellowship House
945 L. Street, NW

You should arrive at Fellowship House during the
day of Monday, May 1. The first meeting of the Freedom Riders will be held at 7 p.m. James Farmer, national director of CORE, will be the project leader.[1]

CORE enclosed an itinerary. They would be paying the expenses of the trip but not transportation costs to Washington or
from New Orleans. I would need some "pocket money for incidental expenses." Dress expectations were defined:

Participants will be expected to dress neatly at all times.
You should wear a business suit or conservative sport
jacket—preferably with tie. You will need dress-up clothes
for meetings.

Sport jacket and tie would not be a problem. I'd been wearing that to church, I think, as long as my legs reached the floor.
And sport jacket and tie were the dress code of the Atlanta Student Movement for men. We wore suits. The Klan wore robes.
We were nonviolent. The Klan was the Klan. We gave the country a choice. The country would have to decide how that seesaw
tipped. It seemed obvious to us how it should, but add "integration" and "equality" to our side of the scale and "segregation" and
"inequality" to the other, and inexplicably to us—unbelievably
to us—the teeter always tottered back to even at best, to their
direction at worst. Worst was the norm.

The date on the letter was April 25. That was a Tuesday. I
received it on Friday, April 28. I'd have to leave inside of forty-
eight hours. Forty-eight hours to maintain my lies before my

parents would not be able to stop me if they changed their minds.

> If you have any questions please write, wire or call me at the CORE office immediately. . . .
>
> Sincerely,
> Gordon R. Carey
> Field Director

Any questions? I had questions. Why me? was a good one. I'd have selected Frank. I looked up to Frank and aspired to be Frank. Frank projected calmness and self-assuredness. I had insecurities I never detected in him. Frank's confidence was made up of periods and exclamation points. Mine was filled with question marks. Any questions? Yes, I had questions:

They picked me?

Can I really do this?

How do I get to 945 L Street NW once I get to Washington?

Who's going to do all the things Mom does for me?

Mom. What does Mom think of this?

Did they pick the right guy?

Could doing this hurt my family?

Can I back out of this?

Now what?

I did not plan on asking any of them. I was filled with excitement. *They selected me! I get to do this! I'm going to Washington!* I checked to make sure the acceptance letter had my name on it. It did. I was going on the Freedom Ride.

On Sunday, April 30, the irony was clear to me at the Atlanta depot. Here I was in my hometown standing in a segregated bus station where I was about to board and sit in the back of a segregated bus so I could travel to Washington, D.C., and, along the way, deferentially sit in segregated sections of bus depots so that once there I could board another bus (or possibly the same bus) to sit willfully in the front and, along the way, sit purposely in the white sections of the same depots, all so I could get back to where I started.

That irony filled me with anticipation and wonder, confidence and courage, anxiety and puzzlement, worry and guilt.

Anticipation and wonder because this was the adventure of a lifetime. The currents of the Atlanta Student Movement were carrying me toward unknown waters of the national movement. Waters others were depending on me to navigate. The chill running down my neck validated the cool morning temperature, but I don't think Atlanta's weather had much to do with the shiver my body was experiencing. The tingles exhilarated; the shudders provoked.

Confidence and courage because I knew I had this in me. I had sat on a banned cafeteria stool in the Deep South facing a man confronting my friend with a meat cleaver. I had closed down lunch counters with Frank and Leon and been threatened and cursed while doing so. I had spent six days in jail and almost twice as many in solitary confinement. Why shouldn't my confidence be high? I was not going to face anything I had not already seen. Each of these experiences had instilled fortitude in me for the next one. Besides, what healthy eighteen-year-old male is not filled with courage, chutzpah, and cockiness, even if it's misplaced? Not this eighteen-year-old. I had courage and cockiness by the bucketful.

Anxiety and puzzlement because, let's be honest. The bravest lion still turns his head when he hears a squeak. The steadiest acrobat still checks the lines holding up the net. I was excited, and I was confident, but I was not crazy. I had never been on an interstate bus. I had never been out of Georgia. Now, I was in some sense volunteering to be a guinea pig. And as a science student, I knew what happened to guinea pigs. It was never good. So, no matter how much I thought the warnings on the application would not happen to me, I still had a hesitation, a pause, a "hmmm" seeping into the crevices of my being.

Worry and guilt because I had avoided telling Dad and Mom about the real purpose of the trip. I had lied. In my thinking, I did not need them to know what was really going to happen, but I did need them to sign a permission form, and I got them to do it. At least, I got one of them to do it.

Years after the Ride, my sister Carole told me she was present when Dad told Mom my intentions. Tears streamed down Mom's face.

"They'll kill him. They'll kill my Tony," she sobbed.

"Ruby, he'll be all right. He knows how to take care of himself, and he's already been in some hard situations."

"Tell him to stay in school," Carole told me Mom demanded of Dad.

"I can't do that, Ruby. He's eighteen, and he needs to make his own decisions."

"You can tell him anything you want to tell him. He's our son, and he's just a child."

"He's not a child, and he's taking up our fight. I want him to do this."

Both Mom and Dad understood how hard it could go on Negroes "acting up," as whites liked to say. Dad understood and wanted me to step into the struggle. Mom understood and wanted to protect me.

So, here it was. Late afternoon, Sunday, April 30, 1961. Dad dropped me off at the bus station. Lonnie, Frank, Leon, and Julian showed up to see me off. Julian interviewed me for *The Student Movement and You,* and his photographer took my picture. Julian's last words to me were "This will be the last time you ride in the back of the bus."

"Yes, it will," I said in anticipation, wonder, confidence, courage, worry, and guilt. I tried to say it so Julian would only hear the confidence.

I boarded the bus.

Part of me was pure business. Just matter-of-fact stuff. I had to get to D.C. so I could get on with what I had volunteered to do. Part was curious. We all have feelings of being the center of the story we are living. I wondered if folks on the bus wondered why I was traveling alone. Did they wonder where I was going? Did they have an inkling of what I was up to? Decades later I'm thinking they were no more aware of the black kid in the back of that bus than I was interested in them, their destinations or motivations. But I was a teenager then. On my first big trip. My first solo adventure. Doing this meaningful work. Of course they were thinking of me.

I know part of me was thinking historically and metaphorically. I remember choosing to sit in the last row. The very last row. That felt important. In my mind I was more than a passenger. I was a representative. I was not a Negro. I was The Negro. The Negro throughout history assigned to the last row in life, consigned to the back of the bus, resigned to being not just second class but last class. Heading to my seat, I was not only Charles Person born in the Bottom. I was Lonnie King born looking up at the bottom. But I also felt I was mere days away from changing that. A shift was coming.

When I sat in the back—the very back—headed to Washington, D.C., four days before the Ride would begin, in my thoughts I was Jackie Robinson walking into Branch Rickey's office August 28, 1945, in Brooklyn. I was Rosa Parks on December 1, 1955. I was Jack Johnson knocking out James Jeffries. I was Paul Robeson debuting as Othello. I was Marian Anderson singing "My Country, 'Tis of Thee" at the Lincoln Memorial. In my mind, the world was about to shake. And when it did, people would take notice.

In the last seat on that bus was a teenager full of himself, thinking teenage thoughts of heroism and destiny. My sitting in that last row for the last time, as Julian had put it, would be a moment prior to an iconic moment in American history. A bus was a comin' to Washington, D.C., and I was sitting in the back of it. But not for long.

When Julian said, "This will be the last time you ride in the back of the bus," I was on board with that. He was speaking my language. And he was right in the ways he meant it. He meant it in a literal sense as a single trip from Atlanta to D.C.

*Just one more time, Charles. You can put up with it one more time if freedom is on the other side,* his words conveyed.

He also meant it figuratively, psychologically, intellectually, inwardly, soulfully, even spiritually. He meant I would never again, because of my skin color, be imprisoned as inferior to any other person or confined to the caste Southern society assigned me. He meant I would be a fully realized human being as my parents saw me and shaped me before the world of bowling alleys and diners and public transportation and civics textbooks and college admissions and Atlanta jails set about to teach me otherwise. For the last time, Julian was saying, I would comply with subservience.

One way he did not mean it was realistically. Atlanta to Washington, D.C., was not one trip. It was many short trips. Atlanta to Augusta. Augusta to Sumter. Sumter to . . . On it went. Seventy miles here. Ninety-five miles there. One hundred twenty miles. Forty-eight. Each section of the trip, each stop along the way, reinforced the opposite of Julian's Declaration of Independence for my personhood.

Athens: Back of bus.

Augusta: Back there, nigger.

Sumter: Silence. After all, what's there to say when everyone knows his place in the world? Just get back there, black boy.

Rock Hill: Don't try anything here.

Charlotte: Back you go, coon.

So many names—nigger, boy, coon. So little kindness.

Whether spoken or implied, the messages repeated in an endless loop. Verbal utterances tried to diminish me. Silence reverberated. Passengers' visual avoidances stared at me in their own embarrassed ways. Signs reinforced:

THIS PART OF THE BUS FOR THE COLORED RACE

COLORED SEAT FROM REAR

FOR COLORED PATRONS ONLY

Every stop reset the needle on a scratched phonograph record. No, Julian, it would not be the last time I would sit in the back of a bus. It would be the fifteenth to last, the twelfth to last, the third. Not until the last section—Fredericksburg to the nation's capital—would Julian's words become my reality.

And so, I complied and subordinated and deferred and subserved at each stop that last day of April 1961. A new day, not only for me but for America would be coming when the dawn of May 4 broke. It would be another day of awakening, but this time, my fellow Riders and I would be waking up America. The countryside of north Georgia rushed by as I stared out the window imagining the future. I was on my way.

Arriving in D.C., the Greyhound bus drove through the bustle of Monday midday traffic. I had spent most of my ride through the night sleeping, but I was wide-awake as I pressed my face to the window and gawked. There stood Jefferson. There sat Lincoln. There rose the monolith to Washington. We turned north off Constitution Avenue, then right onto New York. The bus pulled into the D.C. station. I exited. Last one off. On purpose. It was symbolic to me.

Outside I looked up at another monolith. In bold, capital letters GREYHOUND rose skyward, one letter atop another towering above me. I felt small. This enormous city in size and meaning could swallow me. I looked straight up at the letters. Beside them was a logo of a sleek, lean, muscular greyhound stretched to its maximum stride as if it were racing away from the station, bounding toward a new destination. In another three days, we would be doing the same. Smooth, rounded corners of this modern bus depot had grooved, shiny metallic, horizontal trim above the entrance. It all created a sweeping sense of motion to the building. This was not a terminal. It was a launching pad to the future. It oozed optimism. In the excitement of the moment, so did I. The outside of the building smiled at me. It said, "Let's go."

I walked inside, and it was as if I were watching *The Wizard of Oz* backward. The living Technicolor of this Oz of a city changed at the doorway to the black and white of the movie's start. The interior spoke of the past or at least of the now. Outside, it was blue and bright. Inside, it was dark and dank. Outside, it smelled of fresh air. Inside, it smelled of cigars and cigarettes and people too close to one another. Crowds cluttered. People crammed facing every direction. The station's purpose was to move people, but immobility prevailed. It seemed more a still photo than a motion picture. Yet, somehow every anonymous person was headed someplace in a picture of patience. Suits and ties, hats and dresses, military men and housewives, businessmen and children, suitcases and trunks, all stood stalled. Some were positioned in endless lines; others rested on endless wooden benches.

I thought of purchasing a local ticket on a city bus to get to

Fellowship House. I asked around and discovered 945 L Street NW was a few blocks north of the station, so I walked. Atlanta's march to freedom had given me plenty of practice walking.

My fears of the nation's capital abated. Cars honked. City noise dominated. It felt like Atlanta. But whiter. Friendlier, too. More smiles on white faces than in Atlanta. That was for sure. At least when looking at me. Maybe it was the tourists. I smiled back. It's my nature. I carried my small suitcase. The letter from Mr. Carey had told me to pack as light as possible. Taxis would not be used in most places, and we would have to lug whatever we brought.

On L Street, I approached a two-story brick house in what looked to me like one of the oldest sections of the city. Before leaving Atlanta, I found out the Quakers owned Fellowship House and used it as a meeting-place refuge for people of peace. I didn't know what Quakers were, so I felt uneasy approaching the building.

The cement sidewalk changed to a brick walkway leading to the front door. As soon as the door opened, the atmosphere changed. A city was behind me. In front stood a woman in a plain blue cotton dress with wrist-length sleeves and calf-length hem. Her fashion was as understated as her voice. Beyond her, I could see the rich, warm, deep, dark colors of woodwork. They contrasted sharply to the cold of city cement, steel, and iron.

"May I help you?" I remember her voice was soothing and soft-spoken.

"My name is Charles Person. I'm here for the Freedom Ride."

Her quiet matched her motion. In an instant, her slow, unconcerned steps made me feel not as if I were a visitor far from home, but as if I were home in the comfort of my own mother's kindness. I liked it.

It took only a moment to discern the heroism I imagined for myself would seem as nonsensical to this woman as it would be to a flower. I was enthusiasm mixed with uncertainty. She was humility mixed with . . . humility, living as God made her—a small, contributing part of His creation. She exuded peace as soon as we met.

I stared at the interior of Fellowship House the way I had gazed at the Greyhound building a half hour earlier. The world inside these walls was quiet and soft. Placid waters resided here, not turbulent cataracts of a cosmopolitan city. Outside, there stood busyness. Inside lay respite.

Then, a man with a bolder aspect approached.

"James Farmer," he introduced himself. "Jim," he said, making it less formal. He extended his hand toward me, an act the woman would not have thought to do. A flower has no need to shake petals with another.

I knew who James Farmer was by sight, by sound, by projection of personality. The head of CORE was the opposite of the woman standing beside him. Here was a man of giant personality and considerable height. I would be looking up to him in at least two ways. His voice as resonant and deep as his personality was tall. His round face was shaped by the fullness of his cheeks, the curve of his wide, black eyebrows, and the sweep of his hairline deep into retreat.

"Charles Person," I responded, matching his enormous smile with my own. My smile beamed as bright as anyone's.

I knew he was at least twice my age. His presence commanded the space in the room and made me think more in terms of "Mr. Farmer" than "James" or "Jim." Standing in Fellowship House between Mr. Farmer and my Quaker host, I felt awkwardly young.

The two directed me to take my suitcase up to the common bunk room where all the men were staying. In quick order, the Riders there introduced themselves to me. I exchanged pleasantries with them as I tried to put names to faces. Walter Bergman looked downright old—almost ancient. Jim Peck. Albert Bigelow. I seemed so out of place. All three were so much older than

I. And all three were white. What were they doing here? All the people in the Movement in Atlanta I had worked with, marched with, gone to jail with, were black. All were from the black colleges of the Atlanta University Center. They, like me, were all frustrated because we could not do what whites could do.

The Whites we encountered in Atlanta were all against us to varying degrees. The hooded ones were life-threateningly against us. They wanted us gone, and six feet under was a way to be gone. The ones with aprons were nervously against us. We were causing trouble at their place of employment. All they wanted to do was scratch out a living, and we were disrupting their opportunity to do that. The ones in suits were politically against us. There were important issues that needed to be addressed, and civil rights was an unwelcomed interruption to their agendas. The ones wearing badges were legally against us. They were paid to uphold the law and maintain the customs. At best, they tolerated our protests in order to make their lives easier. What policeman wants violence to break out when he is on duty? The ones in expensive dresses were outraged or amused by us. Our efforts to infringe in their social territory angered or scared or humored them.

No, I had no experience with white folks stepping forward in the effort to change things. So, why would any of these white people be here? Why would any of *them* want to help *us* make a stand for our right to sit where we wanted on buses or to be served in bus stations?

But there they were, and the three men greeted me with the enthusiasm of friends reuniting. It must have been the building. Fellowship House had a way about it.

"Walter."

"Jim."

"Al."

They each shook my hand as Mr. Farmer had done.

"Charles," I responded, taken aback by the abruptness of

their courtesy. I had never met white people so glad to make my acquaintance.

I chose my bunk and put my suitcase on it, wondering what I had gotten myself into. This was going to be different.

Our first gathering was Monday evening to meet one another, socialize a bit, and get the official welcome from Mr. Farmer. All the Riders assembled as Mr. Carey's letter instructed—coats and ties for men, dresses for women. At least in clothing, I felt at ease. Here, I met the three other white Riders: Frances Bergman, Ed Blankenheim, and Genevieve Hughes. Frances was Walter's wife, and if she had not introduced herself to me that way, I could have guessed it. The two were the oldest among us and looked like people who had been together so long they had grown to look alike. Mrs. Bergman's cat-eye-shaped, tortoiseshell glasses were a match for Mr. Bergman's squarer-shaped lenses. Her short, curled silver hair, and her matronly dress matched Mr. Bergman's gray hair, gray suit, gray everything. The two could hardly have been taken for radical activists. They looked much more like lifelong educators. It turned out they were both. While it was difficult for me to understand why two retired white people as old as my grandparents would fight for my rights, it made perfect sense to them.

"No one has any control over the color of their skin, but everyone has control over how they treat others," Mrs. Bergman told me. "And call me Frances."

I did not think I could call Mr. and Mrs. Bergman "Walter" and "Frances" any more than I could call my dad "Hugh" or my mom "Ruby." I was more likely to call them "Papa" and "Grandma." Whatever I would come to call them, I took an instant liking to them, and they embraced me with the warmth they would give a family member.

Ed Blankenheim and Genevieve Hughes were much closer to my age. Ed, I found out that evening, had joined the Marines at sixteen to fight in Korea. That told me he had gumption and courage. It also told me not hitting back might be a challenge for him. I had thought about joining the Marines ever since Kenneth and I had made that Raid on Peach Tree as children. Ed had done it as a youth. His build was slender and stringy, but muscles obviously hid beneath his clothes. I thought he might be a good choice for me to be with if we were not able to live up to our pledge of nonviolence.

Genevieve was beautiful and accomplished. She had moved up in CORE from volunteer to full-time field secretary. She was a talented organizer and dedicated advocate in the freedom movement. Her shoes were familiar with pavement. Her smile curved upward in friendliness as much as Mr. Peck's was flat and stoic. She, like Ed, had to be a good ten years older than I, but Genevieve caught my attention. Genevieve caught everyone's attention. Mr. Farmer had thought about excluding women in a paternalistic effort to protect them from danger. He also wanted to avoid public accusations of sexual impropriety among Riders. He turned Genevieve down for the Ride multiple times, but her persistence won. With two women on the Ride, one of them married and retired, many of our eyes turned toward Genevieve. All the guys within ten years of her age wanted to pull out her chair and nonchalantly maneuvered to occupy the seats next to her at our meetings.

As I looked around the room at these six white participants mixed in with the other six participants of my skin color, I marveled. "Why are they here?" I wondered. That question was quickly overshadowed as my curiosity turned inward and I asked, "Why am I here?" and "Where do I fit?"

I didn't have time to answer myself. Mr. Farmer started the opening session. He emphasized CORE, the Congress of Racial Equality—its founding, its mission, its reach, its initiatives, its key people.

CORE was founded in 1942, six months before I was born. One of the founders was Farmer himself, and he let us know that. From his telling, he *was* the founder. Sometimes it seemed as if he *were* CORE.

CORE's mission, he lectured, was to bring equality to all people through nonviolent change. It didn't matter what race, what religion, what age, what background. Some of the thirteen of us were relative newcomers to activism, but we all shared exposure to Gandhi's teaching of nonviolence and a connection to working for societal change. Some, such as me, had only a few months of experience at a local level. Others had a lifetime of experience and training and practice. Many of us were brand-new to CORE, while others were veteran members, so these classroom sessions were a bit like church. They were designed to open some of our eyes while serving to remind others of foundational truths they had long ago accepted. This was an organization that really believed all people were created equal. Maybe that's why all these different folks— particularly the white folks—were gathered here for this.

CORE's biggest initiative in its history was something I had never heard of—the Journey of Reconciliation in 1947. Mr. Farmer had been central to that, and across the next two days of classroom work, he would teach us the Journey's importance and connection to Freedom Ride 1961. He talked about key people involved in the Journey. Bayard Rustin. I had heard of him. Irene Morgan. I had no idea who she was.

As Mr. Farmer continued the history lesson, he talked about another key CORE member, a Rider on the Journey— James Peck. Jim Peck. Jim. The white man whose bunk was below mine. That's why he was here. Mr. Peck was continuing a ride he'd begun fourteen years earlier.

There was so much to take in. Mr. Farmer wasn't the only one giving us a crash course that night. He had a lawyer verse us on constitutional law and a sociologist help us understand racial customs and white Southern thinking. Southern thinking was easy enough for me; Southern white thinking had put me in solitary. A social activist explained the dangers of what we were about to face and gave dire—I think most of us thought exaggerated—warnings of the deadly possibilities that lay ahead for us. Death was not out of the question, he asserted. The farther south we traveled, the more dangerous it would become. The Klan, he told us, would not allow our Ride to test their tolerance without giving us a test of endurance.

Mr. Farmer thought it was essential that all of us know the past that had brought us all to this location, this moment, this purpose. Toward that purpose, he would spend time each day teaching us that past as well as preparing us for the challenges ahead. Dates and places mattered to him, but of particular importance were the people who preceded us. They were the real reason we were here. Their sacrifices demanded our respect. Older generations had paid a price; now it was our turn. We were part of a lineage. Our nation had its forefathers. So did CORE. We needed to know their story. So, for the two days before the Ride began, I learned of these people and a history that I had never learned in school but that was shaping my future at that moment. As I learned it, I wondered what exactly I was stepping into, and if my participation over the next two weeks would, in turn, shape history, shape our country, shape the lives of people I would never know.

## Those Who Came Before

What has been will be again,
What has been done will be done again;
There is nothing new under the sun.

—*Ecclesiastes 1:9 (NIV)*[1]

She didn't want to be famous. She didn't want to be a footnote in history. She didn't want to be in the newspapers or make a legal precedent or be the future topic of student history projects. She did not want to be a Marian Anderson, a Paul Robeson, or a Jack Johnson. All Irene Morgan wanted to do on July 16, 1944, was get home. To Maryland. From Virginia. From a two-week visit with her mother. Get home. On a bus. An interstate bus. That's all she wanted to do.

Irene took a seat in the back of a Greyhound bus—third row from the back—in front of a white passenger. That was enough to violate a Virginia law enforcing segregated seating. Three rows from the back. Three rows. That's about as far back as a person can get, but for black Irene Morgan, it was not far enough. Her choice of seat was not a problem until more white passengers boarded the packed bus and wanted Irene's seat. But so did Irene. And she was already in it. That's where the problem started, and that's when the Freedom Ride 1961 actually began. In 1944.

Who had ever heard of Irene Morgan? Not eighteen-year-old college freshmen at Morehouse. At least not this college freshman. High school had taught me history, but it had not taught me current events. Even though Irene Morgan boarded that bus in 1944 when I was two years old, by the time I reached high school in 1956, World War II years were not yet "history." They seemed as current in people's thinking as the recently ended Korean Conflict. No, I did not learn of Irene Morgan in history class. I learned of Irene Morgan at Fellowship House during training for our Freedom Ride. James Farmer made sure of that.

It was six weeks after D-Day when Irene stepped aboard that bus and into the footnotes. Like Rosa eleven years later, Irene stayed seated. Like Rosa, the bus driver summoned the police. Like Rosa, Irene was arrested. Like Rosa, Irene took her case to court. Like Rosa, the case deciding the issue moved up to the Supreme Court.[2] And like Rosa, Morgan won the right to sit where she wanted. Except Irene Morgan won her case ten years before Rosa Parks prevailed in Montgomery. The difference was the Montgomery case was limited to local and state laws and had fifty thousand Negroes marching the streets in a yearlong stand. Morgan's case was obscure and solitary and interstate. In 1946, when the Supreme Court in *Morgan v. Virginia* outlawed segregation on interstate buses, few people took notice. It took two years, but Irene Morgan won her right to sit wherever she wanted when it came to interstate travel.

Kind of.

Something I did not understand when I started at Morehouse but would come to know before freshman year's end is that winning in the US Supreme Court does not mean people will accept the decision. Or that states will abide by the decision. Or that government will enforce the decision. According to the law of the land after the *Morgan* ruling, Negroes had the legal right to sit in any seat on any interstate bus, but that did not mean cities, towns, citizens, and law enforcement would live up to the law of the land.

Would they?

The Congress of Racial Equality (CORE) wanted to know and decided to find out.

Founded in 1942, the same year as my birth, CORE had fifty original members (thirty-three white, seventeen black; twenty-eight men, twenty-two women), committed to using Gandhian-nonviolent, direct-action civil disobedience to challenge oppression.[3] They would create a crisis by staging nonviolent actions that either broke laws they considered to be unjust or that would purposefully and publicly obey new laws that disrupted people's traditions and customs.

James Farmer (black) and George Houser (White) along with four others were CORE's founders, and by our Freedom Ride 1961, the fifty individual members had grown to fifty nationwide chapters.

In 1946, when the Supreme Court announced the *Morgan* decision, CORE decided it would test it by going on a "Journey of Reconciliation," an integrated bus ride through the upper South to find out if people would abide by the new law of the land.

In April 1947 in Washington, D.C., sixteen passengers— eight black, eight white—boarded two buses—one Greyhound and one Trailways—just as we would fourteen years later. Their intent was to travel for two weeks around the states of the upper South to see if the drivers, passengers, locals, and police would comply with the recent ruling.

The NAACP opposed the effort. Thurgood Marshall, a leading NAACP lawyer who would become the first African

American to serve on the Supreme Court, thought the Journey was next to insane and would lead to brutality and lynching. He said, "A disobedience movement on the part of Negroes and their white allies, if employed in the South, [will] result in wholesale slaughter with no good achieved."[4]

There was reason for Marshall's concern. Two months before the Journey of Reconciliation began, a mob of white taxi drivers in Greenville, South Carolina, sought revenge for a fellow cabdriver's murder. They forced themselves into the local jail and dragged African American Willie Earle from his cell. The mob shot and stabbed Willie Earle to death.[5]

There was reason for Marshall's concern. The previous summer, in 1946, a white mob in Walton County, Georgia, dragged two black couples—Roger and Dorothy Malcom and George and Mae Murray Dorsey—from their car, tied up all four, and shot them at point-blank range. Sixty times.[6]

There was reason for Marshall's concern. In 1944, the year Irene Morgan tried to keep her seat on the bus, three white men—one a former state legislator—took fifteen-year-old Willie James Howard from his home in Florida to the Suwannee River at gunpoint. There they bound his hands and feet and gave him a choice: be shot or jump into the river. Willie James Howard chose the river and drowned. Howard's offense was sending a Christmas card to a white classmate expressing affection for her.[7]

There was reason for Marshall's concern. In 1942, two weeks after I was born, a thirty-person mob took Ernest Green and Charlie Lang, two teenage Negroes accused of attempted rape, from the Quitman, Mississippi, jail. After castrating the boys, the mob hanged them from the Shubuta Bridge, known by the locals as the Hanging Bridge.[8] The locals called it that because Green and Lang were not the first, just the latest, to hang from its heights.

South Carolina. Not guilty.

Georgia. Not solved.

Florida. No indictments.

Mississippi. No leads.

There was reason for Thurgood Marshall's concern.

Marshall preferred addressing racial injustice in court-rooms with the force of legal argument rather than on buses, in restaurants, or along sidewalks with the force of public protest.

CORE paid no heed. Without anyone's permission or bless-ing except their own, CORE took to the buses. Across two weeks, CORE's Journey of Reconciliation Riders traveled through the upper South—Virginia, North Carolina, Tennessee, and Ken-tucky. They limited their Journey to those states because they be-lieved Marshall was correct about the Deep South's willingness to kill to protect its customs.

On the Journey, Negroes sat in the front seats; whites sat in the back seats. When confronted by authority, CORE members insisted they had a right to sit where they wanted because of the *Morgan* decision.

It worked. Mostly. But Frederick Douglass was right in 1857 when he said, "Power concedes nothing without a demand."[9] In 1947, power was not giving up.

In Chapel Hill, North Carolina, Mr. Peck took a punch in the side of the head after being surrounded by five angry cabdrivers. Arrests followed. It was the Riders who were arrested. The court ordered four of them to thirty days on a chain gang. Three—Bayard Rustin, for one—served twenty-two days of that sentence.[10]

Despite the violence and arrests, the Journey succeeded. Riders concluded their trip with little controversy. They felt suc-cessful. In the upper South, at least, Jim Crow was in retreat.

But people will find a way.

And after *Morgan*, whites found a way to keep segregation in place. The Supreme Court may have ruled that buses must be integrated, but the ruling said nothing about bus stations:

waiting rooms, restrooms, restaurants. Jim Crow still had his
grip on the terminals. Mr. Greyhound and Mr. Trailways saw to
that. Signs in depots declaring WHITE ONLY, COLORED, NO DOGS,
NEGROES, MEXICANS, remained.

Until.

Until Bruce Boynton challenged the custom in 1958 the
way Morgan had fourteen years earlier.[11] Boynton was a twenty-
one-year-old Howard University student, who, like Irene Morgan, just wanted to get home. He didn't make it. Police charged
Boynton, traveling on a Trailways bus from Washington, D.C.,
to Selma, Alabama, with trespassing at a Richmond, Virginia,
bus stop. His actual offense was ordering a cheeseburger in the
whites-only section of the restaurant. Boynton did not understand or agree with the verdict and chose to do what Morgan had
done fourteen years earlier. He appealed the decision. He lost.
He appealed again. Lost again. Appealed again. And won.

In December 1960, the US Supreme Court reversed the Virginia Supreme Court's decision.[12] Segregation in bus terminal
restaurants, restrooms, and waiting rooms, as in buses themselves,
was now unconstitutional. The Court decided any Bruce, any
Boynton, anybody, could order and eat a cheeseburger anywhere
in a bus depot.

So, where did the idea of Freedom Ride 1961 come from?

The answer depends on who is telling the story. Mr. Farmer
taught us it came from him. He explained that three months before our coming together at Fellowship House, he and Gordon
Carey and Tom Gaither devised the idea after CORE elected him
(Farmer) its national director. The three came up with the name
Freedom Ride because they wanted something short, catchy, and
memorable. From that perspective, the originator of the Journey
of Reconciliation in 1947, James Farmer, was the co-originator of
this latest version. No doubt about it.

But if the question is reframed as who tested the *Boynton* decision first? That has a different answer.

The Court announced the *Boynton* decision December 5, 1960.

The next day—the very next day—Lonnie King held a meeting at Morehouse. In his typical "It's going to be us" form, Lonnie wanted to make plans to see if the country's citizenry would live up to the law's decree. Immediately. Those at the meeting decided to send teams of students to cities throughout the South—Chattanooga, Birmingham, Jacksonville, Athens, and others—to ride buses to see what would happen. Here's what happened. Chattanooga arrested cartoonist Maurice Pennington. Jacksonville arrested Spelman student Norma June Wilson. Athens badgered Morehouse students Charles Black and Otis Moss.[13] The Court may have been ready for desegregation. The South was not.

But before Farmer and Carey and Gaither, before Lonnie and Maurice and Norma June and Charles and Otis, before *Boynton* itself—an entire year before *Boynton*—two college students in Nashville, Tennessee, headed home for Christmas. In December 1959, John Lewis and Bernard Lafayette sat in the first seat on their Greyhound bus directly behind the driver as they traveled to their respective homes in Troy, Alabama, and Tampa, Florida. The driver ordered them to the back. They stayed seated. Furious, the driver pushed his seat all the way back so these two testers of *Boynton* before *Boynton* would be as uncomfortable as possible.[14]

Mr. Farmer concluded his lesson on the debt owed to Irene Morgan and Bruce Boynton. I looked across the training-room table at Fellowship House. There sat John Lewis ready and willing to insist on everyone's right to sit wherever he or she desired on public transportation.

So, who contrived the Freedom Ride? Mr. Farmer, Thomas Gaither, and Gordon Carey. No question about it. Who came up with the name? Same answer. But who tested *Boynton* first? Lonnie King with the students of the Atlanta Student Movement. And who threw the glove of challenge down before *Boynton*? John Lewis and Bernard Lafayette, both members of the Nashville Movement. It all made sense. "It's going to be us" was the clarion call of Lonnie King; "We want our freedom, and we want it now," the clarion call of John Lewis.

I learned none of this in school. Irene Morgan? CORE? Gaither? Terry? I knew none of these names before Fellowship House, but Fellowship House schooled me on all of them—on the people and events that came before Lonnie and John and Bernard, and that came before I became part of the Movement.

These people and this organization, CORE, had made their efforts in my lifetime. My lifetime. And I was blind to it. No more. I wanted to learn more. Lonnie and Herschelle and Julian and the other students who helped me find my heart and provided the kindling for my personal fire all taught me that this effort, this movement, this "stride toward freedom" as Dr. King had called the Montgomery Bus Protest, were not the result of a single person saying, "Enough!" The students of Atlanta and Nashville, like the citizens of Montgomery, were legion. The leaders had nothing without the foot soldiers marching with them.

That's how I saw myself—a single foot soldier in an army of thousands. Now, perhaps, that foot soldier was ascending to a role of minor leader. But perhaps not. Perhaps instead, that foot soldier was on an ascending staircase to his adult sensibilities of justice. Perhaps that foot soldier was on a climb toward understanding the freedom struggle—a climb toward understanding his role and responsibility in it.

I was not leading. I was progressing. I was progressing with my country in the direction of hope. I was progressing toward a destination of, as Dr. King commonly said, a "Beloved Community." That Beloved Community, Dr. King taught and Mr. Farmer reinforced, would be a nation reconciled to love and trust so that peace, nonviolence, brotherhood, and understanding would replace racism, prejudice, hatred, and bigotry. I wanted to be an active participant in that walk, that march, that bus ride to justice, that community of brotherhood.

These heroes of mine—not only Dr. King and Rosa Parks, but Irene Morgan and Bruce Boynton, Lonnie King and Julian Bond and Herschelle Sullivan—all came before me whether by years or by months, but I gladly followed their direction, in step with all of them in seeing every acquaintance as a possible friend. Six decades later, I still do.

# 8

## Training in Washington, D.C.

And before I'd be a slave,
I'd be buried in my grave
And go home to my Lord
And be free.

*—Freedom song "Oh, Freedom"*[1]

"What are you going to do when your bus driver tells you to move to the back?" Mr. Farmer asked.

Silence.

Thirteen of us sat around a table in the Fellowship House meeting room on Tuesday, May 2. People processed Mr. Farmer's question and began to offer replies.

"Refuse."

"Stay seated."

"Look him in the eye and keep quiet."

"No. Avoid his eyes as if you don't hear him, as if he's talking to someone else."

We talked each idea out. All sounded plausible to me,

though I thought the best answer was a nonresponse. We should pay no heed to the words and live our lives as the paying customers we were, with the same rights whites enjoyed. That's what we had done in Atlanta. We ignored the demand by the proprietor and waitstaff to move from the lunch counter until the police came or the counter closed. Then we moved. Only then.

I didn't say that out loud. I didn't think it was my place. It might sound stupid. Though CORE believed in equality, believed every rung on a ladder was equally important and every rung offered stability to the structure, I could not help feeling like the low rung. I was eighteen, the youngest in the room by two years. Sitting right next to me was Walter Bergman, the oldest Rider in the room. I could live my life three times over and still not be his sixty-one years. I sat at that discussion full of wide-eyed optimism; he sat full of clear-eyed pragmatism.

"Speak up," he whispered to me. His gray-haired, square-faced, professorial countenance, complete with the dark-rimmed glasses of the day, encouraged me. It intimidated, too. I stayed silent.

Across the table from me was John Lewis. John was the second-youngest Rider, about two and a half years older than I. I didn't know at the time that he had a wide network across the Movement and came with a reputation of being ardent and intense, determined and unshakable. What I saw was someone just like me. Both of us devoted to the cause, fervent in our beliefs, on fire for justice and equality. My fire was a bright yellow flame. You could hold your hands to my fire and feel the warmth. John's fire was the smoldering red coals of full heat and burn. Hold your hand to that and it blistered. My flame danced; John's smoldered. I smiled. John seethed. John was always serious, always straight-faced, always solemn. For me, the importance of the work was primary, but I also felt a sense of adventure. There was no adventure in this for John. For John, this was as serious as life gets.

In some sense, my facial expressions were putty—pliable and moldable. One minute an energetic, upward crescent creased my face, the next, puzzlement, the next, concern or concentration or consternation; John's demeanor was granite, fixed, immovable. It was hard to see John's teeth, his lips always pursed. It was easy to see mine. My mouth formed a smile of wonder. Both faces had frozen fixtures such as our eyes. His stared straight ahead. They bored into you. They obsessively fixated on an unrealized future because the destination was so far ahead. They focused with a determination to reach it. Mine gazed up seeing all kinds of possibility. I was nervous, but I was excited. John was composed, or so he looked to me. I had no idea if he was nervous or excited. I couldn't see any emotion other than seriousness in his gaze.

"Do I belong here?" echoed within me. "I am so out of my league."

I had to believe I did. Someone had chosen me out of all the Atlanta applicants. "Do I belong?" was the question we insisted on answering yes to in Atlanta restaurants and dressing rooms and restrooms.

"Hell, yes, we belong!" was our adamant cry. Jail cells had not convinced us—solitary confinement had not convinced me—otherwise. I had to believe "Hell, yes!" was the response reverberating in the deepest part of me even though my outward smile must have projected my naivete, and my hesitation to speak, I suspect, projected my fear.

It turned out, all the ideas offered were acceptable. Mr. Farmer's point in his question was to make us consider scenarios and have a reservoir of responses to rely on. Since situations would be fluid, circumstances would require quick thinking. Mr. Farmer wanted that thinking done now, in advance of need, for us to have a variety of tactics at our disposal.

I remember him saying something like "Our strategy is to exercise our rights under *Morgan* and *Boynton* to sit in any seat of our choosing, on buses or in facilities, knowing this. It will create tension. Tension will lead to crisis. When the crisis comes, we must remain nonviolent so any violence that occurs is committed against us, not by us."

It's been six decades, and I don't have a transcript of what Mr. Farmer said, so that is not verbatim, but it must be close. It reflects my memory of Mr. Farmer's sentiments, Mr. Farmer's tone, Mr. Farmer's attitude. He expected it to become our attitude. We were going to remain nonviolent. Period.

He gave us phrases to use. "On buses, say in a calm voice, 'I have the right to sit here on the grounds of the Supreme Court decision in the *Morgan* case.' In stations, calmly insist, 'I have the right to sit here on the grounds of the Supreme Court decision in the *Boynton* case.'" We might substitute "sit" with "order food here" or "use this restroom."

He wanted us to get it right, so he kept having us practice.

"I have the right to sit here on the grounds of the Supreme Court decision in the *Boynton* case."

"Again."

So it went. Mr. Farmer kept hammering into us, "We have a right to sit in any seat anywhere, and we are exercising that right nonviolently."

Around the table, the bus scenarios came. "What are you going to do if the station employees don't know or care about *Boynton*?"

Answer: Be polite. Be insistent. "I have the right to sit here on the grounds of the Supreme Court decision in the *Boynton* case."

"What are you going to do on a bus if the driver summons the police, and the police instruct you to move?"

"I have the right to sit here on the grounds of the Supreme Court decision in the *Morgan* case."

"What are you going to do if the station manager summons the police, and the police instruct you to move?"

"I have the right to sit here on the grounds of the Supreme Court decision in the *Boynton* case."

While I practiced along with everyone, my perspective on this was different. Perhaps it was my youth. I did not see myself saying these words in a confrontation. In my mind, I was not provoking anyone. To me, we were normal passengers living normal lives riding buses to normal destinations. I did not think I was trying to create tension. If anyone got upset about where I was sitting or ordering food, it was their problem, not mine. I felt, and I think we all felt, we did not want anything to happen, but if something did happen, we would face it in a nonviolent manner. We were committed to that.

Mr. Farmer moved the conversation to physical encounters.

"What are you going to do if the bus driver or a policeman takes hold of you and begins to move you elsewhere by force?"

Answer: Be polite. Oblige. Do not resist. Do not pull away. Do not hold on to the seat or the person next to you. Instead, obey.

"You have informed them of your legal right. They are the ones in opposition to the law. Resistance by you in any physical manner will be a violation of your commitment to nonviolence. If any violence occurs—and grabbing you to move you someplace else constitutes a violent act—it must be committed by them. We are nonviolent. We are peaceful. Always."

Classroom discussion ended at lunch and changed to practicing physical confrontation in the afternoon. We left the meeting room and moved to a large room with open space. The room had bookcases with volumes dedicated to peace, artwork portraying pastoral scenes of gentleness, and cushioned chairs designed for comfort. Mr. Farmer meant to disrupt the ambience with pushing and shoving, noise and nuisance, vulgarity and profanity.

We took turns sitting on stools to simulate a bus station

lunch counter. Elsewhere, rows of folding chairs four abreast with an aisle in between replicated bus seating. We broke into groups to practice in the two imagined locations. In both scenarios we alternated our identities.

Freedom Rider. Segregationist.

Freedom Rider. Bus Driver.

Freedom Rider. Policeman.

Freedom Rider. Thug.

For me, all this was new. In Atlanta, we had not practiced nonviolent responses to violent reactions to our activism. We had simply, but seriously, consented to nonviolence. For most of us in Atlanta, nonviolence was a tactic, pure and simple. It was not a way of life. But here, at Fellowship House, walking among us were committed pacifists who had paid a price for their pacifism and suffered for refusing to do harm to another human being under any circumstance. Two of the first three men I met—Jim Peck and Al Bigelow—were both devoted pacifists.

Mr. Peck, midforties, sandy haired, sad eyed, and of gentle build, had a choice in 1942. He could answer the call of conscription, or he could spend three years in federal prison for refusing to fight in World War II. As a conscientious objector, he chose prison.[2] He chose prison over nonviolent options offered him such as serving in a hospital. Could I, at age eighteen, do that? A thousand days in prison for my beliefs? I didn't think I could. Or would. That would have been a whole other level of commitment compared to my sixteen days in jail.

Mr. Bigelow looked anything but a pacifist in my mind. He looked as if he belonged on a fishing trawler. Gorton's frozen seafood must have found someone who looked a lot like Al Bigelow when they came up with their yellow-raincoated fisherman logo. Rugged tenacity. Broad-shouldered posture. Sea-weathered face. Mr. Bigelow had the thickest shock of hair by far of anyone at Fellowship House and a build that said football linebacker. His incarceration did not come during World War II as Mr. Peck's had. Far from it. Mr. Bigelow commanded the USS *Dale W. Peterson*, a navy destroyer escort, during the war. It was the dropping of two atomic bombs that turned an officer into a resister.

"I was in Pearl Harbor when we dropped the atomic bomb on the Japanese, Charles," he told me sometime during our two-week Freedom Ride. "I could not believe my country could kill so many innocent people. My life turned that day."

He joined the Quakers and became a pacifist. He attempted to sail a thirty-foot boat into a nuclear test zone in the Pacific to prevent a nuclear explosion in 1958.[3] That's what landed Al Bigelow and his crew in jail. They served sixty days.

"Nigger!" Dr. Bergman sneered at me as I sat on a stool representing a lunch counter setting.

It meant nothing to me. It was nothing. I had heard that in Atlanta countless times. It meant less than nothing because unlike those yelling at me in Atlanta, I knew Dr. Bergman didn't mean it. He was trying to prepare me for something that was already a part of my natural environment. He might as well have turned an electric heater on me to acclimate me to temperatures in the South. No need. I knew Southern temperatures, and I knew Southern vernacular.

"Nigger lover!" I would scream at him when we switched places. That was odd. It did not make sense to me that a Negro would say that to anyone, but I think the idea was to have us coarsen our language to desensitize us to what might be coming.

It was funny when it was Mrs. Bergman's turn.

"Get your Negro backside to the back of the bus!" she would try to scream at me when I sat in the simulated bus seats. She was too kind to say *nigger*, too refined to say *ass*, too gentle to scream. If she had been ordered to knock me to the floor, she would have apologized and helped me up.

And it was difficult to swear at her. What would my parents think if I swore at a fifty-seven-year-old woman? What would they think if they knew this was the "advanced training in non-violent, passive resistance" I had told them I was learning? But here I was raining vulgarities down on Frances Bergman.

As hard as it was to curse at Mrs. Bergman, it was harder to shove a sixty-one-year-old gentleman—*gentle*man—off a stool and obey instructions to kick him. My pushes were more slow-motion hugs followed by landing him softly on the floor. My kicks were more in the style of a professional wrestler's pretend blows. I did not really kick Mr. Bergman. My parents would have killed me if they knew I had, but they wouldn't because I couldn't.

Mr. Bigelow didn't seem to have such hesitations in knocking me to the floor when I teamed with him. When Al Bigelow pushed you, the floor was your next destination. John Lewis poured ketchup on me. Ed Blankenheim spit on me, or at least on my clothes. Genevieve Hughes swore at me. That was shocking. To me and to her. We were supposed to be serious, but we could not help but laugh when Genevieve used vulgar language. Even John cracked a smile.

As interesting and new as these physical-confrontation drills were to me, I think our orientation practices were disappointing to John. He had gone through the Reverend James Lawson's workshops in Nashville, and I think John found those much more centered and serious. I remember thinking of him as being detached, almost disinterested in practicing at the level Mr. Farmer required. I found it hard to connect with John across the days we were in training. Even though we were closest in age, the two of us didn't spend much time together. I think he felt more kinship with his Nashville friends and colleagues, and as I said, John projected a certainty I did not have. I can't imagine him wondering if he belonged. He belonged. He. Belonged.

An evening meal together and singing followed each day's orientation. CORE wanted a pastor to accompany us, and the Reverend Benjamin Elton Cox fit that bill. Elton was about the same age as Genevieve and Ed. He always wore his clerical collar and did not eat without giving thanks to the Provider of the food, though not everyone joined him. Jimmy McDonald led the singing. To him, music captured every emotion, every circumstance. There was nothing Jimmy could not sing about. Jimmy took a popular song such as Harry Belafonte's "Day-O" and led us in a freedom song version of it.

> Free-dom, Fre-e-e-e—dom,
> Freedom comin' and it won't be long.
> Free, me say free, me say free, me say free,
> Me say free, me say fre-e-e-e—dom.
> Freedom comin' and it won't be long.

Then he would have us ring out other songs such as "Oh, Freedom."

> Oh-h, freedom, oh-h, freedom
> Oh-h freedom over me
> (Over me-e-e-e-e)
> And before I'd be a slave,
> I'd be buried in my gra-a-a-ave
> And go home to my Lord and be free
> (And be free.)

Oh, my. The songs we sang. The heights we reached. When Jimmy McDonald and James Farmer and Elton Cox and John Lewis joined voices, certainty took root, confidence soared, courage surged. It was electric.

The evening sessions also gave me an opportunity to ask my

"Why are you here?" question as a way of meeting my fellow Riders and let them do the talking. That let me hide in my insecurity while they provided their answers. I started with those closer to my age.

"So Reverend Cox, why are you here?" I asked.

"Someone has to do this," he told me. "I can say I will never be a slave, but the truth is, if I had been born two centuries ago, three centuries ago, I would have been a slave. And there would have been nothing I could have done about it. But one hundred years ago, Sojourner Truth and Harriet Tubman and Frederick Douglass and so many others made sacrifices so I am *not* a slave. It's my turn to sacrifice on behalf of someone else. We can sacrifice now, Charles, for those we will never know, who will never know of our sacrifice and will never care we did this. We can sacrifice."

That was the crux of Reverend Cox's answer. When I heard words like that come from him, I wanted similar words to come from me.

For white Rider Ed Blankenheim, it was personal.

"In boot camp, I was traveling in the front of a bus in North Carolina with a Negro friend of mine. The driver stopped the bus and said, 'All you niggers get in the back.' He wasn't talking to me, but he might as well have been. That grated on me. It gnawed at me. There was no reason for it, but I couldn't prevent it. Now I think I might be able to change it."

I liked asking the question "Why are you here?" In those two answers alone, I learned why a pastor and a soldier would commit to this.

When they continued the conversation by asking me the same question, my answer revolved around Mom and Dad:

"My mother is a very intelligent woman. But this world doesn't recognize that. My dad is the greatest man I know, but he's spent his life stepping off of sidewalks and avoiding making eye contact with whites. I love him with all my heart, but I'm not doing that. I'm not going to live that way."

Another among us who was not going to live that way was Hank Thomas. Hank joined us at Fellowship House the last day of orientation, replacing his Howard University roommate John Moody. John was suffering through a cold and became increasingly hesitant to participate in the Ride. When John dropped out, CORE offered the slot to Hank, who had been hoping to participate and had applied.

At nineteen, Hank now became the second youngest to me on the Ride. Hank and I have been good friends for six decades since the Freedom Ride, forever linked by it. But when Hank showed up at Fellowship House, he scared me. He was one more reason for me to question my place. Hank was the tallest, strongest, fastest, most athletic, of any of us. He not only towered over me, he had an edge to him formed from a life far different from mine. I held resentments. We all held resentments. We resented how society treated us. Hank held more. He held the festering anger of enduring an abusive stepfather, of living a migrant life growing up in Florida, of having some value because of his star athletic talent but no value beyond that. Hank added height, weight, strength, attitude, and confidence. I was not sure I did. And he added a singing voice as deep as he was tall. His bass notes resonated in the air and reverberated in the soul. When Hank joined Jimmy McDonald's singing, a joyful noise rose to the Lord. I was glad Hank was with us, but his presence made me want to gravitate toward the Bergmans. I felt more comfortable with Walter and Frances.

That last day of orientation the level of violence we practiced increased. Cigarettes pushed into our flesh. Slaps, punches, and kicks connected, although all of us pulled back before hitting with any degree of intensity. The purpose was to learn how to react to the assault.

"Protect yourself."

"Roll into a ball."

"Cover vital and tender areas."

"Use your arms to shield as much of your head, neck and kidneys as possible."

These are the instructions I recall Mr. Farmer teaching us. In addition, there was always an emphasis on not responding with violence.

"Employ passive resistance."

"Maintain your composure."

"Remain silent."

"Refuse to react in kind."

"Confront their example of violence with your example of love."

Practicing violent scenarios seemed so other. It was so contrary to who everyone was, how we lived, what we believed, where we came from. But it was not contrary to why we did it. We did it because Gandhi had been shot. Dr. King had been stabbed.[4] Sit-in students had been shoved and punched and kicked and spat upon. We did it because we believed practice prepares and preparation protects. We did it because James Farmer told us to do it.

I could not bring myself to address Jim Farmer any way other than with the title *Mr.*, but I could grab him and force him to the floor. I could swear at people who were becoming my friends. I could pour mustard on Genevieve Hughes. That was actually enjoyable until Mr. Farmer told me to quit laughing and smiling. The people doing this to us would not be laughing or smiling, he said with a seriousness my smile said I did not yet have.

Get serious. Get to work.

I did as I was told. We all did, but it was hard to believe our trip would be as dramatic or as serious as what we were practicing.

Mr. Farmer insisted it might. Better to prepare for the worst and be wrong than not practice and be awakened to the world's realities.

Our training drew to a close. As our formal preparation ended, there was one thing left to do. We should write. That meant compose letters to our loved ones. It meant write out our last wills. That was a shock to me. Why would I need to write out a last will? For a bus ride? I didn't own anything worth handing down to loved ones. I didn't have a wife or kids who would need what I didn't have, and I sure didn't have any money to bequeath to charity. But beside that, it seemed unnecessary. Was this another signal that I was in over my head? Had I signed on for something the risk of which I could not imagine? It did not seem possible. But others took the directive seriously. At eighteen, I was not old enough to think I might be wrong; just confident and cocksure enough to be certain I wasn't. I did not write a will.

Writing a will was not a requirement. Providing a next of kin was. CORE needed to be able to contact loved ones if circumstances warranted. My parents did not own a phone. There would be no way to contact anyone at 21 Bradley. It only took a moment to figure it out. I filled in the blank. Next of kin: Lonnie King.

Mr. Farmer took everyone out to dinner at a Chinese restaurant. I also did not join all the other Riders at dinner that night. I stayed back for a few reasons. I wasn't then an adventurous eater and didn't think I could stomach, much less enjoy, anything on the menu. Had I to do it over, though, I might make another decision. Stories of the restaurant that night were delicious enough to leave me with a taste of regret.

We all retired with our own thoughts of what the morning would bring.

For Mr. Farmer, Mr. Peck, Mr. and Mrs. Bergman, and John, it would bring serious, be-aware-of-your-surroundings freedom work.

For Jimmy, it would bring singing.

For Elton, it would bring the next steps in his walk of faith.

For Genevieve, it would bring surprise.

For Hank, it would bring whatever it brought. He'd deal with it as needed, when needed.

For me it would bring optimistic adventure.

It was our last night of known peaceful sleep. Dawn would take us away from the Quakers and move us closer to the quake.

# 9

## First Days

Stand up and rejoice, a great day is here
We are fighting Jim Crow and the victory is near.
Hallelujah, I'm a travelin', hallelujah, ain't it fine?
Hallelujah, I'm a-travelin' down freedom's main line.

—*Freedom song "Freedom's Main Line"*[1]

Around the breakfast table on Thursday, May 4, my colleagues told me of a "Last Supper" they had joked about having at the restaurant. That sounded more foreboding than funny to me. I preferred enjoying this last breakfast of warm smells and Quaker cooking.

We departed Fellowship House at 8:00 A.M. and headed to our respective bus depots. John, Hank, Genevieve, Al, Ed, and Elton entered the Greyhound station. Mr. Farmer, Jim Peck, Jimmy, Walter, Frances, Joe Perkins, and I got dropped off at Trailways. We entered with feelings ranging from excitement to trepidation. I held that entire range just within me.

The Trailways station was crowded with people going about

their day, complete with the emotions a morning at a bus station brings. The wait for the bus. The anticipation of the coming trip. The frustration with late departures. The hidden annoyance at complaining customers. The checking of watches to wonder how it is going. The looking at schedules posted on timetables overhead. Everyone in the station seemed to be living a normal morning with the span of normal feelings. People mostly ignored one another. Passengers went about their own business keeping to themselves, absorbed in their own thoughts, consumed with their own concerns.

Unlike other passengers, we expected to gather at least some notice. Mr. Farmer had contacted multiple press outlets weeks before, informing them of CORE's initiative, but few showed up at the Greyhound station. None showed up at ours. An interview here, a photo there, was about it, the other team told us later. The next day *The Washington Post* had a small article on an inside page giving our identities, our hometowns, our purpose, and our itineraries. An accompanying photo showed Mr. Farmer, Genevieve, Hank, Ed, and Elton looking with eager anticipation at a map.[2]

Mr. Farmer commanded attention at a small press conference he conducted, but Genevieve was the most popular with the press.

"There is a possibility we will not be served at some stops," she said at a filmed interview. "There is a possibility we might be arrested. This is the only trouble that I anticipate."[3]

Mr. Farmer had sent letters to people outside the press he thought should have been interested in what was about to happen—President Kennedy, Attorney General Robert Kennedy, the presidents of Greyhound and Trailways. None paid attention. They were preoccupied by other concerns. The two-week-old fiasco of the Bay of Pigs invasion in Cuba to overthrow Fidel Castro was still news. Alan Shepard's blastoff from Cape

Canaveral on Friday, May 5, to become the first American in space riveted the nation's attention. Our small experiment would not be worthy of importance until our direct-action campaign created a crisis as Mr. Farmer had assured us during orientation. But that was ten days away. On May 4, the political leaders of the country and bigwigs of the bus companies had more important things to do than pay attention to thirteen bus passengers saying they would be testing a Supreme Court decision.

The Black press was different. CORE wanted the Ride documented. Reporters from the Black press were interested in accompanying us on the trip. Simeon Booker, a journalist already legendary in African American circles but probably unknown to White audiences, was on our Trailways team. He had covered the 1955 Emmett Till murder trial for the Johnson Publishing Company, publisher of *Jet* and *Ebony*. Simeon knew how to remain detached from us and unidentifiable as a newsperson. One way was sitting in a back seat with a newspaper fully open, leaving others unaware of any association he had to the Ride. An inconspicuous hole in his newspaper allowed him to keep his reporter's eye on whatever happened while remaining anonymous. We also had a Black photographer, Ted Gaffney, on our bus. Moses Newson, a Black writer for the *Baltimore Afro-American,* and Charlotte Devree, a White CORE activist and freelance writer, were on the other team's bus. If violence broke out, media coverage would be essential in portraying our side of the story. The objective was to have evidence confirming which side perpetrated brutality and which did not if tension moved to violence. Let the American people decide who was right, who was wrong.

At the Trailways station, I was mostly left alone. No one interviewed me, and part of that was by my own intention. I worried that Mom and Dad would face repercussions if my identity got out. The last thing I wanted was a burning cross or worse showing up at 21 Bradley Street. I believed I was prepared to

handle anything that came my way, but it would be hard to live
with my actions hurting my loved ones. I was the last mentioned
in any telling of the Ride, if I was mentioned at all. I think I was
seen as a smiling kid having fun. The Riders perceived as deadly
serious and deeply concerned—they were the ones the writers
and photographers sought.

These side interviews were nothing like the launching of a
ship or a public farewell to troops wishing them well in the battles ahead. We wanted some attention, but the deepest part of us
wanted normality. We wanted to be US citizens traveling from
here to there just like anyone else on our bus. "Here" was Washington, D.C. "There" was New Orleans. We were simply taking more time to get to "there" because we were going to make
stops along the way testing facilities, speaking to church groups,
and spending nights in homes to make connections and grow a
movement.

Our group of seven boarded the Trailways prepared for
our first-day assignments. The idea was to have a Black Rider sit
in front and an interracial pair sit together in a place of their
choosing. One Rider, the "observer," would play the part of a
regular passenger and sit where custom demanded. This was in
the hope of guaranteeing at least one of us would not be seen
as any kind of "agitator." Just a normal passenger minding his
or her own business. But the observer, if needed, could stay in
the town where a Rider was jailed to keep CORE informed. The
observer could pay bail if we abandoned our "no-bail" strategy.
The observer could appear out of nowhere to stand up on behalf
of Riders in extreme circumstances. And an observer could bear
witness from an uninvolved distance if necessary. All other Riders dispersed to seats that either challenged or complied with Jim
Crow expectations.

Jim Peck and I were the interracial pair for Day One. He followed me in line with Frances Bergman behind him. It was all as

normal as could be. I gave the driver my ticket, stepped aboard, and headed to the rear. Passengers paid me no heed. I was where I was supposed to be. But Peck? Jim took his seat next to me, and that captured some notice as he settled in.

The Trailways departed.

Our first day would take us from Washington, D.C., the capital of the country, to Richmond, Virginia, the capital of the Confederacy, via Fredericksburg. The ride was comfortable, but, as Mr. Peck and I sat side by side, White next to Black, looks of confusion and curiosity preoccupied a few riders.

No resistance formed, but puzzled, disapproving glances and stares spoke words I heard with my eyes.

"What are those two up to?"

"Why would they be sitting together?"

"What reason could that White man have for sitting in the back of the bus?"

"What is that *Negro* thinking?"

As a child, I felt my mother's displeasure across a crowded room when my behavior warranted. At times I knew I was doing something naughty, or I was pushing a boundary, but I pretended I was not. Mom's eyes focused and drilled and pierced. Her lips tensed. Her head tilted. Her brows narrowed. Her forehead furrowed. And I could tell all this was happening without looking. I avoided looking. But I sensed it. I felt it. The atmosphere would change as if Mom willed it. It thickened. Dampened. Threatened. A storm front moved in. That was the atmosphere in our section of the bus.

"Are we going to tolerate *that*?"

"Driver, do something!"

"What else are those two going to do?"

"Am I safe?"

Their silence echoed. We ignored it. Or thought we did. But we felt it. At least I did. Jim, somehow, seemed good with it.

Calm. Composed. He could sit with his face impassive, his forehead smooth, his posture relaxed. Jim's eyes ignored cold stares.
His manner displayed indifference. He was a passenger sitting
on a bus. That was about all there was to it for Jim.

I, on the other hand, could feel my face warming. The upward curl of the edges of my mouth flattened. I expect my forehead, though decades younger than Jim's, had creases of worry. My
smile changed to my childhood discomfort of knowing I was being watched in censure. Surprise mixed with concern. Concern
mixed with guilt. I think this was my welcome to the big leagues.
My Freedom Ride was on.

Julian's final words to me in Atlanta, "This will be the last
time you ride in the back of the bus," were not playing out. But
my sitting in the back was by design, not societal dictate. A white
man was sitting with me, and I with him. By choice. I was in the
back, I was a bit uncomfortable, but I was free. It felt rebellious,
and it felt great.

Once we cleared the city, we rolled through the countryside
of Virginia. Gentle hills and farmland in the foreground, and
forested terrain in the distance, zoomed past our window. On
the aisle side, passengers walked past us to access the bus's bathroom. Or stood beside us because a line had formed. Though Mr.
Peck and I sat in the back row, we were not at the end of the
bus. Our seats were not against the back window, but the bus's
toilet. The parade of people, the sloshing of water in the toilet
bowl, the "Excuse me" travelers said to those waiting in line as
they squeezed past returning to their seats, the odor, all made
our back-row seats undesirable.

Maybe that's why white society relegated folks such as me to
where Mr. Peck and I were that day. Where I was compelled to be
every day. Jim Crow said:

"Put 'em where it smells."

"Put 'em in their place."

"We're first. You're last."

"That's the way it is. Live with it."

In one sense it was interesting being by the toilet. Here was the one room in the Trailways and Greyhound bus system that was not segregated. On the bus, it did not matter at all where Negro and white waste went. It went to the same place. Down the same hole. In the depot, the room where our waste went could not have mattered more.

Jim and I did not talk. We were not portraying traveling companions. We were two passengers of different races who happened to be seated together. He pulled out a book. I gaped out the window. The trip, the scenery, the job we were on, all said to me, "Where would you, Charles Person, rather be than right here, right now?" I wanted to take it all in and feel it. Jim's response was more "Sittin' on a bus. So what?" This was nothing new to Jim Peck.

With us being noncommunicative, I began writing in a notebook. My intention was to write throughout the Ride. It seemed worthwhile getting my thoughts down and recording names of folks who stood out to me along the way. I doubted anything would come of my notes, but I thought Mom and Dad would be asking me questions when we stopped in Atlanta, and the notebook might help with details. Especially names. So, I stuck to writing and sightseeing. Jim kept to his book.

Our first stop was Fredericksburg, about fifty miles south of Washington. We expected to see WHITE ONLY and COLORED ONLY signs because Tom Gaither, who'd inspired Mr. Farmer to create the Ride and who coined our name Freedom Ride, had scouted the entire route ahead of our trip. He took notes of what we would encounter. Those notes warned us Fredericksburg still had segregation signs hanging in the depots. But when we got to

Fredericksburg, the signs were gone. Like a restaurant preparing for a health inspector's visit, Trailways and Greyhound cleaned up their facilities prior to the "inspector's" arrival.

Just as we were the interracial pair on the bus, Jim and I were the Day One "testers" for the bus depot facilities. That meant it was up to us to use the opposite-race restroom, sit in the opposite-race waiting room, and order food in the opposite-race restaurant. For the white tester, that presumed stations had Negro facilities. Fredericksburg did.

Mr. Peck tested the colored restroom, I tested the white. I even bought a Coke at the white food counter. Nothing happened. Was it going to be this easy the whole way? Or was this experience in the upper South different from what we would face in the Deep South? After all, water boils from the bottom up; the hottest spot is in the deepest part of the pot. At this first stop, the water was not even warm to the touch. Jim told me it had been the same fourteen years earlier. He had integrated the very same restroom on the Journey of Reconciliation. No problem presented itself then either. We took it as a good sign.

When we reboarded the bus, we were not the only passengers integrating the seats. It encouraged us to see black and white customers sitting together in a few other seats. It looked as if *Irene Morgan v. Virginia* had made a difference on the bus. Would *Boynton v. Virginia* make a difference in the depots, restaurants, and restrooms?

As we moved out of Fredericksburg, I was proud of myself for what I had done. Here it was, the first day of the Ride, and I was stepping up. I didn't say anything to Mr. Peck or the others, but it gave me a sense of purpose. It gave me confidence. I could do this. Back then, I probably thought it was all about me showing what I had to offer. Right then. Right there. Now, in my seventies, I think the older members of the team intentionally selected me as a first-day tester to help me experience the water at the top of the pot before the boil of the Deep South. I never thanked them for that. I wish I had.

I think it was that night in Richmond I asked my first-day seatmate, "Why are you doing this, Mr. Peck?" I asked him with a raised emphasis on *you*. I wanted to express it in a curious tone, not one of bewilderment.

I knew he had been on the Journey of Reconciliation. The only one of us who had. I knew he had been jailed for his pacifism during the war. I knew some of the things he had done in his life, but I did not know *why* he had done them. That's what I wanted to know. Why?

His life could hardly have been more different from mine. He hadn't grown up in the Bottom; he had grown up in the Top. That's what I was thinking. I was thinking if there is any place called the Top, that's where Mr. Peck must have been from.

During orientation, I had learned he had been born in Manhattan and was the son of a now-deceased, wealthy businessman who had left him an estate. He had attended a private boarding school in Connecticut, and he had gone to Harvard. If that's not the Top, it must be close. I did not understand it. This man was already free. If what others had told me of Jim Peck was true, he was a millionaire. A millionaire. He could live with as much comfort as he wanted, and here he was sitting next to me in the back of a Trailways bus on his way to what? If Mr. Farmer was right, the answer was, Jim Peck was on his way to trouble. Why would he do that?

"I think life is made up of Upperdogs and Underdogs, Charles. I got to be an Upperdog. Not by virtue of anything other than who I was born to and the color of my skin."[4]

It didn't take much to figure out that meant I was an Underdog. Before I took offense, he went on, "I didn't have anything to do with my station in life. Neither did you. But I can stand up for those who will never have what I don't care to have."

"What's that?"

"Altitude. The ability to look down on others. My mother wanted me to have everything, and I wanted everyone to have anything anyone else was able to have. That was a problem. I've spent most of my life causing what people like my mom think of as trouble, and I think of as insisting on justice."

I wanted to know why he'd joined the Journey of Reconciliation.

"Why do you breathe, Mr. Person?"

"My name's Charles."

"My name's Jim."

I got his point. Four days after meeting everyone I was still using titles with the older Riders. I decided I'd try calling him Jim.

"Why do you breathe, Charles?" he repeated. "To me the answer is because it is the natural state of your existence. I believe it's the natural state of our existence for us to live in equality and peace. Not everyone thinks that. Lots of people think the strongest should thrive at the expense of others. So, I believe everyone needs to make up their minds on which side they stand. I know which side I stand for, so, I need to stand up for that side. Even if it is at a great cost to me. That's why I'm here. I'm here for the Underdogs."

That's my best recollection of what Jim Peck told me six decades ago, but the next thing he said has stuck with me about as much as a conversation can stick with you with accuracy. It surprised me.

"The problem is, when Underdogs become Upperdogs, they turn against the Underdogs. We have to fight that."

That stood out. It made me wonder if I ever became an Upperdog, would I turn? How would I know if I had or hadn't?

I did not get any sense that white people across my life thought of themselves—or could conceive of themselves—as Upperdogs. They sure seemed like Upperdogs to me.

If Mr. Peck was fighting for the Underdogs in the country, I thought I should start calling him and the other Riders by their first names. *Mr.* sounded too Upperdog after that ride to Richmond. Except for Mr. Farmer. I didn't think I could ever call Mr. Farmer by his first name.

In Richmond, we saw no signs segregating colored and white. But colored and white facilities existed. And it was obvious who belonged where. The waiting rooms for Negroes were tiny and cramped. The white rooms were spacious by comparison. Food in colored waiting rooms was purchased through a cubbyhole that adjoined the main, or white, waiting room. A cubbyhole. Those small openings said louder than words could that we were supposed to be thankful for getting any food at all.

With the lack of signs, I had no problem ordering in the white section. But I was the only African American ordering there. Even in the absence of segregation signs, all the local blacks seemed to segregate themselves. If there were no restrictions, why were they doing that? Why were they choosing segregation?

I think they were making that choice because habit is hard to break. Custom hard to change. Perhaps it was living in long-established ways. Perhaps it was not trusting that it really was okay to live in the white world. When the rotten planks of a wooden bridge get replaced, it takes a while to think the new boards will hold. Sometimes it's easier and safer to let someone else step out first.

The riding portion of Day One ended.

Our nights were to become a routine of meeting in a local black church or black college for dinner, speaking to a gathering about that day's ride, passing offering baskets to raise funds to keep us going, and fanning out into homes of those willing to host us in pairs or as singles.

Our first night doing this proved as discouraging for some of us as the day had encouraged. Low turnout at the Virginia Union University chapel made older Riders wonder if there was any point to our effort. I think Jim found the small audience disheartening. Mr. Farmer found it disappointing. Both had given two decades to the cause of freedom and dignity for all. Both had put in three months of preparation for the Ride. Now a small band of folks show up to hear our story and encourage us on. It was not what they were expecting.

Reverend Cox saw it differently, I think. A single candle, to him, offered light. It offered hope. It illuminated. It was good news. Elton accepted whoever showed up and whatever funds raised as God's provision. It would be enough. "All that we need, His hand will provide," he would say to me. And it was easier to believe when Elton Cox said it.

My memory of the night wasn't discouraging at all. My favorite memory was of the meal and reception afterward. I remember country ham and biscuits—both Southern delicacies. There may not have been large numbers, but at the reception, college women my age cheered us on, encouraged us, saw us as heroes. For the first time since leaving Atlanta, I was having college-age fun. We talked college talk. We laughed college laughs. We danced and goofed off the way college-age kids hang out. The days of training had surrounded me with people who—except for Hank and John—were one to four decades older than I was. And all of us maintained a freedom sense about us. A sense of freedom purpose and freedom singing. It was great, and I loved it, but it was of singular focus. This first-night reception had a sense of fun about it to me. Some silliness to it. It was good to feel more relaxed.

After the gathering ended, people from the local area opened their homes to us, and we left one by one with the families who offered us lodging for the night. This was something we all knew before leaving Washington, D.C. Part of our training had been to go over our itinerary and learn what would happen at our stopping points. Group dinners, evening meetings, and lodging apart from one another had all been explained to us. But as is true of so much of life, learning is just learning until experience makes it real.

Leaving the chapel at Virginia Union with strangers that first night felt, at once, both safe and crazy. Safe, because the institutions along our trip were chosen for sensibilities that matched our own. They were on our side. Why would we not be safe? Crazy, because I was assigned to go with complete strangers. I was by myself at eighteen years old with these strangers in a strange city in a strange car being driven through dark streets to an unknown destination.

The whole experience unnerved me. Driving away into the night made me think of the police driving Dr. King away from Atlanta to Reidsville State Prison. That sounds dramatic, but teenage minds are never far removed from the dramatic. My teenage mind wasn't. My parents had no idea where I was, and once I lost sight of my colleagues, neither did they. I felt unstable. I needed to be on heightened alert. The car ride filled me with caution. I wondered if it showed in my voice when I responded to my hosts' questions.

"How did you come to be part of the Freedom Ride, Charles?"

"I applied." Short.

"Where do you go to school?"

"Morehouse." No elaboration.

"Have you done anything like this before?"

"No." No mention of marching, sitting in, jail time, solitary. Could I have been more social? More outgoing? More appreciative? I don't know. I was eighteen. This was the first night in my entire life I was staying with someone I did not know and had never heard of. My first night at Fellowship House I didn't know anyone personally, but everyone knew James Farmer. At least, everyone I knew had heard of James Farmer. And people in the Atlanta Student Movement knew or knew of students in the Nashville Movement. So, when I heard John Lewis would be on Freedom Ride 1961, I knew someone like me was going to be with me. Going to Fellowship House felt about the same as going to Morehouse. It was excitement mixed with anxiety, but no sense of being unsafe. This was different. This put me on edge. I had no way of knowing how to get out of danger if I found myself in danger. I had no one to lean on.

Two months earlier, in solitary confinement, the bars of the cell and the lock on the door had provided a strange and perverse sense of security. I didn't want to be there, but I felt that nothing bad was going to reach me. This was the opposite. I did want to be here, but I also felt in reach of bad things happening.

It seems silly to me now thinking that I ever felt fearful. These were good people who showed kindness and generosity to me in abundance. My hosts offered encouragement. They were proud of us—proud of me. That emboldened me. I had a room of my own, and my bed was clean and warm and comfortable. The quilt—in May—gave me a good night's rest. It was soft and cool the way a quilt, even though meant for warmth, can be. The concerns of the first-day Ride melted away in the shelter my host family provided.

Our second day—Friday, May 5—our teams switched buses. Now the Bergmans and I, Jim Peck and the rest of our squad, rode on Greyhound. The plan was to switch buses daily and sometimes have Riders switch teams to avoid routine and to avoid being identified as specific groups of "agitators" causing trouble for a particular company. By alternating each day, and traveling relatively short days—after all, Washington, D.C., to New Orleans is not a two-week trip unless you make it that—we would be on different buses with somewhat different teams each day with different drivers. In switching bus lines, we thought we would appear to be regular passengers using the bus line's services, not activists with a perceived "radical" agenda. To us, there was nothing radical about what we were doing any more than it was radical for the driver to do his job or for other passengers wanting transportation to their various locations.

We also changed responsibilities daily. So, this day, I was not in the back with the crowd and the toilet. I was up front, but again sitting with Jim Peck. The first day Jim had been the "agitator" by sitting in back with a black man. This day made me the one "out of line" by taking my "wrongful" place in the front.

The bus drivers were professional in dress and appearance. They did not engage with us in conversation, but we took no offense at that. They had their job to do and did not converse with any customers. Nor did they confront us about our seating choices. They were bus drivers going about their daily work. Most of the other passengers, though, avoided us like the plague. It seemed to me their shoulders had a universal tilt away from us wherever they sat on the bus. They gave us looks, but never said anything to us. Even the little eye contact they offered was fleeting, fearful, and uncomfortable. Like their posture, their eyes said what their words did not: "Keep your distance. We don't want any trouble."

We traveled only twenty miles to Petersburg on Friday. I used the time to write Day One thoughts and Day One appreciations in my journal. I wanted to remember my hosts and a few others I had met in Fredericksburg. Science students are used to tables and charts, so I made a table of acquaintances I could write to and thank at the end of the Ride. I tucked my notebook into my coat's inside breast pocket, where I could carry it easily.

Petersburg, like Richmond, had taken their signs down. Here the citizens accepted the *Morgan* decision. The *Boynton* decision, too. We entered the depot to find we were not testing much of anything. Desegregation already existed. Good. It was heartwarming to see blacks and whites living the way people ought to live. Not separated. Not segregated. Together.

That night was so different from Richmond. A huge crowd showed up at Bethany Baptist Church to welcome us. It made me wonder if churches would draw more supporters for what we were doing than college campuses. I expected it to be the opposite. During our sit-ins in Atlanta, the college kids were driving the change.

But not here. The Reverend Lloyd James, the church's pastor, held the congregation spellbound. As I remember, he spoke on how every person made a difference in the struggle. Every single person. Reverend James made you feel as big as those cubbyholes tried to make you feel small. He had Bethany Baptist standing up for God, standing up for human dignity, standing up for one another, standing up for us. He was a tough act to follow.

I remember Al Bigelow from the other team being the speaker. Being the designated speaker was something I did not look forward to doing. I was proud to be a part of all this, but I still thought of myself as the low person when it came to age, seniority, experience, and accomplishment. Why would people want to listen to me when the likes of Jim Farmer, Jim Peck, the Bergmans, and Al Bigelow were available? I hoped my turn to speak would come nearer New Orleans than D.C. I was glad Al was speaking.

I remember Al being good that night for two reasons. First, he was this tall white presence in an almost all-black environment. The image of him standing up in a black church brought contrast in color. It brought hope. Second, Al had a huge physical presence, second only to Hank's, in our group. But Al was a middle-aged man. His physique had filled out. Hank was tall, but Hank was lanky. Al had a huge physical presence magnified by the softness and quiet of his voice. That brought contrast, too. Where Reverend James's words reverberated and echoed, Al's voice required stillness to hear him. Pin-drop stillness. The church went from raucous to muted.

Here was a man who had put himself on a dinghy in the Pacific Ocean in an attempt to prevent the United States from conducting a nuclear detonation in the earliest years of hydrogen bombs, now putting himself at the pulpit of a church filled with people who did not look like him. He spoke of his desire and the country's need for everyone in that congregation to live a life equal to his. He spoke of the fierce force of pacifism and of what kindness, gentleness, and peacefulness could bring the world. He spoke of redemption and reconciliation. Al was a big, big man that night.

After Al finished, we again departed for the homes offered us. Before we left, though, Mr. Farmer gave us our allowance for the next day. We needed to have enough money each morning to pay for food in that day's station in case we were served. Many Southern cities had vagrancy laws that allowed police to arrest those who did not have at least $10 while in the business district. At our training, Mr. Farmer taught us it was important that we choose jail over bail to increase the tension in the conflict, but it was equally important in any arrest that we have the law on our side. Violating vagrancy laws, despite how out of line those laws might be from our perspective, did not advance our cause. We knew we had to be well-dressed, well-behaved, and respectful of both people and the law so that there could be no sound legal reason to oppose our actions.

Two nights into the Ride, it was becoming obvious we would be spread out each night in houses miles apart. This second night felt much better than the previous one. The first night had proved to me that I was safe with the good people who took me in. Now, for the second time, I found myself surrounded by welcome and comfort and love. Once again, my hosts lavished food, conversation, and emotional warmth that made me feel secure.

Thinking back to my parents' hospitality helped change my perspective. My parents had provided room and board for relatives who were moving from the farm to the city. We had done that often.

I remember one time when some of my father's relatives had to give up sharecropping. I grew up in the Bottom, and we were poor, but not like sharecroppers. One of my uncles worked year after year farming another man's land trying to make a living. No matter how hard he worked, no matter how big the crop, the landowner always required enough to keep him from making any kind of living. The landowner had all the control. He kept the books. He set the prices. He sold the crop. He owned the store where the sharecroppers shopped. My uncle was always beholden to the landowner. He could never get ahead. He knew he had to get his family out.

I do not know who made the plan, but all my family from Atlanta went to help my uncle and his family pack up and move. We did it in the dead of the night. Another rearview-mirror car ride. It was a choice my dad made I've never known a white family to have to make: risk driving in the threat that darkness brings to help someone in need or stay home because of fear, in favor of safety. Dad chose the risk.

Mom welcomed our relatives into our small, cramped apartment. The adults sat in the front room and worked out the sleeping arrangements. I shared a bed with one of my cousins. Mom took some old blankets and quilts and made a pallet on the floor for my brother Jimmy Dale and another cousin to sleep on. Our relatives stayed with us for about a week. The next day Mom was busy in the kitchen making food. Turnip greens. Neck bones. Corn bread. Peach cobbler.

Like the houses I now stayed in, our two rooms were crowded, but we thrived in the company of those with a need. That's what I was each of these first two nights on the road: a person in need. And someone was answering that need.

My hosts' provision covered more than my need. Their provision provided kindness, concern, hospitality, and encouragement. It provided Christian love. John 13:34 love: "Love one another as I have loved you." Matthew 22:39 love: "Love your neighbor as yourself." By the time I closed my eyes for a night's rest on Day Two, my cautions, my concerns, my fears, my insecurities, all diminished to the point of vanishing. My optimism, like Elton's faith, was living itself out more than Mr. Farmer's warnings and Jim Peck's stoicism.

# 10

## Shoe-In

Charlotte was . . . the birth of a new "in," the shoe-in.

—*James Peck, Freedom Rider*[1]

The next morning our hosts brought us together in downtown Petersburg for our Day Three, hundred-mile ride to Lynchburg, Virginia. Switching buses again, my team rode Trailways. Switching roles, I was, for the first time, the observer—a normal passenger riding to a destination. No worries. No trouble. Just get on, sit in the back, be inconspicuous. I could play that role. I'd spent my life playing that role except that day on the way to the bowling alley.

So far, Julian's image of my being done with that role was not playing out. But there was a freedom purpose and a freedom strategy to where each of us was sitting. There was calculation behind our choice of seat. And choices were what we were making. They were not being made for us or demanded of us. Choice felt liberating. It felt important. It made me feel free wherever I was on the bus.

This was the first day I anticipated trouble. Jim Peck informed me it was this day during the Journey of Reconciliation that the first frictions heated up. One of the 1947 Riders was Bayard Rustin, a masterful organizer who helped A. Philip Randolph plan the canceled 1941 March on Washington Movement and would go on, in 1963, to help Randolph and Dr. King organize the realized March on Washington. Bayard served multiple stints in jail across his life for being an overt pacifist, Communist, and homosexual in decades when none of those distinctions was respected and all of them were criminalized. So, Bayard was used to trouble and familiar with the inside of a jail.

A driver on the 1947 Journey ordered Rustin, sitting in the front of his bus with Jim that day, to get his black ass to the back of the bus. Bayard refused. Police came, but nothing happened because of the *Morgan* decision. On the other Journey bus, though, friction turned to heat. Heat turned almost to fire. Prior to that bus's leaving Petersburg, Conrad Lynn, a black Rider sitting in front, challenged his driver's demand to get where he "belonged." White and black passengers both aggressively insisted that Lynn move so the bus could get underway. A hostile crowd surrounded the bus to reinforce the point. Petersburg police arrested Lynn and removed him from the bus.[2] Because of these experiences on the Journey of Reconciliation, Jim thought Day Three of our Ride might bring Tension and Confrontation as passengers to our bus now fourteen years later.

Neither showed up.

Our halfway stop took us to Farmville, a town comfortable with segregation. How comfortable? Consider this. Many people forget or perhaps have never known that following the 1954 *Brown v. Board of Education* decision, Southern school systems did not surrender their viewpoints and principles and accept the Court's judgment. For many, the response to *Brown* was not integration. It was closure. Towns closed their entire public-school system rather than comply with a ruling they did not believe in. Closure made sense to people with a segregationist mind-set. It avoided noncompliance and allowed for the continuation of white societal norms. Many children lost a year or more of education. White children with parents of wealth found or created private alternatives. For the segregationists, society remained stable. A collective "whew" released their fears. Integration had been bypassed.

Closure was Farmville's approach to *Brown*. Farmville's approach to *Boynton* was disregard. Tom Gaither's scouting notes informed us COLORED ONLY and WHITE ONLY signs would greet us along with sufficient testosterone to enforce them.

But when we got to Farmville, no signs, no testosterone.

Single coats of fresh paint covered the segregation commands, but did not make them invisible. Clouded messages remained. Like watermarks on stationery, faint hints provided a message. What did they mean? The words could have been covered completely. Obliterated. But they weren't. Was it haste? Was it murmured warning? Was it grudging compliance? It proved to be the last. Farmville was a continuation of Fredericksburg, Richmond, and Petersburg.

We entered the Farmville depot and found no resistance to using facilities or ordering food. To me, the evidence made conclusions obvious. The country was moving forward. I *was* an ordinary passenger on a bus. New norms existed in a new South. Optimism was alive and well in eighteen-year-old me. Progress was alive and growing in America. We were three years yet from Sam Cooke singing "A Change Is Gonna Come." With two and a half days behind us, it seemed to me it already had.

That's what you feel at eighteen. Optimism. Invulnerability. And why not optimism, if invulnerability is your attitude? Jim and the Bergmans and Mr. Farmer all knew better. But I didn't. I wasn't riding just a bus. I was riding a wave. I was surfing through the Ride with a smile on my face, a whoop in my heart. Surfing. Not bad for someone who couldn't swim. It wasn't a reckless smile or a smirking whoop. It was the yelp of youth. Youth feeling triumphant. This was the journey of a lifetime for me. I felt lucky to be on it. I took pride in playing my part. I was young.

Lynchburg was our stop for the night. And this night was different. Instead of staying together as one group at one meeting and breaking up after the evening gathering, the thirteen of us branched out when we arrived in Lynchburg to address eight different congregations. I went with the Bergmans, where Frances was that night's speaker. Frances blended quiet sincerity with conviction. I cannot remember her words. I do remember her manner. Frances modeled a quiet assurance that kindness and nonviolence must be the path forward for our country. The quieter her voice, the more attentive everyone became. I equated powerful voices as the means to engross an audience. This was the opposite. To me, Frances personified dignity.

Today, I think of Frances when I reflect on what happened in our country in the sixties. Multiple assassinations: Medgar, President Kennedy, Malcolm, Dr. King, Bobby. Violence abundant. Riots in the streets. A hundred cities on fire after Dr. King's murder. A war tearing the fabric of the country apart. In contrast, there Frances stood that night—years before any of those events happened—talking peacefully, calmly. She projected to me a different way to demand change. She projected quiet but determined insistence.

Today, I think of Frances when I reflect on what is happening in our country. Seemingly endless deaths from gun violence. A planet on fire from global warming. Loud voices seeking to dominate, to have their way. Anger directed at those who see the world differently. Lack of acceptance of entire groups of people. And I think there is a different way to demand change from these afflictions. Quiet but determined insistence. I think of Frances.

She and Walter, more than anyone else on the Rides, made me feel accepted.

"We'll look after you, Charles," she had promised me during orientation.

"We'll keep you safe," Walter added. His cardigan sweater, his coat with patches on the elbows, his pipe smoking, added authenticity to the protection he pledged.

I didn't know how they could do that, but their saying so made it feel true.

My anxieties and fears diminished the more time I spent in their comfortable and comforting presence. Frances left me feeling assured that night and throughout the Ride. All would be okay if we persevered together. Her gray-haired experience brought Frances deference from the audience. They listened.

One of the enjoyments of being onstage with a speaker but not being the speaker is the perspective it grants. You get to see the speaker, but you also take in the faces of the crowd. The audience's expressions often say as much as the speaker's words. Frances that night spoke to thirsty, hungry ears. They did more than hear her words. They consumed them. They drank and ate and supped on them. What a view for me. What a desire she created in me to be able to emulate her when my turn came. So, for us, Lynchburg that night followed the pattern of all our previous stops. Warm welcome. Enthusiastic supporters. Excitement abounding.

Later, we discovered the other venues that night were not as welcoming. The other Riders spoke to smaller gatherings. Their congregations questioned Riders' motives. The Freedom Riders' stance was taken to be distasteful. Sour. While my experience matched my idealism, others found their experiences matched their realism. That surprised me when we all reconvened.

I remember looking forward to our Sunday, May 7, ride from Lynchburg, Virginia, to Greensboro, North Carolina. Greensboro had inspired my activism with the lunch counter sit-ins fifteen months earlier. For without Joseph McNeil, David Richmond, Franklin McCain, and Ezell Blair, in February 1960, there would be no Lonnie King or Julian Bond or Herschelle Sullivan or Roslyn Pope or Joe Pierce creating and leading the Atlanta Student Movement. No Atlanta Student Movement, then no me sitting down in Sprayberry's cafeteria, sitting down in solitary confinement, or sitting down on this Trailways bus as we left Lynchburg, Virginia. Greensboro, for me, would be a pilgrimage. I wanted to see what a year had brought to this Lexington of a second American Revolution.

First, though, came Danville. The Greyhound team had already stopped in Danville and moved on. When we stopped, Jim, Walter, Frances, and Genevieve all tried to order in the black waiting room. In being rebuffed, they learned that Ed Blankenheim had been turned away about an hour earlier with the Greyhound team. Why, the Danville manager now wanted to know, did all these whites want to wander into colored facilities? Why would they want to order food through the cubbyholes? Those cubbyholes reminded me of jail in Atlanta. In solitary, the cell door had the smallest oblong opening possible to get food through to me. The tip of a white hand would extend the shortest distance it could to get the plates to the prisoners. That left no risk of that white hand being grabbed. Or touched.

These realities—the cubbyholes, the small waiting rooms, simply the idea that there was a "main" waiting room, and it was for Whites, and it was big—suggested to me that the white world saw Negro lives in miniature. When the world gives adults cubbyholes, it is saying, "We will give you the minimum." That hole in the wall shouts at you. Its purpose screams plain and loud. Those with white skin—unless that skin belongs to a Jim Peck, a Frances Bergman, a Genevieve Hughes—can't hear it and don't see it. But they can build it. I was by birth destined to be short. I did not need height subtracted from me. The cubbyhole made me feel smaller than God intended. Made me feel apart. Even lonely.

That's why on many of the stops these first days, I would go to the jukebox in the colored waiting room. I'd put a coin in. And I would call up a song. In Danville, there were a few 45s from Christmas season. Hard to explain, but there they were, Christmas songs in May. I put my coin in and made my selection: "Blue Holiday" by the Shirelles. A wailing call came from the jukebox. "It's been a blue holiday since you've been gone. Oh, my darling, won't you hurry, hurry home." The plaintive music, the woeful words, tranquilized me. They transported me. "It's been a blue holiday; I'm all alone. You know I, I need your love to keep me warm."[3] I did not have a girlfriend back in Atlanta, but two young ladies I was fond of could not understand why I was so devoted to the Movement. Why the Movement? Why not them? They did not want me to go on the Ride, and at this moment in Danville, I did want them with me.

I was hopeful when the Rides were over, when the victory was won, we could resume our relationships. Maybe reunion would kindle a flame with one of them that would lead to something deeper. It was a hope. A longing. This is why I pushed the Christmas buttons on the jukebox. I pushed the Shirelles because I longed for something I did not have. And I pushed the buttons on the jukebox in part because of cubbyholes.

The Danville manager wanted to know, with "Blue Holiday" playing in the background, why a white passenger would want to order and receive food in the colored section of the depot.

"You can order your food in front," he told Jim Peck.

This was perfect Jim Peck territory.

"I'll take it here," Jim said through the cubbyhole.

"Why? White customers order in front."

"If you are not going to treat my friends equally to me, then I want to be treated equally to them."

Pure Jim Peck.

The cubbyhole replied, "If that's what you want, it's okay with me."

As I watched Jim in action, I understood I was on this Ride to sit where the whites sat, to eat where the whites ate, to order where the whites ordered, and to go to the bathroom where the whites did their business. Jim was on this ride to stand with me because he could not stand people being treated unequally. Jim wanted human beings treated the same and treated well. And he wanted it now. He could not fathom why anyone would serve another human being through a hole in a wall unless everyone was served through a hole in the wall. That would have been okay with Jim. This setup was not.

Given the choice of being treated with convenience and privilege versus being treated with discrimination and disadvantage, Jim would choose to join the discriminated, the disadvantaged, the picked on, the underserved, the Underdog. I was coming to understand that, but I still had trouble comprehending why a millionaire would risk what Jim was risking.

Food came out of the cubbyhole for Jim, Walter, Frances, and Genevieve—all the whites in our group. They accepted it. That moment felt to me like Jesus washing my feet. With no words spoken it was each of these four white Riders saying to me, "I know your situation. I live it with you. I am for you." My "Blue Holiday" seemed brighter. I was grateful. That did not feel like a victory. It felt like unity.

We boarded our bus and headed to Greensboro.

Greensboro was a city of contradiction. On one hand, we encountered the first signs signaling where each race belonged. That hand offered Negro Riders little space, few seats, cubbyhole food, disregard, and disrespect. On that hand, little had changed in the year since the sit-ins. That hand suggested the struggle for freedom would take a longer war than a single battle at Lexington. It would take a revolution.

On the other hand, the reception that night at Shiloh Baptist Church—the church that welcomed the Journey of Reconciliation in 1947, the church that two of the Greensboro Four attended—surpassed anything yet on our ride. A packed sanctuary filled us with encouragement. Exuberance raised the roof. Mr. Farmer's words matched the moment. He spoke that evening of themes he had stressed during orientation in Washington. We, as a united community committed to progress, had to make segregation so expensive economically and societally that the only solution would be to change. Economically, that meant refusing to buy where our jobs could never surpass entry level. We wanted more than work. We wanted the opportunity to advance in that work. It meant boycotting businesses that coveted our dollars and bemoaned our existence. Societally, it meant filling jails and refusing bail to make our confinement an inconvenience for every community. Jim's voice was as bold as Frances's was quiet. His message met with resounding response. Just as Jim and Walter and Frances and Genevieve had demonstrated they were for me earlier in the day, the fervor of the congregants' response to Mr. Farmer's words testified to their being *for* us. Sunday, May 7, was a night that swelled our hearts.

On Monday, May 8, our stop in Salisbury, a short hop from Greensboro, brought both discouragement and hope. Discouragement. Segregation signs were telling us who was welcomed where. Hope. We ignored them, and no one intervened to keep us "in our place." In addition, two fellow black passengers on our Trailways bus—both female, both unassociated with us—followed our lead and ignored the signs on their own. No confrontation took place. Just two women going about their lives not as black women, simply as women. That was an invisible sign that suggested the printed signs were on life support.

Then came Charlotte.

I had been on sit-ins and kneel-ins and pray-ins. I had heard of swim-ins. When I woke up Monday, May 8, I did not know I would be the originator of the shoe-in. They say necessity is the mother of invention. I never knew happenstance was the father. Here's what happened.

In 1961, bus terminals often had shoe shines in them, and Charlotte was no exception. Over the first few days on the Ride, my shoes had gotten scuffed up, so I thought I'd get them shined. Simple as that. I got up on the shoe stand, and the employee told me he could not serve me. My stepping up into that elevated seat wasn't meant as a test of facilities. It was meant as a shoeshine. Nothing more. When he refused, though, I thought I should stand my ground. So, I determined to stay in my seat until he treated me as a paying customer, which I was, or until I got arrested. I could imagine my mother saying, "Charles, get out of that chair." I would have stepped down. But Mom was not there. And I was not going to surrender my right to service.

Before I knew it, police came to see what the disruption was. To my mind, there was no disruption. There was a simple expectation to be treated as anyone else would be. In Charlotte, that meant anyone who was white.

A policeman approached. "What's the problem here?"

"No problem, Officer. I am getting my shoes shined."

"This is a white stand." The officer's tone suggested I should know my place.

I did not move. I thought I should stand my ground with him, too.

"We can go easy here, or we can go hard. Your choice. Step

down and this is all over. Stay where you are and you'll be placed under arrest."

He pulled out his handcuffs and raised them up toward me.

At times in life you don't anticipate what is coming or what is happening. It makes you freeze in the moment. I was not prepared for this. As the day's observer, I was not making a test of anything. It was my role to avoid confrontation. In the moment, I felt I could not disrupt the Ride by getting arrested.

I stepped down.

That de-escalated the situation. I returned to the bus and reported what had happened. We gathered to consider an appropriate course of action, and since Joe Perkins was the designated tester this day, we sent him back into the terminal to take the seat I had relinquished.

Before signing on for the Freedom Rides, Joe had served two years in the army and ten days in jail. The former as a medical technician; the latter for sit-in protests in Florida. So, Joe knew regimen. And punishment. Both had been good teachers. Both instilled in him a penchant for action. He wanted results and was not interested in waiting. He strode atop the shoeshine stand expecting service or arrest. He was served with the latter.

The same policeman who confronted me arrested Joe for trespassing. Trespassing. On a shoeshine stand. In a public facility. It's hard to imagine today. The absurdity of it. It makes me wonder, what nonsensical absurdity do we enforce today with desperate, made-up defenses to protect something we cling to with all the strength our grip allows? What is it we will release a finger at a time that our future selves will wonder, what was that all about anyway?

In 1961, it was about Jim Crow. Can life get any more ordinary than sitting, eating, urinating, and defecating? It can't, but these were the common actions we needed to test on the Ride. If they mattered, and to Mr. Jim Crow they did, a shoeshine could matter. In Charlotte, it mattered. Joe Perkins became the first arrest of the Ride. Accused of trespassing on a shoe stand. Guilty of wanting to wear clean shoes in a Southern city. Happenstance had fathered the first shoe-in in history.

We posted bond for Joe's release, but Joe refused it. He put Mr. Farmer's words to practice and stayed behind bars. It was our first use of Jail, No Bail. I don't know if I would have done that. I like to think I would have—it was what we were supposed to do—but when I think back, it is a simple fact: I had given up my seat on that shoeshine when my moment unexpectedly came. Would I have accepted bail when the first opportunity on the Ride to be released from jail came my way? I think I might have. Not Joe. Joe had eyes that said, "Try me," and a demeanor that said, "You better not." He had a confidence that left footprints.

Our Freedom Ride protocols established in Washington required no Rider be abandoned. We could not leave Joe in Charlotte alone. Ed Blankenheim took the job. Ed would remain to assist Joe any way he could. The rest of us would move on.

Joe's refusal to accept bond that day, even in light of our offering it, steeled something in me. It gave me a specific example of what this Ride was about. An example of living out what we said we would do. An example of being who we thought we were. It gave me an example of what I could be. I don't think I would have done what Joe did that day. I don't think I could have been first. But because of Joe, I think I was now willing to be next. That's what Joe Perkins did for me in Charlotte. When "next" came, I would be ready.

## 11

### Trouble Comes a Calling

Free-dom! Freeeeeeeee-dom!
Freedom comin' and it won't be long.

—*"Freedom Song"*[1]

Bus rides create time. The countryside goes by. Sometimes you see it in a blur; sometimes in focus. Sometimes it's hypnotic like watching a waterfall. You lose yourself in thought and imagination.

Wednesday, May 9, between Charlotte, North Carolina, and Rock Hill, South Carolina, my mind drifted. I wasn't thinking of the elevated, heroic me I imagined when leaving home for Washington. That kid was gone. I was thinking of down-to-earth Joe Perkins and what he had done in Charlotte. Chosen arrest over compliance. Chosen jail over bail. Chosen to be apart from us because equality meant so much. This is what we had done in Atlanta. I had made all of these choices in my hometown. Joe Perkins had made them five hundred miles from his. That seemed different to me.

The landscape went past. I jotted in my notebook, and my mind thought ahead. Rock Hill coming up.

Our scout, Tom Gaither, had warned us this stop would be different and hard. He had cause to know. Three months before our training started at Fellowship House, Tom and eight Friendship Junior College students implemented the use of Jail, No Bail. Just what Joe had chosen for himself.

The Rock Hill group, who became known as the Friendship Nine, were participating in a sit-in at McCrory's variety store on January 31, 1961, to mark the anniversary of the Greensboro Four protests. I didn't know any of the students, but I knew Tom. Approaching Rock Hill, I imagined him marching toward confrontation.

The Trailways kept moving. My mind kept picturing.

I visualized the Rock Hill group planting themselves at McCrory's counter and attempting to order as we were doing in Atlanta. I had no personal experience of being grabbed and floored and dragged away as they were except at the practice sessions in D.C. I was sure my practice did not match their reality, and I wondered if reality was waiting in Rock Hill.

Their judge gave each of them a choice of paying $100 or spending a month on a chain gang. Hard labor. He raised the stakes by upping the fine to $200 if they chose to appeal.[2] They did not have the money to get out, but it did not matter. They would have turned it down if someone offered to pay it.

It was the notable use of Jail, No Bail in the Movement, and it changed the cost of segregation for everyone. For activists, it cost time, exposure to the dangers of jail life, and potential consequences to their futures. It cost the ordeals of hard labor. For municipalities devoted to discrimination, it cost the financial burden of incarceration. That's what Mr. Farmer wanted. Fill jails and move the cost of discrimination to the discriminators. Make government pay the bill instead of the Movement pay bail.

I'd like to think it placed a moral cost of shame on politicians and law enforcement for locking up students for wanting a meal where others could get one, but I doubt that figured into the equation.

As the destination neared, I thought about Joe. I thought about the Friendship Nine. And I thought about my time in solitary. My contemplations fortified me—I hoped they did—for what Rock Hill might bring us.

Tom Gaither's warning proved true. Rock Hill was hard.

Our bus lagged the first by a couple of hours, so I did not witness what happened to the Greyhound Riders. At our evening meeting we got the details. John and Al and Genevieve marched into the Rock Hill depot. A dozen or more tough young white guys blocked the way with their bodies and their words: "Nigger, you can't come in here."[3]

The three kept walking and John said, "I have a right to go in here on the grounds of the Supreme Court decision in the *Boynton* case."[4]

The white guys answered with words of their own: "Shit on that."[5]

One landed a punch to the side of John's face. Another hit him straight on. That's the one that put him on the floor. He curled up in a protective position. Feet kicked him. When Al came to John's defense, fists found his face, too. He refused to defend himself. The punches forced Al to the floor. The men turned on Genevieve and pushed her down with her companions. Three Riders were down before police intervened and told the whites it was time to leave.

That night, after this first violence erupted, I began to see a different side of Mr. Farmer. I saw this tall, broad-shouldered, strong man show fear. The violence against the Riders changed something for Mr. Farmer. His face expressed uncertainty. His voice had hesitation in it. Something like "I wonder if we should rethink this." Maybe it was responsibility's weight bearing down on him. We were responsible to one another, but James Farmer was responsible for all of us. Maybe it was thinking out loud. But maybe it was a leader finding the limit of his conviction. This is when I started thinking of the head of CORE more as my peer than as my superior. I began thinking of him more as Jim than Mr. Farmer. He had insecurities, too.

The stories of what had happened earlier in the day helped me imagine that I could move toward the hazard when my time came. I could see being outnumbered, outsized, outmuscled, outmaneuvered, but still pressing forward.

By the time our bus arrived in Rock Hill, the Trailways station was closed and locked. The area around it was not deserted, though. Cars and people were waiting for our arrival. Some friendly; others not. We disembarked. Local supporters moved toward us and surrounded us in protection. They briefly told us what had happened to the Greyhound group. It looked as if the same might happen to us. Carloads of angry whites glared at us, screaming words and offering gestures I had grown accustomed to since marching the streets of Atlanta.

"Coon!"

"Black boy!"

And always "Nigger."

It never got old for people such as this. Somehow, between infancy and adulthood, someone taught them to speak this way to people they sought to diminish. Words flowed out of these men like water out of an opened faucet:

"Jigaboo!"

"Get the hell out of our town!"

My parents would have washed my mouth out with soap for

using such language. Or beaten my behind. My being eighteen would not have stopped them.

Were we really testing whether we could live on an equal basis with this?

The situation was tenuous. But God has a way. When trouble comes a calling, He sends an answer. In Rock Hill, the answer was the Reverend Cecil Ivory. It was Cecil Ivory who had rallied local supporters to shield us when Trailways dropped us off. Reverend Ivory confronted the hooligans on the other side of the street like a stern parent giving wayward children "the look." Outnumbered, outsized, outmuscled, meant nothing to Cecil Ivory. He didn't cower before anyone. He stared them down by himself while his crew ushered us into cars and got us out of there. A few nights before we arrived, he told us later, an anonymous voice on a phone had promised to bomb his home and kill his family. Ivory snarled back, "Why don't you plant two?"[6]

Reverend Ivory had long led the Rock Hill Movement. In 1957, following the success of the Montgomery Bus Protest, he led a successful boycott of the buses in Rock Hill. In 1960, following the lead of the Greensboro sit-ins, Ivory led the Rock Hill sit-ins. He did all this from the seat of a wheelchair he had been in since the mid-1950s.

The day before I met Reverend Ivory, I had inadvertently invented the shoe-in. I did not know that a year earlier, he had intentionally invented the first "wheelchair-in" at the McCrory's five-and-dime in Rock Hill. During the summer of 1960, Reverend Ivory wheeled into McCrory's and up to the lunch counter to order a meal. Arrest followed, but Reverend Ivory insisted it was unwarranted because he was not occupying a McCrory's chair.[7] Ivory had a broad smile, short-cropped hair, a high, smooth forehead, a wisp of a mustache. He also had a withered, crumpled look about him because of the toll his health took. His body may have looked weathered, but Cecil Ivory's spirit was indomitable.

At Friendship College that night Jimmy McDonald led the nightly meeting in song. Whatever the day brought us in intimidation, Jimmy's guitar and Hank's voice reminded us we would overcome. Song emboldened our resolve and deepened our passion as everyone raised their voices with Jimmy and Hank. We sang every night. It would not surprise me if this day that pitted Reverend Ivory on one hand against the segregationists of Rock Hill on the other set us singing:

> *Which side are you on, boys?*
> *Which side are you on?*

One more highlight brought our Rock Hill day to a satisfying end. Joe and Ed were back. After two nights in Charlotte jails, Joe went to court. Ed sat in the courtroom keeping watch on the proceedings. The judge dismissed the charges. The *Boynton* decision may have been going unnoticed by Southern citizens, but a Southern judge enforced it. The court said Joe was not trespassing on that shoe stand after all. Our two companions left Charlotte and caught a bus to join us. Another reason to sing.

Rock Hill brought the first violence of the journey. The blood and bruises did nothing to deter John or Al. The impact on Genevieve was different. She'd never thought the scenarios at our training would play out on the Ride. The physical assaults stunned her. If Genevieve could keep going despite her shock at the events of this day, we all could. If Reverend Ivory could stand up to bigotry from a wheelchair, my standing questions of "Do I belong?" and "Can I do this?" could take a back seat to a deeper assurance of "I do" and "I can." My unexpressed wondering whether I might let the group down could find its answer in Cecil Ivory's seated courage.

At our gathering that night in Rock Hill, John Lewis got word he was a finalist for a two-year position in India to study the ways of Gandhi. To be considered, he would have to leave the Ride for a few days to go to Philadelphia for a final interview. It was a hard call for John to make. John would be the last of us to leave the Ride if the worst happened. But this was for the best. This was an opportunity to follow in the footsteps of his mentor James Lawson, who had taken the same position before returning to Nashville and teaching John almost everything he knew about nonviolence and civil disobedience. We wanted John with us, but we wanted him to take advantage of the opportunity, too.

He made his decision. He would go to the interview and rejoin us.

Wednesday morning, May 10, we entered the Trailways depot and tested the waiting room and restrooms without any difficulties. As we prepared to leave Rock Hill for Sumter, South Carolina, John left us for the airport to catch a flight to Philadelphia. He'd be back most likely the day after Mother's Day. He would join us in Birmingham or Montgomery for the rest of the Ride.

On road trips children often want to know, "Are we there yet?" For them, destination is primary. For us, New Orleans was the geographic objective of the trip, but the journey itself was the destination. Being able to live in the promise of *Boynton* was the finish line. So, while Sumter, South Carolina, was Day Seven's target, the deeper purpose was to continue testing the facilities everywhere we stopped.

Before reaching Sumter, we stopped in Winnsboro.

In Winnsboro, the call to courage rang for Hank Thomas. Hank was as tall as I was short. Hank was slender as a sapling, strong as an oak, hard as hickory, and erect as a forest pine seeking sunlight. When it came to "buying in" to what we were doing, the rules of the Rides challenged Hank more than any

other Rider. For Jim Peck and Al Bigelow, pacifism was a phi-
losophy; for Hank it was a strategy. For John Lewis and Elton
Cox nonviolence was an attitude; for Hank, it was a tactic. Pacifism. Nonviolence. These approaches to our Rides were contin-
uations of lifelong commitments; to Hank they were short-term
measures. When Hank replaced John Moody on the last day of
training, Hank assured Mr. Farmer he could remain nonviolent.
He meant it. I think. At least he intended to mean it. Let's say, he
would try.

In Washington, D.C., Hank had promised he would not
strike back. But Hank would be the first to tell you he had little
confidence he could or would keep that promise. If someone confronted Jim or Al, if someone struck John or Elton, they would
abide in nonviolence and retain their pacifism to the point of
death, because those characteristics had embedded themselves
in the core of all four of them. They had already been tested on
the trip and passed. But Hank? Well, Hank did not grow up in
nonviolence, did not believe in nonviolence, had difficulty con-
ceiving of nonviolence. Where Dr. King believed in redemptive
suffering, Hank believed in retributive suffering. Hank would
not throw the first punch in a fight, but he would throw the last.

In Winnsboro, a fight was brewing. The Wednesday lunch
stop at Winnsboro proved to be the site of our first arrest for sitting at the "wrong" lunch counter. Hank and Jim Peck tested the
facilities by sitting in the white-only section. Hank soon heard a
policeman call him.

"Come with me, Boy," the officer said. There it was again—a
Southern policeman thinking all black males shared the same
name. The officer arrested Hank, not providing a moment for
him to eat a bite or move to a less "offensive" location.

Jim tried to intervene. "This man has the right to—"

That was enough for the policeman. The cuffs came out for
Jim, too. Off they went, Jim and Hank, each taken to a separate

cell. Neither knew where the other was. Segregation in Winnsboro extended to jail.

Frances was the day's observer, so she chose to stay in Winnsboro to keep account of Hank and Jim as we moved on. Her courage amazed me. Walter and Frances had promised to look after me as the youngest Rider. Now, no one was looking after Frances. She was as alone outside the jail in Winnsboro as Hank and Jim were inside it.

Our buses pulled out of Winnsboro. Walter wanted to be with his wife. I thought I should be with her, too. But Mr. Farmer had anticipated scenarios like this. The Ride was to continue. Riders—get aboard the buses. Those in jail—no bail. The designated observer—stay close by and keep close tabs on the circumstances of colleagues.

I was supposed to be finishing up my freshman year at Morehouse. Two hundred fifty miles from those classrooms, lessons in courage and character were presenting themselves to me daily. First, Joe Perkins on Monday. He accepted Jail, No Bail. Then John Lewis, Al Bigelow, and Genevieve Hughes on Tuesday. They endured punches and shoves that put them on the ground. Today, Hank Thomas and Jim. They sat in jail. Finally, Frances. She was on her own now. Of her own choice. Out of sight. Out of touch. No college classroom could teach me any of this.

Each of these Riders had ridden a literal bus—as had I—to bring each of them to our current location. Each had also boarded a metaphorical bus when it was time to make a stand, accompanied by a personal cost. Boarding the Trailways in Washington, D.C., had been easy. When my metaphorical bus came calling my name—when the bus I was on would say, "It's your turn, Charles"—would I board it? Would I move toward the risk as my colleagues had? The deeper we headed into the South toward the land of my upbringing, the more I felt and feared a bus a comin' for me. I hoped these recent days and the examples of my colleagues would strengthen my resolve to step into real danger if my figurative Freedom Bus melded with my literal one.

Winnsboro disappeared behind us. Both buses pressed on to Sumter, South Carolina, where we were scheduled to take a day off. The planning of this rest day one week into our two-week journey now seemed prescient. John, Hank, Jim Peck, and Frances were gone from us. The extra day could provide time for them to rejoin us or for us to find replacements and restore our troop to full complement.

Waking up Thursday morning in Sumter, I discovered Mr. Farmer was absent, too. Down to eight.

Soon, though, both Jims—Farmer and Peck—drove up in the car of a CORE member. Later, Hank and Frances appeared. Celebrations ensued. Storytelling, too. The previous day had brought them all wild times.

For Hank, *wild* meant "terrifying." For Jim Peck, it meant "crazy." For Frances, "revelatory."

**Terrifying.** In jail, Hank had no way of knowing if Jim was in another cell or that Frances was in town seeking a solution to his situation. He felt alone. Worse, close to midnight, the police informed him he was free to leave. Hank was about to be released in the middle of the night in the Deep South.

The middle of the night. For those with a twenty-first-century sensibility, those words might not mean much, but to a Negro in the 1960s, the middle of the night was charged with menace.

In 1935 in Columbus, Texas, carloads of armed men stopped a sheriff's car transporting two black teenagers to jail. A mob of seven hundred gathered as twenty men led Ernest Collins and Benny Mitchell to a tree and lynched them. No investigation. No representation. No trial. No verdict. The sheriff said he did not recognize a single person in the mob. The lynching took place in the middle of the night.[8]

In 1955, Roy Bryant and J. W. Milam showed up at Mose

Wright's house in Money, Mississippi, and took fourteen-year-old Emmett Till away in the middle of the night. It was the last night Emmett Till would know.

In 1960, Atlanta police took Dr. King away from the DeKalb County Jail to transfer him to Reidsville State Prison. Alone. In the middle of the night. Dr. King had no way of knowing if Reidsville was his real destination or a convenient deceit. No way of knowing if he would make it there or vanish somewhere along the way. Things like that happened in the middle of the night.

The middle of the night was no time to be released from a Southern jail, and Hank Thomas knew it.

**Crazy.** Jim Peck had no reason to feel the terror Hank felt. Jim was white. It was daylight. White and daylight did not evoke terror in Winnsboro. White and daylight brought normalcy. Unless you were Jim Peck. Jim liked to drink. Hard stuff. Brandy. Bourbon. Whiskey. He wasn't alone in our group enjoying drink. In North Carolina, Jim had bought some brandy for the road ahead.

Police dropped the trespassing charges against Jim because they would not hold up against *Boynton*. He was on his way out of the jail when police arrested him again. This time it was the liquor. An obscure state law prohibited untaxed alcohol being brought into South Carolina. Jim's North Carolina brandy was going to cost him more than the sticker price.

The South was good at enforcing obscure laws when it came to civil rights. In 1956 Alabama resurrected an obscure 1921 law banning conspiracies against businesses to impede African Americans in their efforts to boycott the Montgomery city buses.[9] They used the law to arrest Dr. King and dozens of other protesters. The South knew how to use the obscure to solve the problems race presented them. Jim was headed back behind bars.

**Revelatory.** Frances tried to find out what was happening to Hank and Jim. Her efforts opened her eyes to the forces aligned against African Americans. She had made little progress in providing her colleagues help, but she had one idea that might make a difference in the life of her friend. Frances found a pay phone.

**Back to Crazy.** Just when Jim Peck found he would not be in reunion with us, but rather spending more time inside the Winnsboro jail, Jim Farmer showed up with bail money. No shortage of irony there. The man who had taught us a week before we would all live by the tenet of Jail, No Bail now intended to use bail money to spring the person among us least likely to accept it. That's life. Mr. Farmer paid it; Mr. Peck accepted. Jim and Jim and the CORE driver came to Sumter.

This was the second time the idea of bail had been considered. Two days before, Joe Perkins had refused it, choosing principle over practicality. Now, Jim Peck was accepting it. I didn't know what to make of that, but I was glad to have Mr. Peck with us. One Rider was back in the fold.

**Back to terrifying.** Police dropped Hank off outside the bus terminal. Hank found himself on the midnight streets of Winnsboro. A black man standing in the black of night in a town that despised black. At a time when no buses were scheduled. At a time when a mob of white men stood around the station. What to do? Being more prone to fight than flight, Hank walked from jail straight toward the bus terminal, straight toward the white waiting room, straight toward the mass of men. One of them demanded Hank get to the "nigger" waiting room. Hank ignored him and stayed in the white one. Demand changed to reprisal. The men moved toward Hank to teach him the error of his ways. Hank found himself one against . . .

**Back to Frances.** Frances's idea was to call a black pastor she knew in Winnsboro. Perhaps he could intervene on Hank's behalf in a way she could not. It was a hope.

**Back to terrifying.** Hank was brave, but he knew when the odds were too overwhelming. No reason to die a martyr at midnight when no one would see and no one would know. He beat a hasty retreat, but where could he go?

A speeding car pulled up just as Hank exited the depot. It was the black minister Frances Bergman had called. Driving like a madman. The passenger door flew open.

"*Get. In.*"

## 12

### Home in Atlanta

It's a funny thing about coming home. Smells the same.
Looks the same. Feels the same. . . . You realize what's
changed, is you.

—The Curious Case of Benjamin Button, *screenplay by Eric Roth*[1]

Dr. King said multiple times across his career, "The arc of the
moral universe is long, but it bends toward justice."[2]

Hank Thomas did not feel the universe bending in his favor
in Winnsboro. He felt terrified. "Get down!" the minister told
Hank, and Hank did.

The car sped away from the Winnsboro station. The minister checked his rearview mirror the way my father had on that
night we were driving to Atlanta in my youth. Moments earlier,
Hank Thomas thought a lynching could be in his future. Now,
he lay crumpled in the seat of the minister's car, all six feet four
inches of him, speeding away from the threat. No vehicles in the
mirror.

The minister drove Hank thirty miles to Columbia, South

Carolina, so Hank could catch a bus to Sumter and rejoin us. It was the code of the South in the age of Jim Crow. Whites had the Ku Klux Klan and their White Citizen Councils. Blacks had each other. And needed each other. Strangers helping strangers even if it meant a sixty-mile, out-of-the-way round-trip to save a soul.

Confronting meat cleavers.

Sitting in solitary for singing.

Rearview-mirror watching.

Slumping in seats while racing from trouble.

The universe did not seem to have an arc in it. Justice did not seem inevitable. The freedom we sought—to be normal human beings living normal lives—felt distant. Living in a *Morgan* and *Boynton* world, a pipe dream.

The Ride was in flux. Frances found her way to Sumter. Jim Peck and Hank were back with us, too. Only John Lewis was missing from our original crew. That soon changed. Elton Cox needed to leave because of an obligation made before the Ride. He was scheduled to speak at his home church on Mother's Day, three days hence. That would reduce us to eleven Riders, whites outnumbering blacks six to five. CORE wanted African Americans in the majority. After all, it was our freedom we were fighting for.

Gordon Carey, the CORE field director who wrote the letter welcoming me to the Ride, enlisted Ike Reynolds, a twenty-seven-year-old from Michigan.[3] Ike flew down to join us.

Morris College in Sumter provided three more Riders. Mae Frances Moultrie, Herman Harris, and Jerry Moore—all students, all black—responded to our need and stepped up to the Ride.

Our number was up to fifteen. We all attended the mass meeting at Emanuel AME on our second night in Sumter. Frances Bergman touched an emotional nerve for all of us that night, speaking of what she had witnessed in Winnsboro:

"For the first time, I felt that I had a glimpse of what it would be like to be colored. [It] made me realize what it is to be scorned, humiliated, and made to feel like dirt. . . . Anything I can do now, day or night, would not be enough."[4]

Frances reminded me of Grandma Booker. Somehow, Frances could hear the constant repeat of "nigger" directed at us and "nigger lover" directed at her and forgive. She could feel the sting and not retract. Experiencing Winnsboro was more than sting. Stings are surface. You can rub them off. Winnsboro cut.

Our new Riders had no difficulty fitting in. Herman Harris and I hit it off immediately. He was an athlete, so that gave us an instant connection. Jim Farmer put us on the same bus, and neither of us would be the tester or observer until after Atlanta. That let us be regular passengers for the next two days, and that gave us time to connect.

Jerry Moore, at nineteen, needed his parents' permission to join, and he misled them to get approval. That was an easy connection for us. And like me, both Jerry and Mae Frances were experienced at sitting in and marching.

I liked Mae Frances. She was quiet and soft-spoken. Prone to listening more than talking. But she'd had enough of Jim Crow, and her feet were willing to speak her mind. I remember Mae Frances wore high heels on the Ride. Gordon Carey's letter to women had been the same one he sent to the men—"dress neatly at all times," "wear . . . a suit," "preferably with tie." Nothing about dresses or type of shoes. I wondered if Mae Frances wore her high heels protesting on the streets of Sumter. She was on the other team. I never asked her.

We moved on from Sumter. Friday, May 12—Day Nine—took us to Augusta, Georgia, home of the Masters golf tournament, which had been played the month before we arrived. But what was that to us? The Masters had been won by Gary Player, from South Africa, home of apartheid. Player had defeated Arnold Palmer.[5] Both of these golfers—and all the rest—were rich white men to us. So was James Peck, but what a difference. Jim literally "spent" his life seeking to make life equal for all. These golfers, it seemed to us, devoted their lives to kissing a tournament trophy rather than fixing a broken society. These men lived lives we could only imagine. The Masters clubhouse was more off-limits to us than the white waiting rooms we sought to test. Freedom Riders inside the halls of Augusta National golf course? Unimaginable.

Golf was a sport as foreign to us as South Africa. Player and Palmer were giants living in gigantic mansions in the clouds and having a good time doing it; we were trying to climb beanstalks. Augusta. The thought of it seemed out of reach. Masters. The name held a different connotation to men such as Gary Player and Arnold Palmer than it did to us.

Our arrival in Augusta brought a victory. Not a victory as big as Gary Player's, but a significant one to us. For the first time in the city's history, Negroes—all nine of us—ordered and ate in the "white" sections of our respective stations.[6] No trouble. No resistance. Just food. Served as if we were as entitled to it as anyone else. It felt as if we had won something big. If we had been more attuned to the culture of Augusta, we might have held the dishes up and kissed them.

Greyhound stations had Post House restaurants. Drivers liked them because they had a service garage where their bus was washed and refueled while the drivers caught a meal. Customers liked them because they had great coffee—bottomless cup to boot. The food was delicious, too. Fried chicken. Home-style macaroni and cheese. Mashed potatoes. All with service we envied. Every Post House stop we made we saw friendly, attentive waitresses serving food with a smile. Until we walked in. We wanted a chance at that food. We wanted the smiles. In Augusta, we got both. And we liked it. Normal human beings. Them. Us.

Our meal didn't make the newspapers as did Gary Player's victory, but it tasted as good as we could imagine. So good that Herman and Walter went back for dessert later that night just to see if they could. And they did. Augusta offered the taste of hope, the promise of progress. It would be fourteen more years before a black—Lee Elder—would be permitted to play in the Masters Tournament, but on Friday, May 12, 1961, a positive future seemed closer than that.[7]

We were on the second weekend of the Ride now. I had held Saturday, May 13, in my mind since Jim Farmer posted the schedule of the Ride in Washington. Atlanta. Home. Mom and Dad. Papa and Grandma. The rest of my family. Kenneth. Lonnie. I could hardly wait. All along the way we had been treated to home-cooked meals out of the kindness of strangers. This day would bring, for me, a meal cooked *at* home. All along, we had slept in comfortable beds. This night would bring my own comfortable bed. All along, we had been in the shelter of strangers who cared about us. On May 13, I would be in the hold of those who loved me more than anyone else on earth.

To be eighteen and away from home for the first time, to be the youngest on a team where the oldest is sixty-one, to feel the distance of geographic space combined with the inability to connect with a family that does not own a phone is to be vulnerable. This was a day to fill the emptiness. A day to change the color of a "Blue Holiday." Maybe my two female friends would be at the station.

Before Atlanta, we made a stop in Athens, Georgia. Athens was the home of the University of Georgia. Four months earlier, in

January, Charlayne Hunter and Hamilton Holmes had been the first blacks to integrate the university.[8] Both had applied in 1959. Both had been denied. Both kept trying. It took two years, but a federal district court ruled both had the right to attend. Charlayne and Hamilton transferred from their current colleges to UGA. Not without tension, protest, and upheaval.

The white South in the fifties and sixties must have liked mobs. They formed so many of them. The University of Georgia contemplated closing in response to two blacks enrolling. It stayed open. Charlayne and Hamilton started classes. That's when the mobs showed up. They started lobbing words and moved to throwing bricks. To their credit, UGA's faculty overwhelmingly supported the integration of their school, and the mobs dispersed.

Given the resistance to Charlayne and Hamilton, we thought our arrival in Athens would be met with proportionate protest. It wasn't. The mobs of January were missing in May. We tested the facilities during a quick stop and, as in Augusta, found no resistance.

Fourteen years earlier, the wheels of Mr. Peck's Journey of Reconciliation bus did not dare tread in Georgia. Now we were witnesses to change for the better. Augusta and Athens were breaths of fresh air.

This was not the Georgia I knew in Atlanta. It was not the Georgia I knew existed just three counties over. Forsyth County, Georgia, lay adjacent to Atlanta's Fulton County. No segregation signs existed in Forsyth County. But not because of positive change. It was because in 1912 whites had "cleansed" the entire county of every black citizen. All eleven hundred of them. Of us. A young white woman had been brutally attacked. She lingered for a week, then died. The word spread it was Negroes who had attacked her. It did not matter the word was incorrect. Within two months, one lynching and two court-appointed hangings later, whites had expelled all Negro presence, eliminated all Negro businesses, and seized all Negro property. There were no segregation signs in Forsyth County because there was no perceived need for segregation in Forsyth County. Forsyth was pure white.[9]

So, we were under no illusions about Georgia. But Augusta and Athens surprised us. They were not the Georgia I expected, or the Georgia I knew, but on these two days of the Ride, they were a Georgia I hoped to live in someday.

There were no more stops between home and me. Atlanta, the "city too busy to hate,"[10] as Mayor William Hartsfield called it, had its gravitational pull on us.

We pulled into our respective Atlanta bus stations. It sounds crazy, but I thought I could smell Mom's cobbler. I turned my head looking out the window hoping to see Mom there. My face must have been a light of anticipation. I could feel my smile lifting my whole face as I looked over the crowd outside the bus. No Mom. No cobbler. Imagination and yearning can create mirages of your senses. My gaze searched now for Lonnie and Julian. Frank and Leon. Herschelle. Either of the girls I was longing to see.

My anticipation faded. My smile drooped. I did not know anyone waiting outside the bus greeting the passengers as they stepped down. I got up from my seat and moved toward the door. The flutter in my stomach was hope mixed with impending disappointment. I stepped off the bus. No one I knew was there to greet me. How could it be? I picked up my luggage and gathered with my companions to hear the plan for the rest of the day.

Taxis whisked us off to Paschal's restaurant. Robert and James hosted us for dinner that night, once again demonstrating their commitment to the Movement. Dr. King and his staff joined us. Dr. King was in high spirits. He told us how proud he was of us. What a model we had been. Models of nonviolence, of direct action, of redemptive suffering. He spoke of God being for us. Of God's truth marching on. We were, he told us—black and white together—champions of moral courage. He filled us with pride.

Then, he took time to talk to each of us, but more so to listen. When it was my turn, Dr. King asked me how I was holding up. I told him about the shoeshine incident and how I was able to learn from the experiences of James Peck, Joe Perkins, and Walter and Frances Bergman. He told me it was now my turn to be an example, as they had been examples to me.

Full of great fried chicken and buoyed by the conversation, we all walked the few blocks to Clark, one of the Atlanta University Center colleges where all the Riders but me would spend the night. I led the way. This was familiar ground.

We approached Clark and there they all were: Lonnie, Julian, Frank, Leon, Herschelle. Students galore from the Atlanta Student Movement joined us to cheer the Ride, voice their support, and hear our stories. I was glad for the location they had chosen. No bus station—even Atlanta's—felt like home to me. This did.

My night at Clark ended early. Even though I was feeling at home with my friends at the college, I was spending the night at my real home, and I was eager to get there. Getting home meant one more bus ride. I stepped off the bus near home and tried to smell my mom's cooking from a distance the way I had as a kid. It didn't work. Maybe my childhood senses and memories were imagination. I was ready to embrace my siblings and feel wrapped in the familiar warmth and clamor of my family.

We lived in a downstairs apartment at 21 Bradley Street now. After my sisters Joyce and Susan came along, and Mom was pregnant with Michael, we knew 5B couldn't hold us. We moved to a three-room, downstairs unit where all the kids bunked together in the bedroom. Mom and Dad still took the living room, and we had a kitchen that could be a kitchen. I stood for a moment outside our door and took a deep breath. I had only been gone a week, but it felt longer. I felt changed.

I knocked on the door. I could have walked in, but I wanted someone to open it. It was Mom. She pulled me into her embrace. I felt her arms. I smelled her hair. I pressed her cheek. She didn't need words to say hello. When she let go, I looked over her shoulder. I couldn't keep the smile out of my voice. I sang out, "I'm home." Joyce and Susan came scrambling out of the bedroom, ready for bed in their pajamas, but wide-awake wanting to catch a glimpse of me during my brief visit.

Even though I had already eaten and it was well after suppertime, I was not about to turn down a chance for my mom's sweet-potato cobbler. When you are eighteen, you can get away with a full meal of great fried chicken with a chaser of cobbler. And that's what I did. In one night, I had the best restaurant food in Atlanta and the best meal my mom could make. Home.

Dad asked, "What have you been doing, Charles?"

I hesitated, unsure of what parts of the Ride to tell them about, wondering if I should leave off the parts where it had turned dark and violent.

"We are riding through different states and staging sit-ins each place we stop."

That was the simplest way I knew to explain the Freedom Ride. Explaining the Ride as a continuation of sit-ins felt as if it would help Mom allow me to continue.

"I believe in what I'm doing, Mom." I spoke to her because I was confident in Dad's approval. I didn't think his "Get on the bus" sentiment would have changed since he said it.

"Is it all right with you if I continue with my friends? We get back on the buses in the morning."

"Tony, what has this been like for you?" Mom tried to hide the concern she couldn't keep out of her voice.

I told them about the shoeshine incident and how their son was now the originator of the shoe-in. Dad laughed. Mom asked more questions.

"Are you eating okay?"

"Have you been to jail?"

"Where do you stay at night?"

"Who have you met?"

"Have you been to jail? Tony? Have you?"

I tried to answer with the most upbeat things I could tell her. I started with a description of the Bergmans, my admiration for them, and my puzzlement over why they would join us when the fight was not really theirs. I told them about Quakers. I even told them about Genevieve swearing at me. I tried to explain Jim Peck.

Mom was as intrigued as I had been about why these whites were joining our cause. I think knowing an older couple was with me on the Ride and watching out for me helped tip the balance for Mom. I pulled the little notebook from my jacket and flipped through it to tell Mom and Dad about the kind people from churches along the way who had taken me in, fed me, and sheltered me for the night. I slipped the notebook back into my pocket, took a deep breath, and with a slight hesitancy said what I thought would gain me the permission I needed to continue the Ride.

"We met with Dr. King tonight. I think he's going to go with us on the Ride. Nothing awful is going to happen. This is something I need to finish. I know I'll be fine."

"You can go, Tony."

That was it. Mom gave permission.

"I'll drop you off at the bus station on my way to work in the morning." That was Dad's permission.

Dad understood my need to go on, and he gave me his blessing. Mom did not understand. She gave me her blessing anyway.

I fell asleep that night in my comfort and naivete. I had told

Mom nothing bad would happen, but I had no way of knowing if that was true. Jim Farmer had told us things would get rough the farther south we rode. Just three states left. Alabama. Mississippi. Louisiana. But, the days since Winnsboro had buoyed my optimism. I was excited for what lay ahead.

Sunday morning, May 14—Mother's Day—I rose in a rush to join my fellow Riders. I got out of the car at the Trailways station.

Dad shook my hand. "Do what you have to do." That was my dad. He had gone to war to do what he had to do. He knew it was my turn, and he expected me to step up. I loved him for that. He drove away.

The rest of my team was already there. Walter, Frances, Jim Peck, Herman, Ike, and Jerry came up to greet me, most expecting me. One was surprised to see me. Frances thought my mom might prevail in keeping me home.

I'd been away from my colleagues for only a few hours and was amazed to discover what had transpired since I left. What they knew that I did not.

I did not know Dr. King would not be joining us on the rest of the Ride.[11] I thought he would. His words of encouragement suggested he would board one of the buses with us to help finish what we had started. It was not going to happen. Dr. King had told reporter Simeon Booker he'd received information that we had not. The Ku Klux Klan was waiting for us in Alabama. Dr. King thought we should all stop in Atlanta and claim success, having proved a point. It would be both reckless and dangerous for us to continue into a known threat of violence. He would not do it. We should not do it.

I did not know Jim Farmer had learned of a threat facing us and had urged Genevieve to abandon the trip. Jim told her that as the only young, single white woman among us, she would be a specific target if violence broke out. Jim implored her to heed his caution. Genevieve would have none of it.[12]

I did not know that Jim Farmer himself had determined to leave. His father's health had been precarious from the start of the trip. Jim had received word of his father's death. He had to decide whether to leave immediately and attend his father's funeral or stay with us as we headed into a perilous portion of the Ride. He chose to leave. Joe Perkins would take over as the leader of the Greyhound bus; Jim Peck would lead those of us on the Trailways.[13]

I did not know Dr. King had told Simeon Booker, "You will never make it through Alabama." Or that Simeon joked in response not to worry about him because all he had to do was stick near Jim Farmer. Simeon could outrun the large, slow leader.[14] It was Farmer who needed to be concerned. That was a nice laugh line, but with Farmer now gone, it lost its humor.

How did all that happen in less than twelve hours?

Here's what I did know.

Buses were a comin' to pick us up for the next legs of the Ride. Those legs would be propelling us into the deepest part of the Deep South. Jim Farmer, John Lewis, and Elton Cox would not be with us. Circumstances had taken them elsewhere. All planned to rejoin us soon. Mae Frances Moultrie, Ike Reynolds, Jerry Moore, and Herman Harris now rode in their place.

At the Greyhound station, Hank, Genevieve, Al, Ed, Joe, Mae Frances, and Jimmy readied themselves. At the Trailways station, James, Walter, Frances, Jerry, Herman, Ike, and I would leave an hour later. But the day was upon us. The time was now. Our buses were no longer a comin'. Our buses to Alabama were here.

## Mother's Day

If the Lord could save me through this, I am here for
the duration.

—*The Reverend Fred Shuttlesworth*[1]

Jim Peck broke the news to our Trailways group at the Atlanta
station Sunday morning, May 14.

"We're in trouble," he told us. "The Klan knows we're coming. Reverend Shuttlesworth says a mob is going to be at the bus
depot to 'welcome us' in Birmingham."

Peck had been on the phone with Fred Shuttlesworth, pastor
of Bethel Baptist Church in Birmingham, and, as we all knew, the
most courageous—some said craziest—man in the entire Movement. Shuttlesworth stood up to threat the way people stand up
to lions in zoos. He seemed unmindful of the danger. The difference is there is a barrier between a lion and a zoo patron. Fred
Shuttlesworth's barrier was his faith. Reverend Shuttlesworth
smiled and laughed at threats made against him because he felt
the certainty of God's hand protecting him.

Jim Peck told us Reverend Shuttlesworth wasn't laughing on the phone. If Fred Shuttlesworth was worried about this mob, we should be, too.

We huddled as we had in Charlotte and Rock Hill to speak in quiet tones, express quick thoughts, formulate a plan, and move. Voices uttered suggestions.

"Wait them out. Frustrate them."

"Take a later bus. They'll go home."

"Bypass Birmingham. Head to Montgomery."

No one wanted delay. Little consideration was given to bypassing the largest city in Alabama. We simply sought any idea. I had not heard of "brainstorming" in 1961, but that's what we were doing.

"We are staying on schedule," Jim Peck said. "The others are underway. They have no way of knowing what Fred told me. We are not abandoning them."

Reverend Shuttlesworth's phone call was further affirmation of Dr. King's warning Saturday night: "You will never make it through Alabama."

We had not made it *into* Alabama. But we had all committed to facing hate eyeball to eyeball if necessary. It was beginning to feel as if this might be a day the eyeballs met. We boarded the bus.

Our Greyhound colleagues were an hour ahead of us. Tom Gaither had warned them Anniston, the second stop in Alabama, would not accept a busload of Freedom Riders into their town without exacting a toll. He did not mean money.

All signs pointed to danger. The warnings at Paschal's. The refusal of Dr. King to join us. The phone call urging caution from a man who threw caution to the wind. The notice given from our Freedom Ride scout that one of our first stops in Alabama might be our last.

All these said, "Stop." Our collective response was not flippant. We did not think, "Never!" We thought, "We must continue."

We had to carry on the Ride to compel the government to ensure the rights the Supreme Court said belonged to everyone. We had to stand up to those who insisted on keeping us down. The atmosphere among us was serious; the temperament, earnest. Tight-lipped concern replaced my first-day smile in Washington, D.C.

The concern justified itself as we stood in line to board the bus. Over at the ticket counter, most of the regular passengers were stepping out of line after a group of white men spoke to them. The men replacing the departing passengers looked big to me, rough, dangerous. Why, I wondered, would they get on a bus that others were choosing to abandon? That scene created eerie sensations. I don't remember feeling scared, but the hairs on the back of my neck were trying to communicate something to my brain.

Journalist Simeon Booker was in our line and no longer had Jim Farmer to hide behind or outrun, joke or no joke. Farmer wasn't with us. But Jim Peck was, and Jim was imperturbable. His resolve quieted the pounding of my heart. His confidence relaxed my neck. At least the hairs on my neck. There was no hesitation in Jim. No fear visible on his face.

Herman Harris and I boarded the bus and took the same seats we had occupied since Wednesday when Herman joined us in Sumter. First row, right side, diagonal to the driver. Jim, Walter, and Frances headed to the back. Ike Reynolds and Jerry Moore sat in middle seats.

The men I saw in the ticket line now boarded the bus. Their eyes projected shock, anger, and eagerness. With four black Riders—Ike, Jerry, Herman, and me—ignoring the segregation standard, we tweaked a sore spot in these men already provoked by their bigotry. Their world must have seemed upside down, completely backward. Three white Riders in the back of the bus; two blacks in the front seat; two others intermingled in the middle with white passengers. The exact opposite of what they could tolerate.

The Bergmans told me later that as soon as the wheels on

the bus began turning, the men started in with hate-dripping words.

"You niggers will be taken care of when we get to Alabama."[2]

I didn't hear the threat. I was too consumed in thoughts fluctuating between family and my immediate future:

"I told Mom I'd be fine."

"Why are those men on the bus? What are they going to do?"

"I lied to her again."

"What's the plan? What's the plan?"

Our only stop in Georgia before crossing the state line was in Tallapoosa. As a man got off, he looked at Herman and me in the front row and sneered, "You niggers had it good here in Georgia. You just wait till you get to Alabama."[3]

Herman and I kept silent. The bus moved on. Out the front window, a sign drew near: WELCOME TO THE HEART OF DIXIE. Herman and I looked at each other. Alabama. The men must have seen the sign, too. I now heard their words. Loud. Clear.

"You niggers think you're hot stuff. You are nothing to us."

"Hey, nigger lovers, you'll be getting yours soon."

Then the swearing.

"Shit. You motherfuckers don't have any idea what's comin' your way."

On it went. Threat. Epithet. Taunt. Vulgarity.

Their intensity, their volume, brought intensity and volume to my thoughts:

"If these guys mean business, what do I do?"

"Calm. Calm. Do not hit back."

"What am I going to tell Mom? And Dad, too?"

"I can take this. Whatever comes, I can take it."

Talking to Herman even for assurance and comfort seemed too risky to me. It must have seemed the same to him. Perhaps unnecessarily provocative. But staying quiet heightened anxiety. I chose anxiety over provocation. I kept my eyes up and forward.

I think Herman did the same. As we moved toward Heflin, the first stop in Alabama, their verbal anger echoed in my ears and my verbal silence shouted in my brain.

"Assholes. You listening to me?"

*I have the right to this seat. They have no right to keep me from it. How's Herman doing? What's going on in the back?*

"Get your black asses out of those seats."

*Here it comes. It's coming. I'm sorry, Mom. I'm sorry.*

One encouragement we had was that nothing bad had happened to the first bus. If it had, we might have encountered the Greyhound alongside Highway 78, or we might have heard something in Heflin. But no. Nothing. Nothing bad in Heflin. No bad news.

And these thugs were not backing up their words with action. Maybe my mind was being overactive, overconcerned. Still, I could not silence it:

"Ignore them. Ignore them. Look straight ahead. Straight ahead. Do not provoke. Do not provoke."

Perhaps the tough talk was bluff and bluster. Maybe nothing was going to happen.

Then we pulled into Anniston.

If you want to know what Anniston felt like when our bus arrived, go to the deadly sites—the deadly nights—of the Civil Rights Era. Go to what's left of Bryant's Grocery and Meat Market, near Money, Mississippi, where Roy Bryant and J. W. Milam killed Emmett Till three times over in the earliest hours of August 28, 1955—shooting him in the head, strangling him with wire, drowning him by attaching a cotton gin pulley to his neck that sent him to the bottom of the Tallahatchie River.

Go to the site on the backcountry road outside Philadelphia, Mississippi, where Ku Klux Klansmen executed James Chaney, Andrew Goodman, and Mickey Schwerner in the darkness of the first night of Freedom Summer in June 1964. The murderers shot all three, but they chain-whipped Chaney, the only African American of the three, before firing the shot that killed him. Find these spots. Fix your thoughts on what it must have been like on each of those solemn, horrific, now sacred, nights. Stand still.

A palpable density presses on you. Suspicious sensations start at your neck and move down your back and arms. Time slows. Your surroundings whisper, "Watch your back, your front, your sides."

This is how it felt in Anniston. But here, there were visible indications of impending threat. Temporary, hastily written signs declared the depot closed. Angry faces lingered in the street.

"Why would the station be closed when our bus is scheduled to arrive?"

"Why does everyone look so irate?"

The driver hurried off the bus as soon as he opened the door. Walter and Jim stepped off to pick up sandwiches for the ride to Birmingham. The white thugs made their exit as well. With the station closed, Walter and Jim made their way to a sandwich shop while the driver met with a police officer. Nearby stood a group of young men, who looked as though trouble might be entertainment for them. Tough guys all. Sleeves rolled up tight above their biceps. Hair slicked back with Brylcreem. Cigarettes hanging from lips. Facial expressions of magma bubbling. They had the kind of look that creates a stereotype. I had no way of knowing what Herman was thinking, but my mind started imagining scenarios of trouble coming our way and flashed back to orientation sessions of what our response was to be. I tried to steel myself by repeating one thought in my mind:

*Stay nonviolent. Stay nonviolent. Stay nonviolent.*

Ambulance sirens broke the thought echoing in my head and raised my anxiety. Multiple sirens. It seemed they might be headed to the Anniston station where we waited in eerie anticipation . . . of what?

Something was wrong.

It was in the air.

Walter and Jim reboarded the bus, handing us our sandwiches almost secretively as if food were not allowed. The conversation outside broke up. The driver now came aboard. The driver, standing beside his seat and facing us, announced with a tone of straightforward fact more than concern, "We have received word that a Greyhound bus has been burned to the ground. Passengers are being taken to the hospital by carloads."[4]

Herman and I looked at each other. Or *ambulance-loads*? The sirens now made sense. The news stunned me. *Burned to the ground?* Did that mean Genevieve, Hank, Al, Joe, Jimmy, Ed, and Mae Frances were all dead? Were they the ones being taken to the hospital? Who made it? Who didn't?

"A mob is waiting for our bus and will do the same thing to us unless we get these niggers off the front seats."[5]

*Niggers.* Always *niggers.* That's what we were to them. That's how they saw us. It didn't matter whether it was a bus driver or a tough guy or a police officer or a politician or a white mother or father. I was—we were—*niggers.* And as understandable as that word's meaning was to them, it was as puzzling, perplexing, and insulting to us. I could not imagine seeing anyone with white skin in any comparable way to how they categorized me, categorized us with a single word. *Nigger.*

Then the driver's tone changed to command: "All right, let's move."[6]

He was not talking about the bus moving on to Birmingham. He was talking to Herman and me. We stayed put, choosing instead to force him to react to our inaction. He shrugged his shoulders and tipped his head in a have-it-your-way gesture and stepped off the bus as if he had given us our chance to move.

His exit brought the entrance of the rolled-up sleeves. As if orchestrated, the hooligans rushed the bus. I could see hatred in their eyes. I could read intent in their attitude. I could sense fury in their clenched fists. I knew eyeball to eyeball was coming my way.

They streamed aboard. I had nothing to say to them. Nothing. But, if I had, they gave me no time to say it. A crushing blow to my temple snapped my head sideways. Then, one of the men grabbed my tie to control my body, and his fist slammed straight on into my face.

Herman was next. Fists smashed into his head. Collectively, the thugs pulled us to where they wanted us—out of our seats into the aisle.

James Peck came rushing up with Walter Bergman behind him saying, "These men have the legal right—"

I don't think he got much farther. A blow to his face sent Jim backward across two seats. At sixty-one, Walter did not need and could not take as sharp a blast, as strong a blow as Jim, a decade and a half younger, had just received. He got it anyway. A fist flew into his face.

Picture a bus aisle. Narrow. Confined. Yet in that small space the hoodlums proceeded to punch, kick, shove, kick, club, kick, beat, kick, mug, and kick us toward where they thought we belonged. Where we always belonged in their minds. Back in the back.

How is it possible a mob even fits on a bus? Yet there it was. Language accompanied their physical force.

"Niggers, get back," they said to Herman and me. "You ain't up North. You're in Alabama, and niggers ain't nothin' here."[7]

Whether we wanted to or not, Herman and I were moving via their power to the back of the bus. Ike and Jerry were already there. I have no recollection of their travails, but blood smudged their faces, their clothes, too.

Half of the thugs fixed their attention on Jim and Walter. Two Klansmen held Jim's head in their hands and delivered hit after hit. I had never been punched in my face, but as violent as that was, the men amplified their fury even more toward these two white men who, in the view of our attackers, were betraying white values. Peck lost consciousness. Bergman already had. As Walter lay faceup unresponsive, his assailants stomped on his chest, still venting their wrath on his unmoving body. That's what did Mr. Bergman in. Walter was defenseless.

His wife, Frances, rose from her seat in the rear of the bus and begged.

"You're killing my husband. Stop. Please, please, stop!"

The thugs met her plea with words of their own.

"Nigger lover, get back there where you belong."

Frances was helpless.

One of the muggers ended the assault saying, "Don't kill him."[8]

The bludgeoning of Walter Bergman ended with words spoken out of calculation more than sympathy. Injuries from a fistfight provoked by outsiders are more easily defended than a murder charge. Even though that murder charge in a Southern court would turn to manslaughter, then to accident, then to "What could we do?" and then to "Not guilty." From a Southern white viewpoint, we started it; they ended it. "And the losers got hurt, Your Honor." That's about all there would be to it in Alabama.

Dr. King had been right: "You will never make it through Alabama."

We were barely in Alabama.

Walter Bergman's body lay in the aisle. Jim Peck's, too. Jim was a bleeder. Blood from his head flooded the floor, making it wet and slippery. His blood did not deter the thugs. They deposited Herman and me in the back seat, dumping us there like trash in a dump. Walter and Jim came next. Their limp bodies landed on ours, their blood staining our clothes. Now, we were pancakes. Piled high. One on top of the other.

My troubles—Herman's, too—were now compounded with the weight of our two white friends lying on top of us, so I doubt I had this thought at the time, but today—all these decades later—I still puzzle:

What was a millionaire doing on the floor of a bus bleeding as profusely as Jim Peck was—perhaps bleeding out—on behalf of me? On behalf of 19 million Negroes who didn't know who he was, had never heard his name, and would think he was a fool for doing what he was doing?

Why are there Jim Pecks in the world? I still wonder. And why are there people willing to punch, kick, beat, bruise, batter, and bludgeon the Jim Pecks of the world?

I did not understand it then. I do not understand it now. But I am grateful there are Jim Pecks. And I was grateful for it then.

The policeman boarded the bus. It was an opportunity for order to be restored, for law enforcement to enforce, for Justice to remove her blindfold. But no. The officer expressed no distress, no recognition over what had transpired on this bus. Instead, his attitude seemed dismissive. He directed his words to the thugs: "Don't worry about any lawsuits. I ain't seen a thing."[9] That was all. He turned and left them and us as he had found us.

The driver reboarded the bus, faced us again, and told us how it would be:

"A mob is waiting down the road for our bus. We're going to take another route to Birmingham, and you niggers are staying put."

He started the bus and headed out of Anniston.

The ride to Birmingham was incredibly tense. All the tough guys now blocked access to the front of bus, enforcing what Trailways bus lines had not when we boarded. It was as if they were their own WHITE ONLY sign. I suppose from the Klansmen's perspective, they were defending Southern honor, Southern customs, Southern norms. But I grew up in the South. They were not defending anything I believed in. They cursed and badgered us all the way into Birmingham. Jeers, glares, hostile postures, and enraged expressions outmatched our nonviolence and our attempts at civility. Vulgarity and anger were not the only tools the men wielded. Raised fists held pipes. One held a gun.

For our part, insisting on the legal rights *Morgan* afforded us became a low priority. Stopping the bleeding and de-escalating the violence took precedence. With no hope of relief present on the bus, submission to their intimidation was our only prudent choice. We took no offensive or defiant action. There was no point. We complied. As our bus ride of the obscene moved westward toward Birmingham, we were not alone in the back-row pile. Legal Right and Reason joined us in the heap of the discarded.

The events stunned the few regular passengers seated elsewhere on the bus into obedience, too. We rode the rest of the way to Birmingham in silence, not responding to the verbal hate and anger directed at us.

The violence of Anniston filled us with dread of what lay ahead. The Greyhound destroyed. Our colleagues hospitalized at best, perhaps dead. Our Trailways team engulfed in brutality. Reverend Shuttlesworth's warning to Jim Peck had been of Birmingham. After Walter and Jim regained consciousness, we had two hours to contemplate what waited for us there. Two hours to collect ourselves enough to be able to carry on with our mission. That became our job in those two hours. Collect ourselves.

We pulled into the Trailways station in Birmingham around 4:00 P.M. No sooner did we stop than the doors opened. All of our attackers raced off the bus spewing final words of wrath and satisfaction our way. They were gone. That was the good news. The bad news was a much-larger mob of men filled the station.

Here we were characters in the absurd. Here we were looking out the window of our bus outnumbered and outmatched.

Here we were dressed in our best clothes stepping into a mass of men gathered to do us harm. Yet, here we were, history and moral obligation and commitment pulling us with inexorable force toward a danger we could not avoid.

Photographs exist in abundance of public lynchings across our nation's history where a community assembles as if attending a social event. The killing of a black man provides the town its entertainment for the night. Smiling faces, curious faces, engrossed faces, express amusement, satisfaction, and fair warning to others who might find themselves future "fun" for those townsfolk. You see photos like that, and you wonder, Who can those people be? Where can that have taken place?

This day, we needed no picture to prick our imaginations. The smirking, the curious, the engrossed awaited us. The place was right outside our bus.

We disembarked and stood on the landing dock.

Jim and I were the designated testers for the day. That meant it was up to us to head into the white waiting room and restaurant. But Jim looked like hell. It did not seem to me he would be able to conduct the test of the facilities as planned. He looked at me, and for the first time since I had met Jim, his eyes had a hint of hesitation in them, a shadow of weariness, a kernel of doubt. It was a look I took to mean, "We don't have to do this." I understood. He was far more injured than I. But we had a job to do. I looked him in the eyes.

"Well," I said, "let's go."

In my high school baseball days as a catcher, I had prepared myself for "gonna hurt" moments when runners would plow into me trying to reach home base. That's what I thought now. *Gonna hurt.*

Jim and I walked into the waiting room. At first—just for a moment—everything seemed okay. We were allowed to enter. Then a whole wall of men—no women, just men—moved toward us. The wall surrounded us. Enveloped us. The men saw Jim's bloodied face.

"Get the nigger that did that."

"Teach that nigger a lesson."

"Show Blackie what happens when niggers do this."

They assumed I had beaten my own colleague. We witnessed Fury's rise for the second time in a day.

"That son of a bitch is gonna pay."

"Send him on a one-way ticket to hell."

"Kill 'em."

Jim intervened.

"He didn't do it!" Jim yelled.

It didn't matter that I didn't do it.

"Leave him alone."

His words meant nothing. When blood swirls in the water, sharks don't leave anything alone.

"Before you get my brother, you will have to kill me," Jim blurted.

That was the worst thing Jim could have said.

As if by command, they attacked us. Jim went down immediately. I lost track of him. I'm sure he lost track of me. Each of us had our own specific troubles. As for the others—Herman, Walter, Frances, Jerry, and Ike—I had no way of knowing anything of them.

It seemed as if the mob had all kinds of weapons. The men had pieces of pipe and sticks, and some bystanders said they saw brass knuckles and a gun. Blows rained down. Voices spitting anger kept accusing me of having injured a white man to the point of bloodshed. The white man they accused me of hurting was the same man they were attacking along with me. The blows continued.

I tried to make progress toward the white-only restaurant. I may have moved the circle around me at least a few steps. I like to think I did. But let's be clear. I did not get anywhere close to the food counter. Any movement in that direction stopped. The mob pushed me the opposite way. Out of the waiting room. Into the hallway. Attackers pulled my suit coat up over my arms and head, I think, to keep me from fighting back, which I had no intention of doing. I had promised to remain nonviolent. I don't know how long they beat me. It seemed an eternity.

The taste of blood made me aware, for the second time this day, how much trouble I was in. I spread my feet to give myself a sturdier foundation. Not that I could have fallen anyway. They held me up to have a better target. A camera bulb flashed.

That was a godsend.

The Klan hated "niggers" and "nigger lovers." But they hated cameras even more. Cameras held evidence. Pictures could identify faces beyond a reasonable doubt. A "nigger lover" could identify an assailant. That wouldn't matter. A white judge or white jury would ignore the charge. A "nigger" . . . well, a "nigger" would never have a chance to identify a white assailant under oath. So, accusations made by us would not be a problem in the South. Accusation made by photograph, though? That could be a problem.

The mob gave up on me and moved toward the flash.

One picture survived the attack in the Trailways bus station. In it, six men are viciously pummeling someone. Two of the assailants are seeking to control the victim's body. Two others are leaning into the victim delivering kicks and punches. One of those wields a lead pipe in his right hand. Two others are slightly removed, one with his hand in a fist. All six have eyes fixed on the victim. The hallway is filled with other members of the mob. The victim is unidentifiable. His back is to the camera, and his body is at an angle that conceals his face behind one of the attackers.

While there is controversy surrounding the identity of the victim in the photo, I believe it is me.[10] I look at the photograph, it sure feels like me. The clothes seem like mine. The surroundings seem like mine. The image matches my memory of what happened to me. But what happened to me, also happened to Jim Peck, and Jim thought it was him in the middle of that mob.[11]

In some sense, it should not matter because Tommy Langston's single photograph captures a moment that happened repeatedly that day. What matters more is that at least six men in the photo are plainly identifiable. Not one of them was held accountable in any meaningful way. Three of them faced token charges of disorderly conduct and paid small fines. The man with the lead pipe? A serious charge faced him: assault with intent to murder. But Southern Justice brought multiple hung juries and zero days in jail. Nothing mattered. My word would not have mattered. Jim Peck's word would not have mattered. And Tommy Langston's photograph did not matter. The picture, it turned out, did not cause a problem after all.

But the flash of the camera may have saved my life.

The attackers left me to go in search of the cameraman. That created opportunity. It allowed me to walk away. I rose and sought escape. During the ordeal, I didn't run, I didn't cry out, I didn't cover up, and, for some unknown reason, I felt no pain. Maybe it was shock. I slowly walked from the station until I reached the street. As luck would have it, or fate, a city bus came at that precise moment. I got on. I had no idea where I was or where I was going. The driver looked at me in astonishment. His eyebrows rose. Alarm showed on his face. I looked at the driver.

"Take me somewhere."

# 14

## Mother's Day, Part II

The Lord knew I live in a hard town, so he gave me a hard head.

—*The Reverend Fred Shuttlesworth*[1]

Anyone who spent time in the Movement knew the name Fred Shuttlesworth. Reverend Shuttlesworth committed his life to fighting injustice in Birmingham, where segregation was more than idea and policy. Segregation stood tall and fixed. Inflexible as steel. Immovable as a mountain. Birmingham was the most segregated city in America, the toughest bastion of racism in the United States. Whites called it the Magic City; blacks called it Bombingham.

Reverend Shuttlesworth was crazy bold because he intended to "kill segregation or be killed by it."[2] And he was willing to face Goliath alone. He announced civil rights actions he intended to take in advance, and then he took them. Consequences be damned.

In 1956, the week the Montgomery Bus Protest ended in

victory, Fred Shuttlesworth announced he would lead Birmingham's Negro citizens onto city buses the day after Christmas. It was the direct opposite of Montgomery. Instead of boycotting buses, Reverend Shuttlesworth would flood them with black passengers. They would sit in any seat they chose. Shuttlesworth was saying, "Here we come."

Christmas night—twelve hours before execution of the plan—Reverend Shuttlesworth's home blew up with him in it. Sixteen sticks of dynamite blasted the parsonage into oblivion. Neighbors rushed from their houses to see their pastor's home in ruins. Police approached the crater. So did members of the Klan. Parishioners gathered to mourn their minister's death. Police and Klan to celebrate it.

Out of the rubble climbed Fred Shuttlesworth in pajamas. Untouched. Unscathed. To Reverend Shuttlesworth, it was God's hand on his life. Shadrach, Meshach, and Abednego survived the fiery furnace of Nebuchadnezzar. Daniel survived the lion's den. Now, God was saving Reverend Shuttlesworth from Bombingham's dynamite. He approached a policeman he knew to be a member of the Klan. The policeman spoke first.

"I did not think they would go this far, Reverend. I'll tell you what I'd do if I were you. I'd get out of town as quick as I could."

"Officer, you're not me. Go back and tell your Klan brothers that if the Lord could save me through this, I am here for the duration. The war is just beginning."[3]

Nine months later—September 1957, the same month the Little Rock Nine captured the front pages of America's newspapers—Reverend Shuttlesworth announced, a week before the start of school, that he would enroll his daughters in a white school. Within days, a carload of Klansmen accosted a young black couple walking a local country road. They pistol-whipped the man. They told him to relay a message: "Stop sending nigger children and white children to school together . . . or we gonna do them like we're gonna do you."[4] They stripped the man naked and castrated him with a razor blade.

Only one man in Birmingham was planning to integrate city schools. Fred Shuttlesworth. This act of profound violence was a telegraphed message to the only man I can think of who would be undeterred and uncowed by such threat against him or his family.

What would I have done in that horrific circumstance? Not what Fred Shuttlesworth did. The first day of school, Reverend Shuttlesworth walked his daughters, Ricky and Pat, toward the all-White school. A mob surrounded them.

"We've got this son of a bitch. . . . Let's kill him."[5]

The mob pounded Reverend Shuttlesworth and beat him and chained-whipped him and pummeled him and tried to kill him. He just did not die.

Now, the Freedom Ride was in Fred Shuttlesworth's city. The need was great, and a great man was available to answer the need.

The door closed. The bus lurched forward. I held on to a pole and steadied myself. Eyes stared at me. I ignored them. I stayed standing where I was. I had started the day at the front of a Trailways bus. I wanted to end the day at the front of a bus. The White driver looked ahead and drove. I don't know how long. The bus slowed to a stop. I had no idea where we were. He opened the door and looked at me almost with compassion.

"I'll let you off here. Head across those tracks." His voice had empathy. He wasn't ordering me off or telling me where I should "git" to. He was offering me something. A sense of direction. Like a compass.

"Thanks," I said, returning his gentleness with a tone of gratitude. I stepped off.

It was such a brief exchange. He didn't charge me anything. He didn't snarl or bully or mutter indignantly. He was kind. It was so different from what I had experienced all day—the nicest thing that had happened to me since entering the state of Alabama.

As a child, I reveled in choo-choo trains, huffing and puffing and billowing thick black smoke. Kenneth and I would sit down as close as we could to the rumbling iron so we could feel the ground shake as trains passed. We loved the smell of burning coal and the sight of something so big and powerful.

My parents commanded us not to cross the tracks. It was too dangerous. We thought they wanted to keep us safe from the train cars. And they did. But as I grew, I came to understand "Don't cross the tracks" was a different instruction from "Don't play on the tracks" or "Don't walk on the tracks." I came to understand Mom and Dad were protecting Kenneth and me from what was on the far side of the tracks.

That's what the driver was doing. Taking me to the tracks. Protecting me. He and I both knew the other side of the tracks meant the Black section of town—"my" section of town—where people like me would take care of people like me. In other words, the poor section, the area of urban blight that my social studies book at David T. had taught me about. In Atlanta, I lived on "the other side of the tracks." He was dropping me off in the same relative place in Birmingham. In his kindness to me, he was saying all I had to do was cross them and I would be okay. I'd be safe.

I crossed the tracks and spotted a phone booth. All of us on the Ride were required to carry pocket change, so we could place phone calls if needed. This was my day to need the change. I picked up the receiver and inserted a coin. The voice on the other end was Fred Shuttlesworth.

"What do I do?" I said. My thoughts fuzzy, my surroundings unfamiliar. I had just escaped and was in a strange city. Now what?

It was a question familiar to Fred Shuttlesworth.

"Where are you?"

"I don't know. The tracks."

That could have been anywhere. Birmingham's industry guaranteed railroad tracks. My memory of this is in pieces, but I must have given enough landmarks.

"Stay there. Help's coming."

Birmingham was Fred Shuttlesworth's city. He knew how to find people in trouble.

I felt light-headed. Unsteady. I sat down on the tracks. And waited. Cars passed. None slowed. My head felt wet. I didn't care. I cared about a car stopping.

One did. Who knows how long it took? Two men got out. The driver didn't. They introduced themselves. I don't remember their names. Deacons from Reverend Shuttlesworth's church, they said. They checked me over and looked alarmed. The top of my head, they told me, had a gash. That's why my fingers were wet. I don't remember reaching up to feel it.

"You need to see a doctor."

We drove off. Time disappears when you're in shock. Feeling wet doesn't matter. You think of minor stuff and ignore the major.

"Where's my coat? What happened to my coat?"

That's what you think. The blood doesn't matter, but who the hell took my coat?

They gave me a towel and told me to press it against my head. We pulled into a driveway. The men told me to stay put. I don't know how long I waited. They came back and started the car.

"What was that about?"

"He's not going to see you. We're moving on to the next one."

Two more stops. Two more "moving on."

There were three black doctors in Birmingham, I found out that day. All were afraid to treat me. The doctors saw us as "outside agitators." Birmingham's segregationist propaganda had

seeped into the black community. That's the depth of fear Birmingham fostered. Members of my own community saw me as
trouble. For them.

Thugs on a bus. A mob attack. Now, Negro doctors refusing to treat me, a Negro patient. This day told me in Birmingham there lived a different brand of segregationist. The whites
of this city saw war coming to their community, saw me as an
invader. They were prepared to defend their city. Or at least
their lifestyle, their customs, and their prejudices. They were
prepared to defend them with deadly force. The blacks lived in
tangible fear of the consequences of getting "out of line" with
white standards.

"What now?" I asked.

"We're going to the church."

Bethel Baptist Church stood on Twenty-Ninth Avenue in Birmingham. The other side of the tracks from where the bus driver
let me off. A double staircase rising from the sidewalk to a single front door took parishioners to a long lengthwise sanctuary
with tall, arched stained glass windows. Beautiful. Majestic. I
had never been to Birmingham, so I had never seen it. Beside it,
the parsonage, rebuilt after the 1957 bombing took Fred Shuttlesworth from bed to crater, provided church-supported housing for the pastor and his family. Ruby Shuttlesworth loved her
husband, but years of confronting Birmingham's racism was
taking a toll on her and her children—Fred, Jr., Ricky, Carolyn,
and Pat. When the deacons couldn't find a doctor to treat me, it
was Bethel Baptist's parsonage they headed for.

I held the towel to my head. By the time we arrived at Bethel,
blood had begun to soak the towel. The deacons led me inside
the parsonage. Reverend Shuttlesworth came to my aid. One

look at my head put him on the phone for a doctor. I was starting to pay attention to the wet. My fingers were slick and sticky
simultaneously.

A nurse in the congregation said she could bandage my injury with a patch that would pull the open wound together until
we could find someone willing to treat it. She cleaned the area
and bound the wound. Knowing the blood flow was stopped relaxed me. I was grateful.

Jim and Walter arrived. Bethel members rushed to help Jim
into the parsonage, his forehead a mass of red. Both men looked
awful. Jim saw me and shook my hand. It might have been re-
flexive. He didn't seem much aware of what he was doing.

Reverend Shuttlesworth switched tactics. Not able to find
a doctor to help with my wounds, he turned to calling for an
ambulance to aid Jim. No ambulance would come. White emergency providers had no intention of coming to the other side of
the tracks. Black providers balked. It was the doctor scenario all
over again. Fear. Concern for their own safety. Worry over arrest.
Worry for their families. Birmingham's oppression mired an entire community in a bog of inaction. Reverend Shuttlesworth
was furious. He bristled at their fear. He thought it cowardice.
He thought it contemptible.

My wound seeped. Jim's practically gushed. I had no way to
see my injury; Jim's skull was exposed from his.[6] He was in far
worse shape than I was.

Somehow Reverend Shuttlesworth prevailed. An ambulance
was on its way. So were the police. They challenged Reverend
Shuttlesworth to turn our white Riders over for arrest. Segregation laws extended to residences. Walter and Jim were breaking
them.

Where had the police been earlier in the day when we
needed them? Even *The Birmingham News* wanted to know the

answer to that. "Where Were the Police?" was the headline on the front-page editorial on Monday, May 15.[7] We later found out the commissioner of public safety, Bull Connor, had given the Klan fifteen minutes free rein to do whatever they wanted before he would bring his forces to the bus stations and stop them. Connor could get away with it. It was Mother's Day after all. He could claim it took time for his officers to report in from their celebrations. And no one would question Connor's authority.

Except Fred Shuttlesworth.

Reverend Shuttlesworth challenged back. He wasn't surrendering Riders to police when what Jim needed was medical care. The police backed down and left. Fred Shuttlesworth was accustomed to intimidating the police as much as they tried to intimidate him. Finally, an ambulance took Jim to the hospital. My bleeding was sufficiently stopped that I stayed at the parsonage.

All the Riders in our Trailways group found a way to Reverend Shuttlesworth's church. Simeon Booker showed up, too, and we all started to piece together our individual experiences of the day. Each had a story to tell. Herman and Jerry avoided the melee at the Birmingham bus station by escaping moments before the violence began. Frances, too, dodged disaster by taking a city bus, at Walter's insistence, away from the trouble before it started—as I had done after it ended. Walter, himself, chose to stand with Jim and me. I did not know it, but Walter followed us into the station disregarding his injuries. It was a near-fatal decision. The mob descended on this older, already-wounded gentleman with ferocity. He did not remember what had happened, but Simeon witnessed it.[8] The mob hammered Walter till he collapsed to the floor. A new layer of bright, fresh blood lined his head atop the dried blood from the bus ride. Walter crawled and pawed the floor like a stunned, wounded animal seeking safety.

Jim was beaten unconscious by the mob that encircled him. But more than that, Jim's head was busted open, his nose crumpled, his face gashed, his clothes soaked with blood. That was when Simeon knew he had to leave to get help.

When Walter awoke from his stupor on the floor of the station, the depot was almost empty. The storm had passed. The mob gone. He stumbled upon a nearly incoherent Jim. Together, the dazed pair succeeded in hailing a cab with a black driver who brought them to Bethel. To Fred Shuttlesworth.

Ike Reynolds was roughed up and deposited in a Dumpster much the way we all had been deposited in the back of the bus in Anniston.[9] He was injured, but nothing like Jim or Walter or, for that matter, me. CBS newsman (and future anchor of ABC's national news broadcast) Howard K. Smith was coincidentally in Birmingham filming for a special documentary called *CBS Reports: Who Speaks for Birmingham?*[10] Having been tipped off to the coming violence, Smith was on-site during the riot. Smith came across Ike and took him to a hotel room to get a firsthand account for the evening news. Somehow Smith's report and Ike's testimony never made it on air. Ike got to Bethel Baptist thanks to Smith's news team.

As Jim headed for medical help, the caravan carrying our Greyhound companions from Anniston arrived at Bethel Baptist. Hank. Genevieve. Relief replaced our fears created earlier in the day by the ambulance sirens we heard and the ominous words of our bus driver. Al. Mae Frances. Stunned and battered. But alive. And mobile. To us they seemed resurrected from the dead. Jimmy. Joe. Ed. We were so glad—and so thankful—to see them. All were present and accounted for. Joy abundant. Grace overflowing.

Details emerged as each of them related the difficulty of their day and the fate of their bus.

When the Greyhound stopped in the alley adjacent to the bus station in Anniston, Hank told us, the scene was as tranquil as . . . well, as Mother's Day. Anxieties the Riders felt seemed misplaced. Quiet and calm and Sunday-in-May serenity pervaded the air. Then, it didn't.

From nowhere Anger surrounded the bus. Clubs. Chains. Bats. Sticks. Hatred smashed against windows. Outrage beat on the body of the bus. Testosterone spewed venom. It was madness. Genevieve could not believe her eyes or her ears. Hank felt caged. The bus started rocking. One man lay down in front of the tires to block the bus from leaving. Others stabbed at the tires with blades to keep the bus from leaving.

A half hour of trapped terror ensued. Riders watched with the horror of fatal inevitability. A window shattered. An object hit the side of the bus. Another thud. Another. Hank and Genevieve and Joe and Mae Frances looked through windows in shock at Anger screaming at them to come off the bus. Another window shattered. Hatred demanded Al and Ed and Jimmy to get off the bus. Their fear commanded them to stay on. They stayed on. Fists pounded the bus, bats struck. More windows broke. More shouts. Riders were powerless against the violence. The confusion of yells and thuds, the vibrations and rocking of the bus, the shattering of more glass added to the terror, to the inexplicable vehemence of pent-up, now-outpoured, aggression.

Then it was over. Police sauntered in and made a show of restoring stability. They cleared enough of a way for the bus to leave. The driver backed out of the alley. It drove—more like limped—away.

But not alone.

Cars and trucks followed. Some passed the bus then slowed to keep the bus from speeding up or getting away. As if it could with punctured tires. A bizarre and dangerous caravan of vehicles left Anniston heading west down Highway 202.

Riders wondered what possible path to safety could be available. Then they found out.

None.

Five miles out of Anniston, the Greyhound's tires lost all air. Riding on rims, it lost the ability to continue. The driver pulled over at an intersection with a lone country grocery store, Forsyth and Son. He abandoned the vehicle, leaving Riders and regular passengers at the mercy of men intent on teaching the Riders the last lesson of their lives: *Don't.* Don't think of changing our ways. Don't dare to try your laws in our state. Don't ever come this way again.

Men beat the bus with arms and fists and crowbars and pipes and chains. One man tossed an incendiary device through a broken window. It went off. Smoke filled the cabin. Passengers coughed and panicked.

Where to go?

What to do?

Genevieve bent low to let the smoke rise over her. Hank, too. First, he crouched. Then, he lay in the aisle. He could try to make it out of the bus and into the mob. Or he could die. He could save himself from murder by choosing to suffocate to death. He could fall asleep from breathing smoke, or he could die at the hands of a mob. Fear of the mob surpassed fear of the smoke. He chose asphyxiation. Hank determined to stay down.

Genevieve chose life. She told us she shouted out, asking for direction, "Is there air anywhere?" No reply.

Smoke turned to fire. Panic turned to desperation.

That's when Genevieve acted.

Genevieve rose from her knees and sought a window to slip through. She squirmed and writhed her way out and down to the ground. There she saw Jimmy and Charlotte Devree, the journalist. They had wedged their way out of windows, too. They all crawled, then scooted, as best they could from the bus now turning into flame.

Hank discovered his instinct for survival overcame his inclination to die. He rushed for the front door and pushed with all his considerable strength. That's when the voices lashed out.

"Let's burn them niggers alive. Let's burn 'em alive!"[11]

Hank pushed. The mob pushed harder. Stalemate. The door did not budge.

Nowhere to go. No way out. Hank could not fit through a window. His first decision to choose death on the bus would end up matching the mob's final verdict. Smoke or heat or flame would suffocate or burn him to death.

Then something remarkable happened.

An explosion in the back of the bus. Where the fuel tank was.

A mob, prepared to burn human beings alive, was not prepared to suffer the same death. They backed away. The door opened.

Hank tumbled out the door, followed by a chain of passengers hurrying from the flames, stumbling to the ground. Confusion consumed the dazed escapees. Fire consumed the bus. Thick black smoke billowed from windows. Yellow flame flew up. Clouds of charcoal and ash and dust and soot climbed skyward. The broken front windshield served more like a train's smokestack, allowing massive plumes to rise. Hank, Mae Frances, Joe, and Ed sat in enfeebled fatigue looking back at the conflagration. The bus was a furnace. The door from which they'd escaped now engulfed in incineration.

Hank told us a man approached him expressing concern.

"Are you okay?" the man asked as if he meant it.

Hank nodded yes, and a baseball bat struck his head. Now he wasn't. The bat flattened him to the ground.[12]

Mae Frances was grounded, too. Lying prone in her white dress, weakened from smoke inhalation, Mae Frances needed help. Her face pressed against the grass and earth. In that moment of need, help showed up. No adult. A child.

While adults conspired to kill, a child tried to save. Janie Forsyth, twelve-year-old daughter of the owners of Forsyth and Son, brought life-restoring water. She was old enough to know she was supposed to be against those lying on the ground. She helped anyway. People needed water. She provided it. Glass after glass.[13]

Hank and Joe told us what happened next.

Police broke up the crowd. A white couple took Genevieve to a hospital. An ambulance came for the white Riders, but would not take our black colleagues anywhere. The driver finally relented and took everyone to the Anniston hospital.

In a sense, the hospital was simply a larger version of the bus. Riders inside. Mob forming outside. Buildings don't rock as buses do, but they can burn. Our Greyhound colleagues feared another fire might be set. Joe Perkins saw the writing on the wall and called for help. He called Reverend Shuttlesworth.

Reverend Shuttlesworth would have driven two hours to Anniston and headed into the threat of the mob without wavering, but we were already at his parsonage, and we needed his help. Instead, he sent his longtime bodyguard, Stone Johnson, with carloads of deacons telling them they must remain non-violent in the face of any violence perpetrated upon them. All agreed. But Stone Johnson believed in maintaining equality, or at least equilibrium, with what he called his "nonviolent .38."[14] Fred Shuttlesworth may not have known it, but his bodyguard was not about to sacrifice himself at an altar of pacifism. He was a bodyguard for goodness' sake.

Others riding in the caravan brought shotguns. They drove up to the hospital, confronted the antagonistic crowd, picked up the Riders, and raced back to Bethel Baptist in Birmingham.

When they arrived, their guns were gone. Stone Johnson's form of nonviolent, direct action had provided safety and rescue.

Everyone except Jim Peck was back in the fold at the parsonage.

At the church that evening, a crowd filled the sanctuary to capacity. It was an emotional meeting. Thirteen of us sat in a line of chairs across the front facing the congregants. We must have looked like a ragtag, beaten bunch. Blood still caked our skin. Bruises by then were fully swollen, tender, and dark. I remember that Dr. Bergman spoke, and a lady in a faded gabardine dress sang a song—a plaintive, mournful hymn—that filled the room with energy. We listened to Scripture and joined together in hymns and freedom songs.

Then it was Reverend Shuttlesworth's turn.

He rose from his seat and to the occasion. Only Fred Shuttlesworth could stand among the beaten, the bloodied, the injured, the fragile, the defeated . . . and smile. He smiled a smile so broad the ocean could fit inside. He smiled a smile that made you feel as if God Himself saw your suffering and saw such purpose in it as to say, "Well done, good and faithful servants."

Reverend Shuttlesworth looked out at the gathering that night and looked down upon us.

"When white and black men are willing to be beaten up together, it is a sure sign they will soon walk together as brothers."[15]

Fred Shuttlesworth could see defeated, beaten men and women sitting in shock and yet project a message that essentially said, "Now we are getting somewhere."

After the meeting, Reverend Shuttlesworth assigned deacons to protect us wherever our night's rest was. The deacons brought their weapons. I found it comical that we nonviolent warriors were being protected by Fred Shuttlesworth's nonviolent men armed to the teeth with guns.

I slept well that night. Everything was over. I had guards

guarding me. I had a great meal in me. And I was exhausted. The events of the day had drained me, but I had—we all had—done something. I had—we all had—made it plain: we belonged. I had—we all had—kept moving forward and lived up to what we sang: "Ain't gonna let nobody turn me 'round." And I could rest knowing that CORE had contacted my next of kin—Lonnie King—so I knew he would let my mother know I was all right.

Mother's Day came to an end. I've never had another one like it. I hope I never do.

## The Day After

Precious Lord, take my hand
Lead me on, let me stand
I'm tired, I'm weak, I'm worn
Through the storm, through the night
Lead me on to the light
Take my hand, precious Lord, lead me home.

—*Thomas Dorsey, "Take My Hand, Precious Lord"*[1]

Where the hell was my coat?

I remember the mob pulling it over my head to control my arms. I wasn't going to use my arms to protect myself or my fists to hit back at my attackers. But they did not know that. I doubt it would have mattered if they had. I remember the coat being stripped from my body as the arms of my muggers thrashed to hurt me. In a fire, a person's priorities are to leave things behind and get out. In the fire of the Birmingham bus station, my mind wasn't on my coat. The heat was on, and I needed to get away. The required dress code would, for me at least, have to be excused.

It wasn't the dress code that bothered me. It was the coat's contents.

My notebook was gone. All the information. All the names of those who had housed me and helped me. All the people I had hoped to keep in touch with or at least thank at the end of the Ride. Gone.

The assault. The grabbing. The punching. The semiconsciousness. Somewhere in all of it, my notebook had disappeared. My recollections would have to serve as my memory of these past ten days in my life. The lumps on my face. The cuts. The bruises. The gash on the top of my head. All these ached Monday, May 15. But none bothered me, as I recall, more than the notebook lost. It was gone, and it was not coming back.

On Monday morning, May 15, we all reassembled at Bethel Baptist. After the Mother's Day service, some of us had fanned out to stay with members of Reverend Shuttlesworth's congregation, but many in his church were scared and not able to risk taking us into their homes. So, the rest of us had to make due at the church or the parsonage. Reverend Shuttlesworth's daughter, Ricky, woke on Monday morning to find sheets soiled with Freedom Rider blood.[2] While that should have been shocking to a normal teenager in a normal house in a normal city, little was normal about being the daughter of Fred Shuttlesworth. Sheets soiled with blood were not far out of the ordinary for Ricky and her siblings.

The biggest surprise Monday morning was Jim Peck being back with us. Jim had required extensive medical treatment at the Birmingham hospital. Reporters had gathered in his room to get his story. Amazingly, he responded to one of their questions about the Ride, "The going is getting rougher, but I'll be on that bus tomorrow headed for Montgomery."[3]

Fifty-three stitches kept Jim at the Birmingham hospital till

2:00 A.M. when Reverend Shuttlesworth and one of his deacons picked Jim up to return him to us. Even that did not go without incident.

First, police threatened Jim with arrest for vagrancy as he waited outside the hospital for Reverend Shuttlesworth to arrive.[4] When Jim tried to avoid arrest by heading inside, the hospital refused him readmittance. They had discharged him. He had no cause to reenter. That refusal had nothing to do with his status as a patient; it had everything to do with his being a Freedom Rider, a troublemaker, an outside agitator, a nigger lover.

When Reverend Shuttlesworth's car arrived, Jim got in, and it pulled away. The confrontation was not over. Police stopped the car under the bogus accusation of its being stolen.[5] *Driving while black* may be an expression coined in recent decades, but it is far from a modern phenomenon.

When Jim showed up at our meeting Monday morning, he looked as if a hurricane had hit him. It had. Huge bandages framed two black eyes and covered his forehead, his temple, and one cheek. Teeth were missing. Gauze stuck to his face, but it was hard to know if it was glue or Jim's blood serving as the adhesive. The back of his head was a patchwork of white compresses soaked in blood against the darker backdrop of his hair. I was in awe of the man. The most beaten among us, the most gravely injured, was this enormously wealthy, white man.

My parents had taught me jealousy is not a good thing. Proverbs says, "Envy rots the bones."[6] Still, my mind had often wondered what I would do if I had money beyond imagination. Help my parents? Buy a mansion? Do whatever I pleased? Never did I consider the possibility of fortune living itself out in the manner that sat before me in the crumpled, battered, broken, still-bloodied form of Jim Peck. This millionaire was willing to surrender his life so I could wonder and imagine and perhaps someday do whatever I pleased. How could it be that going through what he had endured in the past twenty-four hours was what Jim Peck pleased to do?

The Bergmans, too. There at the table sat Walter and Frances, two of the kindest people I had ever met. Both were retired educators from Detroit. I don't remember hearing the word *retirement* growing up. If I did, the word referred to the wealthy of the world. It did not apply to people in the Bottom. In the Bottom, age and disability made people stop working. But, retire? I was decades away from living in a country where that word could apply to people of my heritage.

It was not a word unfamiliar to the Bergmans. They had worked across their careers and now had the opportunity for a life of leisure. Some leisure. Like Jim, they were joining in that morning's conversation as if the previous day was what they had signed up to do. Not that they welcomed the violence, but that they had always known Jim Farmer's orientation warnings were distinct possibilities, even probabilities. Tom Gaither's scouting report had proven accurate. The Bergmans had known it could. Knowing it, they had boarded a Freedom bus anyway. For ten days.

Across the trip, the Bergmans had assured me they would protect me. On Mother's Day, Walter had tried. He had come to my defense twice. On the bus in Anniston and in the Birmingham station. This teacher, labor activist, and civil rights advocate had spent a day of his retirement being pummeled twice on my behalf.

The willingness of the white Riders to fight, even at great cost to themselves, for something they already had—and were in no danger of losing—on behalf of millions who did not have it amazed me.

We discussed how to move forward given the setbacks of Mother's Day. There was no way to know what awaited us if we returned to the depots. If one of the gentlest holidays of the year—Mother's Day—brought bloodshed and destruction, what would a workday bring when Birmingham's streets would be filled with the same types of people but more of them? It was obvious we were vastly outnumbered by the Klan, the police, and the general population, who had little concern for our well-being and few boundaries on their behavior. We felt safe and secure at Bethel Baptist, but our objective was not Birmingham; it was New Orleans.

That Monday morning, we were not thinking about New Orleans. We were concerned with returning downtown and with the upcoming stops on our itinerary—the state capitals of Montgomery and Jackson, and the smaller towns along the way.

We discussed the practicality of continuing. Was it even possible to move on? Two Riders were more shaken than others: Jimmy MacDonald and Mae Frances. Both were weak from smoke inhalation on the Greyhound and filled with trepidation from the trauma of the previous day. Genevieve, also, had apprehensions after being shell-shocked by Sunday's horrors. Years later, she would say, "I'd learned to be afraid overnight. I was no longer so interested in dying for the cause. I appreciated being alive."[7]

Beaten as he was, Jim Peck made the most impassioned plea to continue. A man accustomed to professional dress, Jim sat at the meeting looking disheveled and wan. If the most severely beaten of us were to quit, he told us, violence would win. All the segregationists would need to do would be to react with more violence anytime we challenged the status quo even if we had the law of the land on our side.[8]

I agreed. We had faced arrest in Charlotte and Winnsboro. We had faced violence in Rock Hill, Anniston, and Birmingham. Papa's question to me after Georgia Tech denied me admittance and his irritated demand both sounded in me: "What are you going to do about it?" "Do something!"

We took a vote. By a two-to-one margin, we agreed the Ride must continue.[9] We would take one bus and stay together the rest of the way. Tired and weak, we had been through the storm. Battered and beaten, we had made it through the night. We hoped the light of righteousness and justice awaited us this new day.

Members of the Bethel Baptist congregation drove us to the Greyhound station to catch an afternoon bus to Montgomery. The events of Sunday had gained national—even global—attention. A photo of the burning Greyhound bus blazed across front pages of newspapers throughout the country and the world. National news organizations were descending on Birmingham. Given that, we thought police protection would accompany us to guarantee our safety. America was supposed to be "the land of the free," and here was a mob setting fire to a bus trapping American citizens inside. Surely, city, state, or national government would not allow a repeat of violence with the nation and world watching.

One by one, we climbed out of the caravan of cars that carried us to the Greyhound bus station. We tried to move with resolute purpose toward the station despite being stiff and sore from our wounds. Even the bandaged Jim Peck refused to limp or grimace. The police decided—or were ordered—to do their duty. They formed a barrier and held up their arms to keep this day's mob away from us. As the current group of Anger hurled hateful words at us, we sought to stay calm, but we had to be on high alert. The two beatings I had received the past day made it difficult to keep my eyes focused forward. I wanted to ignore the threats, but a movement here, an action there off to my side, I'm sure, drew involuntary physical responses. A slight turn of my head. An unintentional tremor.

Their shouts and jeers reached us, but that is all. Violence boiled in their words, and I could feel the thoughts of the men lined up eager to strike more blows. Police in my line of vision wore sneers. The protection they offered did not mean they were suddenly on our side. They were doing the least they could to prevent physical violence, it seemed to me, while enjoying the verbal thrashing we received.

Once we were in the station, police threatened Reverend Shuttlesworth with arrest for staying with us as we huddled together and waited for our bus. Another case of vagrancy in their minds. So, Reverend Shuttlesworth did what he always tried to do—solve the problem by being more obstinate than his opponents. He purchased a ticket he had no intention of using.[10]

For a man committed to nonviolence, Reverend Shuttlesworth was a master counterpuncher. He tweaked and poked, goaded and prodded, the inflexibility set against him with annoying intentionality. Boarding the Birmingham buses rather than boycotting them back in 1956 was not breaking the law. He was following the law set by the *Browder* decision. Taking his girls to Phillips High School in 1957 was not illegal. The *Brown* decision had made it legal. By defending us on our Freedom Rides, Reverend Shuttlesworth was standing up for the law under *Boynton*. Now, by purchasing a ticket to Montgomery, he was doing it again. He was no vagrant. He was a passenger. By blatantly obeying the laws, Fred Shuttlesworth could not have been a bigger irritant to Birmingham's bigotry.

We sat together in the white waiting room. In Birmingham, Alabama, Hank, Herman, Jimmy, Joe, Jerry, Ike, Mae Frances, and I were seated in the bastion of Bull Connor's segregation. On Sunday, the forces of segregation had hammered us. On Monday, taking our seats and keeping them felt like victory. Tenuous, fragile victory. But victory.

We sat. We waited. We read. We waited more. We experienced the tedium boredom offers in the downtime of waiting in a transportation terminal. And we did it in what up to this day had been the "white" waiting room of the Birmingham bus station. Oh, that we could live in such boredom without police protecting us. Oh, that these seats had never had rules about whose tedium was allowed to occupy them. Glorious boredom. Wonderful tedium.

It is the human condition, I suppose, to be dissatisfied. Our inactivity stretched beyond our expectation. Our afternoon tickets to Montgomery turned out to be tickets to nowhere. A three o'clock departure came and went. No bus driver was willing to take us to Montgomery. While most of us, including me, sat and sat and sat some more, Reverend Shuttlesworth was a whirlwind of activity as he demanded accommodation.

Since earlier in the day, Attorney General Robert Kennedy had been in personal contact with Simeon Booker and Reverend Shuttlesworth to navigate through the crisis. By afternoon, Kennedy had given Reverend Shuttlesworth his private phone number.[11] Now, Reverend Shuttlesworth considered himself to be on a first-name basis with the attorney general of the United States.[12] At least to us. "Bob," he told us, had to get us a bus driver, and he would. "Bob" had to get us police protection beyond the city limits all the way to Montgomery, and he would.[13] Reverend Shuttlesworth did not want us continuing without a guarantee of our safety.

Our time in those seats reminded me of Atlanta's lunch counters. Hours of staying in place while being denied service. In Atlanta, the lunch counter service never came. At least not as of May. In Birmingham, bus service to the state capital still hung in the balance. And so, we sat, and we waited.

Then the announcements came. There would be no guarantees. There would be no bus driver.

Alabama governor John Patterson was not budging, and he was certainly not offering promises. He would provide police escort to the city limits, and even to the nearest border to get us out of his state. He was not going to have local or state law enforcement provide a convoy to Montgomery. "Rabble-rousers," he called us. He had neither interest nor inclination to side with rabble-rousers.

There would be no driver either. Demands from Reverend Shuttlesworth to Attorney General Robert Kennedy led to demands from Kennedy to the head of the Greyhound station. Get a driver. But no driver would yield to being ordered into obedience. None would risk his life driving a bus destined for destruction. Then get a Negro driver, Kennedy ordered. As if there were Negro bus drivers in the Greyhound system.

Hours passed full of negotiation between Reverend Shuttlesworth and Robert Kennedy and Greyhound officials and Jim Peck and Joe Perkins. Disappointment began to replace the small sense of victory we took in integrating the station. Earlier satisfaction began to deflate. Reality was setting in. Our effort to continue the Rides would be in vain.

We needed a Plan B. We gathered to consider our options and decided we would fly out of Birmingham to get to Montgomery. This was not what we wanted, but we were stalemated. We saw no practical alternative. The bus station eagerly refunded our money, and CORE staff members purchased airline tickets for us.

By now it was late afternoon, and when we left the terminal, the crowd was small. I thought we had waited them out. I thought they had given up. Since we did not have to put on a show of fortitude for a mob that was not there, we straggled out of the terminal to Reverend Shuttlesworth's caravan waiting to drive us to the airport. The hours of sitting and waiting had stiffened sore bodies even more. We each had specific wounds that created their own hardships. The gash on my head was bandaged and sore. Jim and Walter looked awful from the neck up, but their gait spoke of broader injuries. We hobbled and limped and grimaced as we climbed back into cars. Sinking into my seat, I lay back, closed my eyes, and felt grateful for the reprieve from another threat. The gratitude was short-lived. At the airport, the threat reappeared. Another gauntlet of frenzy waited for us. The crowd had not dispersed. The mob had not given up. It had relocated.

A large, angry crowd waited for us. The intensity of those incensed at our being in their city—even as we sought to leave it—at once bewildered and worried me. My memory of driving past those eager to get to us is in freeze-framed images. Eyes ablaze. Freeze. Muscles tensed to full strength. Freeze. Veins bulging from throats. Freeze. Fists too clenched to pry apart. Freeze. Jaws locked. Teeth bared. Why such anger? These people did not know us. We did not know them, and we did not feel any of what they felt. How could our existence in their city bring such visceral hostility? It was like watching a movie in slow motion and being unable to push play or fast-forward. The images we passed made no sense. But there they were. I think of them today, some six decades later, and there they are again. There they will be as long as I live. Anger directed at me by strangers just for being me. It was the same as the day before, but with the protection of the police, this day's mob could not reach us.

We made it inside the airport fatigued and frustrated that we were leapfrogging on to Montgomery, but relieved at having a course of action. We were prepared to put the events of the previous and current day behind us. When we were allowed to board the plane, we had to walk out to the tarmac, past more ill-wishers who screamed yet more words that had by now become both familiar and requisite. We heard words no mother wants her children to hear, words no one wants directed at him or her. As epithets and vulgarities filled my ears, I preferred to fill my mind with words more meaningful to me: Precious Lord, take my hand. Lead me on, let me stand.

Our day had brought one roadblock after another to the

continuation of our journey. As soon as we settled in our airplane seats, a new means of stopping us arose. The pilot announced a bomb threat. The plane could not fly under that circumstance. We would not be getting out of the burning bus that was Birmingham after all.

We deplaned and returned to the terminal. Another wait brought another plane. Another plane brought another bomb threat. Discouragement rose to new levels as we wondered what Plan C would be.

Unknown to us, Robert Kennedy had rushed a representative of his office to navigate and accompany our departure from the city. John Seigenthaler, a soft-spoken, tough-minded mediator with a strong Southern drawl, arrived as we sat dispirited in the terminal following the second canceled flight, and he tried to assure us all would be okay. Seigenthaler negotiated with the airlines to try to arrange a third plane. Despite his encouraging presence, the events of the past two marathon days were leaving us sapped, almost disoriented. Each of us tried to project confidence, but a bus burned, multiple riots, multiple muggings, canceled buses, gauntlets of fuming madness, and two bomb threats all warred against endurance. How would this day end?

At day's start, we had voted to move on to Montgomery by bus. Near day's end, we were taking a new vote, and that vote found a new outcome. Every effort to reach Montgomery had been thwarted. We were barely on our feet. We feared Montgomery would be a repeat of Mother's Day, and we could not survive a repeat of Mother's Day. Jim Peck could not. Walter and Frances could not. Mae Frances and Genevieve could not. I could not. And we were not only responsible for ourselves. Other lives were on the line. Journalists who had been with us for the entire Ride were at risk. Other passengers and bus drivers were at risk. Our photographer, Ted Gaffney, overheard a bus driver say, "I ain't no Freedom Rider. You ain't gonna kill me."

We changed our minds. Our flight's destination would not be Montgomery. It would be New Orleans, the final destination for the Ride.

I was one of the changed votes. I was exhausted. Given the choice of flying to more rabid crowds in Alabama or flying to the finish line, my decision was easy. Though it would end the Freedom Ride, I chose with the majority. "For God's sake," I thought, "let's get on a plane and get to the end."

Joe Perkins was irate. How could we cave to someone as craven as Bull Connor? How could we surrender to injustice and wrong? How could we give up? He raged into the white Riders, whom I had grown to respect so much. Like the wealthy and comfortable people they were, he bristled, they could opt out of their circumstances anytime they wanted. And now they were. He could not. He was forever a black man who had to fight for those who could never withdraw to the lap of luxury. How dare they change their minds. How dare they end the Ride.

I understood Joe's anger. Little more than twenty-four hours earlier, I had looked into the eyes of a bludgeoned Jim Peck, who had looked back at me with an "It's okay if we do not do this" expression, and I had said, "Let's go." And into the conflagration we moved. Now, we were spent. Jim Peck, Walter Bergman, Mae Frances, Genevieve, Ike Reynolds, and I were barely standing. Frances Bergman had no business placing herself in any more danger. We had done our best. Our best had exposed Bull Connor to the world. Our best had revealed the hearts of those willing to murder and maim, and the hearts of those willing to take a beating and not strike back. Our best had been offering ourselves for slaughter so the eyes of the country would see and the minds of the country would understand the level of hatred leveled against human beings for being born as God made us. Our best had been to create a crisis that would force the nation to come to its senses. Our best had confronted violent hatred with nonviolent love. It was time to get to New Orleans.

It was almost into tomorrow when Mr. Seigenthaler arranged for another plane to take us there. No announcements to the press. No answering phones to accommodate threats, fake or authentic. Just get on the plane and get in the air.

My Freedom Ride had started with the first bus ride of my life out of Georgia. It would end with my first plane ride. With midnight closing in, we again boarded a plane. Black Freedom Riders. White Freedom Riders. Kennedy man, John Seigenthaler. Simeon Booker. Others in our entourage. All climbed aboard.

I think almost everyone breathed a sigh of relief. The state of Alabama and the Kennedy administration were happy to have us on our way to our final destination. The segregationists, no doubt, were satisfied, perhaps even proud. They had chased us away. I'm sure Reverend Shuttlesworth was relieved we were safe. But those of us who had tried so hard to prevail against Jim Crow racism were disappointed. We were simply unable to carry on the fight in the condition we found ourselves.

Our sigh was both relief and rest. There was no sigh coming from Joe Perkins. The abandonment of a commitment made unto death and our surrender to exhaustion and injury infuriated him.

The plane was an Eastern Airlines turboprop, and I was thrilled, as any first-time air passenger would be, when the plane accelerated down the runway and took to the sky. I looked out my window into the dark of night and watched Birmingham disappear from view. I watched the engine all the way to New Orleans.

# 16

## Resolution

We're going to keep coming until we can ride from anywhere in the South to anyplace else in the South . . . as American citizens.

—*Jim Zwerg, Freedom Rider*[1]

The Kennedys thought Freedom Ride 1961 was over. Mine was. But unknown to them or to me, Fisk University student Diane Nash, in Nashville, Tennessee, was not thinking "over." She was leading Nashville SNCC students in an emergency effort to replace our halted initiative and renew the bus journey to New Orleans. Freedom Ride 1961 was about to go plural. The Freedom Rides were about to begin. While we were in the air to New Orleans, Diane already had plans underway to meet Southern violence with more nonviolence. The Kennedys had no clue.

In January, when the Friendship Nine sat-in at McCrory's in Rock Hill, South Carolina, and were assaulted and arrested and jailed, Diane Nash said from over two hundred miles away at a SNCC meeting in Atlanta, "We have no alternative other than to join them."[2] She traveled to Rock Hill with three others, got arrested, refused bail, and served hard labor to stand up to injustice. Now, she was again over two hundred miles away from the injustice. And, again, she saw no alternative.

On Mother's Day, as we were being burned and beaten and battered, Diane was at a picnic with fellow Nashville students. She was celebrating the Nashville Movement's achievements thus far—the desegregation of Nashville movie theaters, the admission by Nashville's mayor, Ben West, that he was not opposed to desegregating local lunch counters,[3] and the Freedom Ride itself. These were all reasons to celebrate. John Lewis, by coincidence, was at the picnic while he stopped in Nashville before intending to rendezvous with us in Montgomery.[4]

The mood at the picnic changed in a moment. Over the radio, the story of Anniston and Birmingham halted the celebration. It was another "We have no alternative but to join them" moment. Diane Nash intended to finish, with a Joe Perkins mind-set, what we had started. She was committed unto death.

It took an hour for our plane to reach New Orleans. Entering the New Orleans airport felt a lot like leaving Birmingham's. A ring of white police officers, dressed in riot gear and compelled against their natures, greeted us in the same style Birmingham's had bid us farewell. Sneers engraved their faces. Contempt gleamed from their eyes. Unlike in Birmingham, here law enforcement joined the public in addressing us with the language to which we had grown so accustomed across our lives and across our Ride: nigger, nigger lover, spook, coon.

Not all the public was against us. A small contingent of CORE members greeted us with celebration. Loud cheers. Warm embraces. Congratulatory handshakes. We had reached our destination a day ahead of the seventh anniversary of *Brown*. We had tested the *Boynton* decision enough to learn the Deep South was unwilling to accept integration and quite willing to defend segregation to the extreme. We were walking models of that extreme.

CORE whisked us away to Xavier University, where most of us spent the night—really, the wee hours of Tuesday, May 16—sleeping in dormitory rooms, and where a news conference later in the day brought media attention to each of us.

As we were giving interviews in New Orleans on Tuesday, Diane Nash, Jim Bevel, and Bernard Lafayette were finalizing plans in Nashville to send ten replacement Riders—eight black, two White—to Birmingham to pick up where we had been forced off. Robert Kennedy learned of the new effort. As soon as he did, relief in Washington, D.C., changed to distress. The Freedom Ride crisis was supposed to be behind him.

Reverend Shuttlesworth learned of the new Riders when Diane called him to say they would be on their way soon. His relief over our safety in New Orleans turned, at first, to anguish over new bus passengers heading toward their deaths, then to acceptance when he realized he could do nothing to stop them. Diane Nash was employing his own tactic. She had announced the plan she intended to execute. Now, she was acting on it. No permission asked. No permission needed.

Seigenthaler and Shuttlesworth both implored, begged, and warned Diane not to move ahead with such a dangerous and deadly plan.

"Don't you know they will kill you if you come?" was a common refrain.

"Then others will follow" was Diane's unshakable response.[5] Buses were coming whether others liked it or not. New Riders would be on their way to Birmingham. Better get you ready, oh, yeah.

Wednesday morning, May 17, John Lewis, Bill Harbour,

Catherine Burks, Lucretia Collins, William Barbee, Paul Brooks, Charles Butler, Allen Cason, and two white students, Jim Zwerg and Salynn McCollum—all between nineteen and twenty-two years old—left Nashville. No sooner did they arrive in Birmingham than Bull Connor put most of them in jail.

I woke up May 17 in the home of a Honduran family. After our first night in New Orleans, some of us fanned out for the final time into the homes of strangers, while some stayed in dorms at Southern University. For me, it was the first time I had ever stayed with someone from a foreign country, and many of their habits fascinated me. The children in the family all drank coffee. That was different from anything I knew growing up. In the morning, they all put warm milk on their cornflakes. Different. But tasty.

Later that day saw a crowd of hundreds—maybe as many as a thousand—cram inside and spill outside New Zion Baptist Church to celebrate the anniversary of *Brown,* the completion of our Ride, and the goodness of God. About half of us were able to attend and speak to the congregation. Walter, Al, Ed, Joe, Ike, Herman, and I told of the experiences of the past two weeks and the challenges faced the farther south we traveled. Jimmy McDonald led us in song. And song. And song.

Hank and Jim Peck had left for New York City to keep the nation's attention focused on the Ride. They were picketing outside the New York Port Authority bus terminal on this seventh anniversary of *Brown.* Jim and Hank were unaware that Nashville had intentions similar to their own. Keep the Ride alive.

Genevieve and Frances were too troubled by the horrors of Anniston and Birmingham to attend New Zion. Mae Frances had left our group in Birmingham because of respiratory problems.

Jerry Moore had left because of the death of his grand-father.[6]

Inside New Zion, the white Riders among us were proud to speak to this African American congregation. After explaining the pummeling he had taken at the hands of his own race, Walter Bergman spoke of his black eyes being the one part of his body he could be proud of. Al Bigelow appreciated the black soot that covered his body from the flames of the burning bus in Anniston.[7] When it was my turn to speak, I talked of walking together with Jim Peck into the maelstrom in Birmingham. Why shouldn't I walk into a bus station together with Jim? The mob had its reasons. Why shouldn't I walk together with anyone I pleased? Birmingham had its reasons. The city had overpowered us. Police, doctors, hospitals, and regular citizens had all conspired to defeat us. Why could they not tolerate us?

The end of my talk at New Zion Church ended my Freedom Ride 1961. My Ride concluded the day it had been planned to end, May 17. The Freedom Rides would last across the summer. They were just getting started.

The stories of the rest of the Freedom Rides—the fulfillment of our Ride—are best told by those who rode them. Bill Harbour. Catherine Burks. Jim Zwerg. Hank Thomas. Bernard Lafayette. And others in the first wave of our replacements. They have such stories to tell.

They found violence in Montgomery equal to ours in Anniston and Birmingham. Beatings and bludgeonings. Besiegement. In Montgomery, alone, some three thousand whites entrapped twelve hundred blacks—including Dr. King, including Reverend Shuttlesworth—inside First Baptist Church. Torches threatened immolation. Overturned cars in flames heightened the threat. The Kennedy brothers had to send troops to rescue them.

Like us, injuries forced some replacement Riders to abandon the effort. Jim Zwerg was beaten as badly as Jim Peck. Like Peck, Zwerg spoke words of conviction to the press from his hospital bed.

"We're dedicated to this. We'll take hitting. We'll take beating. We're willing to accept death. But we're going to keep coming until we can ride from anywhere in the South to anyplace else in the South . . . as American citizens."[8]

Both Jims intended to continue their Freedom Ride. Neither could.

But most did continue as far as Jackson, Mississippi. In Jackson, they were jailed at first and then imprisoned in the notorious Parchman Prison Farm. In Parchman, with no recourse left, with no way to continue, the Riders chose to sing. Their song began with a promise.

*Buses are a comin'*
*Oh, yeah.*
*Buses are a comin'.*
*Oh, yeah.*
*Buses are a comin'.*
*Buses are a comin'.*
*Buses are a comin'.*
*Oh, yeah.*

They had no way of knowing if their words were true. How could they? The only ears hearing their lyrics belonged to prison personnel and themselves. But their words steeled their own resolve and infuriated their jailers. From promise, the song moved to threat.

*Better get you ready.*
*Oh, yeah.*

*Better get you ready.*
*Oh, yeah.*
*Better get you ready.*
*Better get you ready.*
*Buses are a comin'.*
*Oh, yeah.*

The jailers punished them for their singing and disruptiveness by blasting them with water, spraying them with insect repellent, and taking their mattresses from their cells. Instead of silencing themselves, the Parchman Riders changed the lyrics, and, in doing so, increased the threat by adding the single word *but*.

*You can take my mattress.*
*Oh, yeah.*
*You can take my mattress.*
*Oh, yeah.*
*You can take my mattress.*
*You can take my mattress.*
*But, buses are a comin'.*
*Oh, yeah.*

And the buses came.

## 17

### Aftermath

They shall mount up with wings as eagles;
they shall run, and not be weary;
and they shall walk, and not faint.

*—Isaiah 40:31 (KJV)*[1]

With replacement Riders incarcerated and under hard labor in Parchman, the call went out across the country. From pulpits. From SNCC. From CORE. From *The Student Voice*. The call went out to replace the replacements. Come to Jackson. Descend on the South. Choose two cities. Ride from one to the other. Ride with a person of another race. Sit in the front of the bus. Integrate a terminal. Enter a forbidden restroom. Order food from an off-limits restaurant. Get arrested. Do not pay bail. Stay in jail. Stay. In. Jail.

Hundreds answered the call. And the buses kept a comin'.

Across the summer of 1961, over four hundred Americans gave up what they were doing and chose to ride. Chose arrest.

Chose jail. Chose to make equality a priority in their lives. Chose to make it *the* priority in their lives.

Jackson, Mississippi, was the center of the target for the Freedom Rides. Most Rides started or ended there. But other cities found Freedom Riders a comin' their way. Washington, D.C., to St. Petersburg, Florida. Atlanta to Montgomery. New York to Little Rock. New Orleans to McComb, Mississippi.

On they came. On it went. Sixty-three Rides. Four hundred thirty-six Riders. About half black; about half white.

Students.

Ministers. Priests. Rabbis.

Lawyers. Journalists. Office workers.

Longshoremen. Teachers. Artists.

Carpenters. Homemakers. Laborers.

Engineers. Writers. Social workers.[2]

People of all stripes, from all regions of the country came and exercised their citizenship. They have incredible tales of courage, service, and sacrifice challenging our country to live up to our traditional motto: *E pluribus unum*. From many, one.

One people.

Indivisible.

One people.

Living in concert with one another.

One people. Offering respect and dignity and equality to all people.

I got to be on the first Freedom Ride. The honor of a lifetime. Those who followed became heroes of mine because they finished the work I could not. My part was responding to the indwelling of Papa's message to me: "Do something." Others responded to the calls within them. They were able to finish the journey because the prisoners of Parchman were correct. Buses *were* a comin'. And a comin'. And a comin'.

When Robert Kennedy sought a "cooling off" period, James Farmer replied, "We have been cooling off for three hundred and fifty years. If we cool off any more, we will be in a deep freeze."[3] James Farmer wasn't cooling off. He was doubling down. He went to Parchman. As did John Lewis. As did Hank Thomas.

From New Orleans, I flew back to Atlanta. I thought I would rejoin the Rides and rejoin James and John and Hank. That did not happen. I did end up in Montgomery when they were in Montgomery, but my visit would be across town from the bus depot. I would be in a courthouse in answer to a subpoena.

In Atlanta, my parents and siblings celebrated my "safe" return. Hugs, tears, kisses, handshakes. But also, questions. Why the gash on the top of my skull? Why the welts under my eyes? Why the swelling of my face? I told them I was fine. I told them I would be returning to continue what had to be completed.

Mom wanted no more of it. She had seen the photo of the burning bus. She had seen the photo of me in the middle of the mob. Now she saw the results of the beating. Her happy-go-lucky, brimming-with-optimism son was standing before her still full of optimism, still confident, still committed, but far less happy-go-lucky. Far less "It will be okay." Maybe it would not be okay.

A white man named John Doar came to our apartment at 21 Bradley. We had never heard of him. Today I look back, and I am in awe of the man. Doar was the deputy assistant attorney general of the United States, and he would become a rock star in the Justice Department. He defended us on the Rides in 1961. He accompanied African American James Meredith to the doors of the University of Mississippi to integrate that school in 1962. In 1963, he stood up to a mob gathered outside Medgar Evers's house the night Medgar was ambushed and slain.

Doar prosecuted the 1964 killers of James Chaney, Andrew Goodman, and Mickey Schwerner. Doar prosecuted the murderer of Viola Liuzzo, a white woman who was shot and killed after marching with Dr. King at Selma in 1965.[4] Like Jim Peck and the Bergmans, like Genevieve Hughes and Al Bigelow, like Ed Blankenheim, Doar stood up with unequivocal courage for equality under the law even though, as a white person, he already enjoyed it.

John Doar came to take my deposition on the events leading to the violence of Mother's Day. We sat on the porch in the wicker-backed chair drinking mom's lemonade, and he asked me what happened in Birmingham. He had a couple of pictures. He wanted personal testimony. I think he expected this to be a slam dunk of a case, but this was his first case in the South, and he had never prosecuted a case involving blacks in front of an all-white jury. In this instance, he discovered having all the facts in his favor did not mean victory. He discovered having all the facts did not mean a thing.

I went to the trial, but they never called me as a witness. While replacement Riders were being confronted and battered and bloodied across town, I spent the whole week in a chamber room waiting to testify in court. This was the South. I never took the stand. The jury exonerated my attackers.

After the trial, I returned home to 21 Bradley. Mom understood I wanted to continue in the Movement. But in the past four months alone, I had spent ten days in solitary confinement, two weeks on my Freedom Ride, and one day facing death at the hands of my countrymen. She wanted me to pursue a different path.

Mom encouraged me to enlist in the army. She thought I'd be safer serving my country in the military than serving in the Movement. This time I obeyed. Almost. I chose the Marines instead. That change in trajectory in my life led me to being on the ground in Cuba *during* the Cuban Missile Crisis of 1962. It led me to Vietnam, where I was among the early deployments of marines to land in 1965. It led me to twenty years of service to a country—my country—that tried to kill me for the seat I claimed on an interstate bus. Imagine. Safer serving in Cuba, safer serving in Vietnam, than serving on my own country's soil in the effort to overcome the disease of racism. Hard to believe.

Hank Thomas went to Vietnam, too. All these decades later, Hank tells the story of revisiting both Anniston and Vietnam after the battles ended. In Anniston, some twenty years after the Freedom Ride, no one would shake his hand. In Vietnam, his former enemies, once sworn to kill him, hugged him. That is an America Hank Thomas knows exists.

And yet.

Hank knows he lives in an America far different from that, too. After returning from Vietnam, Hank has gone on to own multiple Marriott hotels in Atlanta and multiple McDonald's restaurants. Hank speaks with gratitude and pride of his rise from being the son of an impoverished sharecropper in Florida to being a wealthy, highly respected business executive in Georgia. When he does, my friend concludes by saying, "Only in America."

By the fiftieth anniversary of the Freedom Rides in 2011, Anniston welcomed us with open arms. And in 2017, the Freedom Riders National Monument opened in Anniston. The monument has two sites. One is at the downtown bus station. The other is five miles outside the city where on a day long ago tires went flat, a mob attacked, and a bus burned.

A national monument needs a keynote speaker for its opening. Anniston, Alabama, invited Hank Thomas as that speaker.[5]

Only in America.

By September 1961, the government relented. On September 22, 1961, the Interstate Commerce Commission issued another desegregation order. By November 1, WHITE and COLORED signs would have to come down, passengers could sit anywhere they pleased—anywhere we pleased—on interstate buses and trains. Depot waiting rooms, restaurants, and restrooms would have to be desegregated. Drinking fountains would have to be integrated to be available to anyone, anytime.

By November 1, the signs were gone. The Freedom Rides reached their conclusion by permeating America's consciousness. They arrived at their real destination. Not New Orleans, but equal accommodation on public transportation and equal access to public facilities.

Today I do not ride a bus, but I travel other modes of public transportation, and no one considers it anything other than normal to sit next to anyone of any race. It pleases me that no one has to worry about being consigned to a seat based on race.

Did we belong where we thought we belonged in 1961? Of course, we belonged. Do you belong where you think you belong today? Of course, you belong. But "Do I belong?" is a universal question asked in every generation by those who feel they do not. It is a question resisted by those who think others do not belong.

In every era, it takes a bus of change to lead the way to new senses of belonging. Thankfully, a change bus is always a comin'.

In 1960, in the Atlanta Student Movement, my bus came. I got aboard.

In 1961, on the Freedom Ride, my bus came. I got aboard.

Later that year, when the Marines called, another bus stopped to pick me up. I got on board and stayed aboard for twenty years through the Cuban Missile Crisis, into Vietnam, and beyond.

By boarding my buses, I tried to serve my country—and did serve my country—to the best of my ability. I love America for what it is, but I love it more for what it aspires to be: a country where all *are* created equal; a nation out of many, one; a government of the people, by the people, for the people; a place where justice rolls down like waters and righteousness like a mighty stream.

To reach those aspirations, others must board the bus a comin' for them. The ride will not be easy, but it will be necessary. It always has been. It always will be.

# EPILOGUE

## The Cost of the Ticket

Tired now of the bitter river,
Tired now of the pat on the back,
Tired now of the steel bars
Because my face is black,
I'm tired of segregation,
Tired of filth and mud,
I've drunk of the bitter river
And it's turned to steel in my blood.

—*Langston Hughes*[1]

Halfway between the Washington Monument and Lincoln Memorial in Washington, D.C., beside the Tidal Basin, and facing the Jefferson Memorial, stands Martin Luther King, Jr. He is thirty feet high. He is stone and immovable as his determination. The King Memorial is a monument to a man who belongs among the giants remembered in our nation's capital. Carved into the memorial's base are words from Dr. King's triumphant speech at the 1963 March on Washington for Jobs and Freedom: "Out of the mountain of despair, a stone of hope." Surrounding his stalwart frame, fourteen quotes from the twelve years of his public career capture his short life's work and his long-term vision for America and the world. Words such as:

> "I believe that unarmed truth and unconditional love
> will have the final word in reality."
> "Commit yourself to the noble struggle for equal rights.
> You will make a better person of yourself, a greater nation of your country, and a finer world to live in."
> "Injustice anywhere is a threat to justice everywhere."
> "True peace is not merely the absence of tension; it is
> the presence of justice."[2]

Dr. King stands arms crossed in fortitude, eyes fixed on Jefferson, the author of "We hold these truths to be self-evident, that all men are created equal" and the owner of Sally Hemings. The memorial to Martin Luther King, Jr., is spectacular. It is inspiring. It is beautiful.

But, I'd rather have him alive.

If Dr. King were alive, there would be no monument, no holiday, no fourteen quotes carved in stone. There *would* be volumes more of his thoughts for us to absorb. Decades' more discomfort from him for aspirations not met by us. Mountains more challenges for everyone to welcome. Or reject.

I'd rather have him alive.

Dr. King would be in his nineties now had our nation allowed him to live. But it did not allow him to live. *We* did not allow him to live. Night after night of the final years of his thirty-nine-year life, Dr. King faced phone calls spewing death threats at him, his wife, and his children. Day after day, he experienced the perils faced when a dangerous man with a dangerous message makes dangerous, public appeals. Appeals for nonviolent change. Calls for the Beloved Community. Demands for an end to war. Proposals for economic justice. Ideas to end racism. Ideas such as "Give us the ballot"[3] and "The time is always right to do what is right"[4] and "Hate cannot drive out hate; only love can do that."[5]

Simple in content. Hard in practice. Deadly when pursued seriously.

Those who live north of the Mason-Dixon Line seem to think racism and bigotry have always thrived far away from them. But in 1966, King took his fight to Chicago, where he absorbed threats, faced white backlash, recoiled from explosives, and was struck with bottles and bricks. From this experience, Dr. King wrote, "I had never seen, even in Mississippi, mobs as hostile and hateful as in Chicago."[6] So much for the Mason-Dixon Line.

Dr. King is dead now—it might be said, safely dead—and has been for over a half century. So, we can honor his disruptive life and celebrate the change he brought even though much of the country was not excited about that change or him during his lifetime.

Such is the cost of boarding the bus. Such is the cost of the ticket. The trip is never free for stepping on board the bus that moves America forward.

For me, the cost of my Freedom Ride ticket and the price of my Atlanta Student Movement activism, as it was for so many in the Movement, was dropping out of college, personal injury, and lifelong physical issues. The gash on my head, given to me on Mother's Day 1961, became a lump on the back of my neck as fluid drained from the wound over the years. I was able to have it removed in my sixties. The cost of my service in Vietnam was exposure to Agent Orange, which has required me to use a walker for the last decade. The Veterans Administration provides medical resources to me, and I am grateful for the care and attention.

But like my desire to have Dr. King still with us, I'd prefer to have full use of my legs. There is always a cost to service.

For Dr. Bergman, the cost of the ticket was spending the rest of his life in a wheelchair. Within weeks of his Mother's Day beating, Walter suffered a stroke that doctors attributed to the Freedom Ride violence. He was never the same after the mobs of Mother's Day were finished with him.

For Janie Forsyth—now Janie Forsyth McKinney—the price of the water she provided the Greyhound Riders as they suffered on the road outside Anniston was relocation. Her family could not stay in Anniston following the threats and intimidation that followed her acts of kindness.

The cost for our replacement Riders was enormous. I knew few of the replacement Riders in 1961. Today, many are good friends.

For Bill Harbour, the cost of the ticket was expulsion from Tennessee State University for his activism followed by an inability to return home after his release from forty-nine days in Parchman. It was too dangerous, his mother said, for him to come back to Piedmont, Alabama, twenty-five miles from Anniston. Better stay away.

For Jim Zwerg, the cost of the ticket was loss of relationship. His father gave Jim a choice. If you go on the Rides, we are finished. Jim went on the Rides. He and his father never reconciled.[7]

Many white Riders were disinherited. Some have died living in poverty or are living in poverty today. There is a cost to the ticket.

In every generation, some do not enjoy the full citizenship, the full freedom, we each want. Today, people of color are jailed and murdered at disproportionate rates. Schoolchildren practice active-shooter drills. Women experience sexual harassment and assault. The LGBTQ community encounters inequality. Each time injustice rises restricting whom we long to be, a protest rises. #BlackLivesMatter. #MarchForOurLives. #MeToo. #LoveWins. People board a bus.

African Americans board a bus because we are tired of knowing police might be called on us while bird-watching in a park. We are tired of knowing we might be attacked and killed minding our own business in our own apartments by those who have sworn to serve and protect us. We are tired of knowing knees might be pressed against our necks to the point of death or multiple bullets might be shot in our backs from authority. We are tired of not being able to jog in a neighborhood without threat of violence against us or to stop and look at a house under construction as so many others are able to do.

Langston Hughes was "tired . . . of the bitter river" when he published those words the year I was born.[8] Martin Luther King, Jr., was tired of "people . . . being trampled over by the iron feet of oppression" when he spoke those words in Montgomery in 1955.[9] We Freedom Riders were tired of being denied access to seats on buses, in waiting rooms, and in restrooms in 1961. In 2021—almost eighty years after Hughes, sixty-six years after King, sixty years after the Freedom Rides—we are still tired. Tired. And so, protest comes. People march. Buses come. People get on board. Change comes, too.

In 1961, our change took days, then weeks, then months. We started with thirteen Riders and ballooned to over four hundred. It took beatings. It took action at the highest level of government. It took court rulings. It took the force of nonviolence. It took me.

In 2021 and '31 and '41, it will take you. Nothing will change if you, my reader, my friend, my fellow American, if you do not take Papa's advice and "do something." Look around. What injustice do you see? What change needs to happen? Get on the bus. Make it happen.

There will be a cost. Agents of change pay a price. But the present moves on. The future holds almost unanimous approval of those who make a stand today in favor of a better tomorrow. Of those who board the bus. Be on the lookout for your chance. It will happen like this. A bus will pull up and stop. It will open its door. You'll wonder if you should get on. You'll wonder if you can get on. You will hear a song emanating from inside. The words will offer hope if it is your bus to board. The same words will sound like threat if it is not. But the words will be plain, distinct, and bold. And here is what they will say:

Buses are a comin'
Oh, yeah.
Buses are a comin'
Oh, yeah.
Buses are a comin'
Buses are a comin'
Buses are a comin'
Oh, yeah.

# ACKNOWLEDGMENTS

Thank you to the team that brought this story to publication:

Agent Greg Johnson, president of WordServe Literary, who championed this project's path to publication from the moment he heard of it.

George Witte, editor-in-chief of the St. Martin's Publishing Group, whose guidance gives confidence, whose kindness exudes warmth.

Kevin Reilly, Rebecca Lang, and Alyssa Gammello of St. Martin's, for shepherding the project with guidance and forbearance.

Steve Boldt, whose copyediting taught us lessons we did not know and corrected errors we could not see.

Thank you to those who inspired and educated us:

Janie Forsyth McKinney, who knew what to do and did it.

Reverend Fred Shuttlesworth, whose single-handed courage and indomitable determination was and is a model for championing equality.

Raymond Arsenault and Derek Catsam, who educate new generations about the Freedom Riders through the excellence of their research and writing and the infectiousness of their enthusiasm instilling hunger and curiosity in their audiences for more.

Heather Shumaker and Kristin A. Oakley, for their mentoring and expertise.

Christy Wopat and Shannon Ishizaki, for their enthusiasm for this project.

Charles acknowledges and thanks:

My wife, JoEtta, whose faithful support, ongoing encouragement, and careful eye kept me on track.

My friend Richard Rooker, who heard my story of living in the Bottom and gave it life.

Richard acknowledges and thanks:

Charles and JoEtta Person, who invited our family into their home, into their lives, into their hearts.

My wife, Nancy, without whose abiding love, patience, encouragement, and support this book would not exist.

Our son, Zack, who made a telephone call in 2007 that started us all down a path to today.

# NOTES

## PROLOGUE: A MOTHER'S ARMS

1. Victor Hugo, *Les Misérables,* trans. Isabel F. Hapgood (New York: Thomas Y. Crowell, 1887), bk. 4, chap. 1, "One Mother Meets Another," https://www.gutenberg.org/files/135/135-h/135-h.htm.

2. Freedom Rider Hank Thomas tells the story of the bus attack at West Point Center for Oral History, https://archive.org/details/CSPAN3 _20180219_034600_Oral_Histories_Hank_Thomas_West_Point _Interview/start/1500/end/1560, at 11:11.55. Also, Thomas tells the story of the bus attack at the dedication of the Freedom Riders National Monument, May 13, 2017, in Anniston, Ala., https://www.youtube.com/watch?v =oTMswW40I7M&t=22s, at 2:12.

3. https://www.youtube.com/watch?v=HPOUDSxbrDs, at 2:17.

4. Andrew Manis, *A Fire You Can't Put Out: The Civil Rights Life of Birmingham's Reverend Fred Shuttlesworth* (Tuscaloosa: University of Alabama Press, 1999), 190; Diane McWhorter, *Carry Me Home* (New York: Simon & Schuster, 2001), 177; "'Bull' Connor Again," *Afro-American,* June 17, 1961, 4, https://news.google.com/newspapers?nid=UBnQDr5gPskC&dat =19610617&printsec=frontpage&hl=en.

5. This quote and all subsequent quotations from the inaugural address of John F. Kennedy, January 20, 1961: http://www.americanrhetoric .com/speeches/jfkinaugural.htm.

6. Quotation from the Declaration of Independence: https://www

.archives.gov/founding-docs/declaration-transcript; quotation from Fourteenth Amendment: https://www.archives.gov/founding-docs/amendments-11-27.

7. *20th Century Day by Day* (New York: Dorling Kindersley, 2000), 872.

8. https://www.ranker.com/list/best-movies-of-1961/ranker-film.

9. Robert F. Kennedy (US attorney general), interviewed by Peter Maas, "Robert Kennedy Speaks Out," *Look,* March 28, 1961, 24.

10. https://kinginstitute.stanford.edu/encyclopedia/sit-ins.

11. Most famously, John Lewis spoke these words at the March on Washington, August 28, 1963. See John Lewis, *Walking with the Wind* (New York: Harcourt Brace, 1998), 220; http://voicesofdemocracy.umd.edu/lewis-speech-at-the-march-on-washington-speech-text/.

12. What is called the Montgomery Bus Boycott today was called the Montgomery Bus Protest by the participants because a 1921 Montgomery municipal law banned "boycotts."

13. https://kinginstitute.stanford.edu/encyclopedia/browder-v-gayle-352-us-903.

14. https://kinginstitute.stanford.edu/king-papers/documents/i-have-dream-address-delivered-march-washington-jobs-and-freedom.

## 1. LIFE IN THE BOTTOM

1. https://rosaparksbiography.org/bio/let-us-look-at-jim-crow-for-the-criminal-he-is/.

2. https://www.biblegateway.com/passage/?search=joshua+1&version=KJV.

3. https://www.pbs.org/wgbh/americanexperience/features/flood-klan/.

4. Methodist preacher William Joseph Simmons led a group of fifteen to the top of Stone Mountain, burned a makeshift cross, and named himself the Imperial Wizard of the Invisible Empire of the Knights of the Ku Klux Klan: http://content.time.com/time/subscriber/article/0,33009,898581,00.html.

5. https://www.smithsonianmag.com/history/what-will-happen-stone-mountain-americas-largest-confederate-memorial-180964588/.

## 2. AWAKENINGS

1. https://www.ncpedia.org/listening-to-history/forbes-david.

2. Rosalind Rosenberg, *Jane Crow: The Life of Pauli Murray* (New York: Oxford University Press, 2017), 267; also, https://www.newyorker.com/magazine/2017/04/17/the-many-lives-of-pauli-murray.

3. https://www.archives.gov/publications/prologue/2008/spring/robinson
.html; also, https://www.pbs.org/wnet/african-americans-many-rivers-to
-cross/history/was-jackie-robinson-court-martialed/.

4. https://www.dignitymemorial.com/obituaries/springfield-va/marcelite
-harris-8045674; also, https://www.af.mil/About-Us/Biographies/Display
/Article/106829/major-general-marcelite-j-harris/.

5. *Foot Soldiers: Class of 1964, an Atlanta Story That Changed the
World* (Atlanta, Ga.: An Alvelyn Sanders Production, There Is a River, Inc.,
2012), DVD.

## 3. DO SOMETHING

1. *February 1, 1960: The Story of the Greensboro Four,* https://www
.youtube.com/watch?v=X5s3WEYt4_Q, at 23:08; also, Christopher Wilson,
"The Moment When Four Students Sat Down to Take a Stand," *Smithsonian Magazine,* January 31, 2020, https://www.smithsonianmag.com
/smithsonian-institution/lessons-worth-learning-moment-greensboro
-four-sat-down-lunch-counter-180974087/.

2. Rosa Parks with Jim Haskins, *Rosa Parks: My Story* (New York:
Puffin Books, 1992), 116.

3. *February 1, 1960,* at 27:00.

4. https://www.crmvet.org/info/sitins.pdf.

5. Many resources are available online to learn about Lonnie King and
the Atlanta Student Movement. Two excellent extensive video interviews
with Lonnie King are available. At https://www.loc.gov/item/afc2010039
_crhp0090/ is a two-and-half-hour video interview for the Library of Con-
gress conducted in 2013 by Dr. Emilye Crosby, with an accompanying transcript.

https://tile.loc.gov/storage-services/service/afc/afc2010039
/afc2010039_crhp0090_King_transcript/afc2010039_crhp0090_King
_transcript.pdf. At https://soar.kennesaw.edu/handle/11360/2400 is a
one-hour video interview for the Atlanta Student Movement Project, the
*Dr. Lonnie King Interview,* conducted by Jeanne Law Bohannon on July
19, 2017, and transcribed by Ella Greer. A one-hour oral interview with
accompanying still photos titled *An Interview with Lonnie C. King, Jr.,*
conducted July 24, 2018, by Gregg Ivers for the Julian Bond Oral History
Project, is at https://www.youtube.com/watch?v=V0OIb03TKck–. A transcript of an August 29, 1967, interview of Lonnie King by John H. Britton is
at https://www.crmvet.org/nars/6708_lonnie_king.pdf. "The Atlanta Sit-In

Movement, 1960–1961: An Oral Study," a master of arts thesis, May 1980, by Vincent D. Fort is at http://digitalcommons.auctr.edu/cgi/viewcontent .cgi?article=3957&context=dissertations.

6. Different versions of this conversation exist. Often the words between Lonnie and Julian are quoted as Lonnie saying, "Don't you think something like Greensboro ought to happen here?" Bond replies, "It probably will," and King responds, "We ought to make it happen." The stories I remember have Lonnie saying, "It's going to be us."

## 4. THE LEADER OF THE PACK

1. https://www.themusicallyrics.com/h/351-hamilton-the-musical -lyrics/3703-the-story-of-tonight-lyrics.html.

2. See Crosby, https://www.loc.gov/item/afc2010039_crhp0090/.

3. Ibid., 2.

4. Ibid.

5. Ibid., 3.

6. Ibid.

7. Ibid.

8. Ibid., 10–11.

9. Ibid., 17.

10. http://okra.stanford.edu/transcription/document_images/Vol03Scans /71_5-Dec-1955_MIA%20Mass%20Meeting.pdf.

11. Crosby, 17.

12. Slightly different versions of "An Appeal for Human Rights" can be found at https://www.crmvet.org/docs/aa4hr.htm and https://www .historyisaweapon.com/defcon1/anappealforhumanrights.html.

13. Brief explanations of many of these shootings can be found at "14 High-Profile Police-Related Deaths of U.S. Blacks" at https://www.cbc.ca /news/world/list-police-related-deaths-usa-1.4438618 and https://www .buzzfeednews.com/article/nicholasquah/heres-a-timeline-of-unarmed -black-men-killed-by-police-over and https://newsone.com/playlist/black -men-youths-who-were-killed-by-police/item/10. Jemel Roberson shooting available at Holly Yan, "'Hero' Security Guard Killed by Police Was Working Extra Shifts for His Son's Christmas," CNN, https://www.cnn.com /2018/11/15/us/chicago-area-security-guard-police-shooting/index.html.

14. This and all subsequent quotations from the Declaration of Independence at https://www.archives.gov/founding-docs/declaration -transcript.

15. Governor Ernest Vandiver's comments on "Appeal for Human Rights" are available at http://crdl.usg.edu/cgi/crdl?format=_video;query =id:ugabma_wsbn_42211.

16. https://www.archives.gov/founding-docs/constitution-transcript.

17. Edward A. Hatfield, "Atlanta Sit-Ins," *New Georgia Encyclopedia*, March 13, 2019, https://www.georgiaencyclopedia.org/articles/history -archaeology/atlanta-sit-ins; Benjamin E. Mays, *Born to Rebel* (New York: Charles Scribner's Sons, 1971), 290.

18. https://soar.kennesaw.edu/bitstream/handle/11360/2404/pope -transcription.pdf?sequence=2&isAllowed=y, 5.

19. Crosby, 21.

20. Ibid., 28.

21. Ibid., 30; Mays, 295–96. Mays says it was Wheat Street Church, not Ebenezer.

22. Crosby, 30; Mays, 295.

23. Crosby, 31.

24. Ibid., 33.

25. *The Student Movement and You*, circa June 1960, 1, http:// digitalexhibits.auctr.edu/exhibits/show/seekingtotell/item/26#?c=0&m =0&s=0&cv=0&xywh=-542%2C0%2C2394%2C2135.

26. Jared Keller, "The Strange History of the October Surprise," *Smithsonian Magazine*, October 11, 2016, https://www.smithsonianmag.com/history /strange-history-october-surprise-180960741/.

27. Hatfield, "Atlanta Sit-Ins."

28. Crosby, 36.

## 5. MAN OF MOREHOUSE

1. https://www.morehouse.edu/about/college_hymn.html.

2. http://asmhistoricaltrail.com/atlanta-student-movement-1960/.

3. Crosby, 53. The multilevel glass "bridge" connected both buildings of Rich's department store across Forsyth Street; also, Howard Raines, *My Soul Is Rested: The Story of the Civil Rights Movement in the Deep South* (New York: Penguin Books, 1977), 90.

4. For a detailed explanation of the complex and consequential politics of Senator Kennedy's telephone call, see Taylor Branch, *Parting the Waters: America in the King Years, 1954–63* (New York: Simon & Schuster, 1988), chap. 5, "A Pawn of History," 351–78; Crosby, 54–55; Raines, 89–90.

5. George B. Leonard, "The Second Battle of Atlanta," *Look* 25, no. 9 (April 25, 1961): 36; complete "Oath to Non-Violence" at https://www.crmvet.org/docs/62_atl_training.pdf.

6. Leonard, 36.

7. Ibid., 32. I remember the manager telling Leon to get his hands off the menu. *Look* magazine quotes the manager as telling him to get his hands off the counter.

8. Ibid.

9. https://www.crmvet.org/nars/lonnie14.htm.

10. To learn more of the Paschal brothers' role in the Movement, see The HISTORYMAKERS: The Nation's Largest African American Video Oral History Collection, https://www.thehistorymakers.org/biography/james-paschal-41.

11. Raines, 92; Crosby, 62.

12. Raines, 92; Crosby, 62; Branch, 397.

13. Branch, 397. In September, the merchants kept their word.

14. https://www.crmvet.org/docs/sv/sv6103.pdf, 7.

15. CORE—the Papers of the Congress of Racial Equality, 1941–1967, reel 44, #456, accessed at Valparaiso University Christopher Center Library, Valparaiso, Ind. The CORE papers are available on microfilm in approximately thirty locations around the country.

## 6. ON MY WAY

1. CORE, reel 44, #456.

## 7. THOSE WHO CAME BEFORE

1. https://www.billboard.com/articles/news/6576161/jidenna-janelle-monae-wondaland-classic-man-interview.

2. The case deciding the Montgomery Bus Protest (*Browder v. Gayle*) did not include Rosa Parks in it. The defendants were Aurelia Browder, Claudette Colvin, Susie McDonald, Jeanetta Reese, and Mary Louise Smith. The Supreme Court summarily affirmed the district court's ruling in the case, meaning it confirmed the lower court's decision without hearing additional argument. The Supreme Court then denied rehearing the case, ending the litigation.

3. August Meier and Elliott Rudwick, *CORE: A Study in the Civil Rights Movement* (Champaign: University of Illinois Press, 1973), 8.

4. Derek Charles Catsam, *Freedom's Main Line: The Journey of Reconciliation and the Freedom Rides* (Lexington: University Press of Kentucky, 2009), 23.

5. Dan Howard, "The Lynching of Willie Earle, SC's Last, Foreshadowed Changing Times," *Greenville News,* April 9, 2018, https://www.greenvilleonline.com/story/news/local/greenville-roots/2018/04/09/lynching-willie-earle-scs-last-foreshadowed-changing-times/499199002/.

6. Matt Stevens, "Secrets of 1946 Mass Lynching Could Be Revealed After Court Ruling," *New York Times,* February 12, 2019, https://www.nytimes.com/2019/02/12/us/moores-ford-lynchings.html; also CBS News, "Ruling May Help Unlock Answers to Notorious 1946 'Moore's Ford' Lynching," https://www.cbsnews.com/news/moores-ford-lynchings-ruling-unlock-answers-notorious-1946-rural-georgia-slaying/.

7. http://www.pbs.org/harrymoore/terror/howard.html.

8. Jason Morgan Ward, "The Infamous Lynching Site That Still Stands in Mississippi," *Time,* May 3, 2016, https://time.com/4314310/hanging-bridge-excerpt-mississippi-civil-rights/.

9. https://www.blackpast.org/african-american-history/1857-frederick-douglass-if-there-no-struggle-there-no-progress/.

10. Catsam, 37, 40–42; Raymond Arsenault, *Freedom Riders: 1961 and the Struggle for Racial Justice* (New York: Oxford University Press, 2006), 53–55; Meier and Rudwick, 38.

11. https://www.al.com/news/2018/05/he_wanted_a_cheeseburger_but_h.html; Catsam, 63–64.

12. Arsenault, 93.

13. Crosby, 56–57.

14. Lewis, 89.

## 8. TRAINING IN WASHINGTON, D.C.

1. https://www.lyrics.com/lyric/1093302/Pete+Seeger/Oh%2C+Freedom.

2. James Peck, *Freedom Ride* (New York: Simon & Schuster, 1962), 39.

3. Randy Kennedy, "Albert Smith Bigelow, 87, Pacifist Who Tried to Halt Nuclear Tests," *New York Times,* October 8, 1993, D17, https://timesmachine.nytimes.com/timesmachine/1993/10/08/619493.html?pageNumber=108; also http://ivy50.com/blackhistory/story.aspx?sid=3%2F11%2F2009.

4. Dr. King was stabbed in 1958 at a book signing event by a forty-two-year-old African American woman, Izola Curry. See https://mashable.com/2016/01/18/mlk-stabbing/.

## 9. FIRST DAYS

1. http://20thcenturyhistorysongbook.com/song-book/race-relations/the-freedom-riders/.

2. Elsie Carper, "Pilgrimage Off on Racial Test," *Washington Post,* May 5, 1961, B4.

3. Video clip of Genevieve Hughes interview available at Freedom Ride section of National Center for Civil and Human Rights, Atlanta, Ga.

4. James Peck published an uncopyrighted biographical manuscript, *Underdogs vs. Upperdogs,* in April 1969.

## 10. SHOE-IN

1. Peck, *Freedom Ride,* 118.

2. Arsenault, 44; Catsam, 25.

3. https://www.lyrics.com/lyric/3035284/The+Shirelles/Blue+Holiday.

## 11. TROUBLE COMES A CALLING

1. "Freedom Song" lyrics are an adaptation of Harry Belafonte's "Banana Boat Song," also known as "Day-O," https://www.lyrics.com/lyric/29226328/Harry+Belafonte/DayO+%28Banana+Boat+Song%29.

2. Catsam, 122.

3. Raines, 111.

4. Lewis, 137.

5. Ibid., 138; Raines, 111.

6. Arsenault, 123.

7. http://leadonnetwork.org/wordpress/2016/02/07/black-disability-history-reverend-cecil-ivory-naacp-organizer-for-rock-hill-sc-sit-ins/.

8. http://lynchingintexas.org/items/show/512#&gid=1&pid=2; https://calendar.eji.org/racial-injustice/nov/12; https://books.google.com/books?id=BsuqCwAAQBAJ&pg=PA592&lpg=PA592&dq=ernest+collins+and+benny+mitchell+lynching&source=bl&ots=tE1NPQleXZ&sig=ACfU3U3aULRfLqJgYvlcFPgciK3WBAAn1g&hl=en&sa=X&ved=2ahUKEwiq-Lq08IznAhWSWM0KHd4IC-EQ6AEwBXoECAoQAQ#v=onepage&q=ernest%20collins%20and%20benny%20mitchell%20lynching&f=false.

9. https://kinginstitute.stanford.edu/encyclopedia/montgomery-bus
-boycott.

## 12. HOME IN ATLANTA

1. http://www.screenplaydb.com/film/scripts/The%20Curious%20
Case%20of%20Benjamin%20Button.PDF, 100.

2. Martin Luther King, Jr., "Out of the Long Night," *Gospel Messenger,* February 8, 1958, starts on p. 3, quote found on p. 14, col. 1; John Craig, "Wesleyan Baccalaureate Is Delivered by Dr. King," *Hartford (Conn.) Courant,* June 8, 1964, 4; Selma March, March 25, 1965, https://kinginstitute.stanford.edu/king-papers/documents/address-conclusion-selma-montgomery-march.

3. Arsenault, 128.

4. Ibid.

5. http://www.augusta.com/masters/story/history/1961-gary-player-first-international-masters-winner.

6. Peck, *Freedom Ride,* 123.

7. https://www.pga.com/timeline-african-american-achievements-in-golf.

8. https://www.blackpast.org/african-american-history/university-georgia-desegregation-riot-1961/.

9. https://www.npr.org/2017/12/08/569156832/the-racial-cleansing-that-drove-1-100-black-residents-out-of-forsyth-county-ga. See also the excellent in-depth examination of Forsyth County's past in Patrick Phillips, *Blood at the Root: A Racial Cleansing in America* (New York: W. W. Norton, 2016).

10. Leonard, 34; also https://medium.com/@johnthebeeler/a-city-too-busy-to-hate-29533b219477.

11. Arsenault, 133.

12. Ibid.

13. Ibid., 134–35; James Farmer, *Lay Bare the Heart* (New York: Arbor House, 1985), 201.

14. Arsenault, 133; Raines, 112.

## 13. MOTHER'S DAY

1. Diane McWhorter, *A Dream of Freedom: The Civil Rights Movement from 1954 to 1968* (Singapore: Scholastic, 2004), 6.

2. Arsenault, 149.

3. Charles A. Person, Freedom Riders 40th Anniversary Reunion Oral History Project, University of Mississippi, November 8–10, 2001, https://vimeo.com/70330473?ref=fb-share, at 11:12; Hollars, 69; Charles A. Person, "Speech at Georgia Tech," meeting with University of Wisconsin at Eau Claire students, Professor Jesse Yang presiding, March 17, 2018, at 9:00.

4. Arsenault, 149.

5. Ibid.; Simeon Booker with Carol McCabe Booker, *Shocking the Conscience: A Reporter's Account of the Civil Rights Movement* (Jackson: University Press of Mississippi, 2013), 191.

6. Booker, 191

7. Arsenault, 149; Booker with Booker, 191.

8. Booker with Booker, 191; Arsenault, 150.

9. Booker with Booker, 192; Arsenault, 150.

10. Historians Raymond Arsenault, Derick Catsam, and Diane McWhorter all state that the photo is of a black bystander, George Webb. Arsenault, 155; Catsam, 164; McWhorter, *Carry Me Home*, 212.

11. Peck, *Freedom Ride*, 128; also https://www.youtube.com/watch?v=4kYZKcVY6_o&t=520s, at 6:27–6:54.

## 14. MOTHER'S DAY, PART II

1. Manis, 153.

2. McWhorter, *Carry Me Home*, 22, 187.

3. McWhorter, *Dream of Freedom*, 6; McWhorter, *Carry Me Home*, 115; Manis, 110.

4. Manis, 147; McWhorter, *Carry Me Home*, 125.

5. McWhorter, *Carry Me Home*, 127.

6. Ibid., 209; Manis, 264.

7. "People Are Asking: 'Where Were the Police?'," *Birmingham News*, May 15, 1961, 1.

8. Booker with Booker, 194–95.

9. Arsenault, 156.

10. Ibid., 153; Catsam, 163–64; McWhorter, *Carry Me Home*, 182–85.

11. https://archive.org/details/CSPAN3_20180219_034600_Oral_Histories_Hank_Thomas_West_Point_Interview/start/1500/end/1560, at 11:11.55; also https://www.youtube.com/watch?v=oTMswW40I7M&t=22s, at 2:11.

12. Arsenault, 145; also related by Hank Thomas in previous citations' videos.

13. Janie Forsyth McKinney, https://www.youtube.com/watch?v
=r1EDOL9II0s, at 2:45.

14. Timothy B. Tyson, *Blood Done Sign My Name: A True Story* (New
York: Three Rivers Press, 2004), 70; https://prospect.org/notebook/armed
-resistance-civil-rights-movement-charles-e.-cobb-danielle-l.-mcguire
-forgotten-history/.

15. Manis, 267.

## 15. THE DAY AFTER

1. A. M. E. Hymnal, "Precious Lord Take My Hand," by Thomas A.
Dorsey, arranged by E. C. Deas, published by the A. M. E. Sunday School
Union, 1954, p. 333.

2. Ellen Levine, *Freedom's Children: Young Civil Rights Activists Tell
Their Own Stories* (New York: Puffin Books, 1993), 72–73.

3. Bud Gordon, "Will Keep Up Fight, Says Crusader," *Birmingham
News,* May 15, 1961, 10.

4. Peck, *Freedom Ride,* 130.

5. Manis, 267.

6. https://www.biblegateway.com/passage/?search=PRoverbs+14&
version=NIV.

7. Video clip of Genevieve Hughes interview available at Freedom
Ride section of National Center for Civil and Human Rights, Atlanta, Ga.

8. Peck, *Freedom Ride,* 130.

9. Catsam, 177.

10. Ibid., 178; Manis, 268.

11. Arsenault, 170.

12. Manis, 270.

13. Glenn T. Eskew, *But for Birmingham: The Local and National
Movements in the Civil Rights Struggle* (Chapel Hill: University of North
Carolina Press, 1997), 159–60.

## 16. RESOLUTION

1. https://www.youtube.com/watch?v=uQbqzaRAql8, at 0:36.

2. "Three Protest Groups Elect Jail; Call Comes from Rock Hill for
Help," *Student Voice,* February 1961, 1, https://www.crmvet.org/docs/sv
/sv6102.pdf.

3. David Halberstam, *The Children* (New York: A Fawcett Book,

Random House, 1998), 234; https://www.tennessean.com/story/news/local /2017/03/02/complete-coverage-civil-rights-movement-nashville/98648442/.

   4. Arsenault, 179.

   5. Ibid., 183.

   6. Catsam, 186.

   7. Ibid.

   8. https://www.youtube.com/watch?v=uQbqzaRAql8, at 0:36.

### 17. AFTERMATH

   1. https://www.biblegateway.com/passage/?search=isaiah+40%3A31& version=KJV.

   2. Arsenault, 533–87. Raymond Arsenault has compiled an outstanding table of all the Freedom Rides and Riders of 1961 with extensive information.

   3. Farmer, 206.

   4. McWhorter, *Dream of Freedom*, 122.

   5. https://www.youtube.com/watch?v=oTMswW40I7M&t=22s.

### EPILOGUE: THE COST OF THE TICKET

   1. https://genius.com/Langston-hughes-the-bitter-river-annotated.

   2. https://www.nps.gov/mlkm/learn/quotations.htm.

   3. https://kinginstitute.stanford.edu/king-papers/documents/give-us -ballot-address-delivered-prayer-pilgrimage-freedom.

   4. http://www2.oberlin.edu/external/EOG/BlackHistoryMonth/MLK /MLKmainpage.html.

   5. Martin Luther King, Jr., *Where Do We Go from Here: Chaos or Community?* (Boston: Beacon Press, 1968), 63.

   6. https://kinginstitute.stanford.edu/king-papers/publications /autobiography-martin-luther-king-jr-contents/chapter-28-chicago -campaign.

   7. Halberstam, 319–20.

   8. https://www.mcgill.ca/poetrymatters/files/poetrymatters/langston _hughes_the_bitter_river.pdf

   9. https://www.blackpast.org/african-american-history/1955-martin -luther-king-jr-montgomery-bus-boycott/

# INDEX

JoEtta Person

CHARLES PERSON is one of two living Freedom Riders who remained with the original Ride from its start in Washington, D.C., to New Orleans. This historic event helped defeat Jim Crow laws in the United States. A sought-after public speaker, Person maintains active contact with schools, museums, and the activist community. He lives in Atlanta.

RICHARD ROOKER is an English and history educator, writing coach, and longtime personal friend of Person. He is an active board member of the Indiana Historical Society.